A-11-74

The Large City: A World Problem

THE LARGE CITY:
A WORLD PROBLEM

Ursula K. Hicks

Macmillan

Ursula K. Hicks 1974

First published 1974 by
THE MACMILLAN PRESS LTD.
London and Basingstoke
Associated companies in New York,
Dublin, Melbourne, Johannesburg and Madras

SBN 333 172132

Printed in Great Britain by
J. W. ARROWSMITH LTD.
Winterstoke Road, Bristol BS3 2NT

Contents

Acknowledgements

My first debt is to the [Canadian] Bureau of Municipal Research which in 1966 organised the establishment of forty multi-interest study groups in Metropolitan Areas of thirty countries, and especially to Simon R. Miles (then Assistant Director of the programme) who brought me in as Fiscal Consultant to the Study Seminar in Toronto in 1967. This assignment first drew my attention to the special problems of urban settlements as distinct from the general organisational and fiscal problems of local authorities in which I had long been interested. Not only was the information supplied by the cities in response to a questionnaire, of great interest, but so also was the opportunity of meeting in Toronto members of many of the city groups and of discussing with them the special problems of their respective cities.

Of other scholars who have helped me I should like to mention Professor Alice Vandermeulen, of the University of California, Los Angeles, who first encouraged me to publication and supplied me with useful contributory material; also Professor Roy Bahl who supplied me with new material and with whom I had interesting discussions in Washington.

In Japan my special thanks are due to the management at the Chunichi Shimbun of Nagoya who financed my visit, and to Professor Fujii of the University of Nagoya who distributed my questionnaire to the large cities and subsequently made arrangements for my interviews with the authorities. I should also like to thank the city authorities in Tokyo, Osaka and Nagoya for the figures they supplied, including unpublished material, and for their patience in answering my questions.

In India my special thanks are due to the Indian Institute of Public Administration where I had many useful discussions, and especially to Drs Datta and Bhattacharya whose work provided me with useful materials and ideas.

Finally, my thanks are due to my lecture audiences in Austria and Italy, whose criticisms helped me to a better understanding of the legal and fiscal difficulties of their respective cities.

U.K.H.

Part I – General

1 Introductory

All over the world the great cities are in trouble. The problem of how to deal with the large urban concentrations of the modern world has not yet been solved. It is a problem which besets not only the advanced countries, but afflicts all areas with dense populations and consequently large cities. The troubles seem to be particularly severe (if one can particularise) in Japan, India and the U.S.A.; very likely also in China, but that is unknown territory. The worst difficulties occur in areas that have populations of one million or over, rising steadily with the size of the population. No country has really succeeded in getting to grips with the socio-economic or even with the sheer physical problems of catching up with the needs of modern communities of this size.

Even in some of the richest and most advanced countries the standard of life is visibly going downhill. Property is not being adequately maintained, much of it is obsolete. Street capacity has not been adjusted to the needs of modern traffic. Housing is fantastically inadequate to accommodate the flow of immigrants and growth of the indigenous population. The resulting congestion breeds physical and psychological strain and disturbance. It increases health hazards for even the most fit. It becomes increasingly difficult to collect taxes from the residents and even more so from the army of commuters who daily surge into the city for work, but live outside its jurisdiction. Services in the city are deteriorating, especially education and public health. Law and order can no longer be taken for granted. In some areas crime is increasing in volume and severity in a quite alarming manner.

3

There is a school of thought which maintains that the cities no longer exist in the traditional sense of self-regarding communities. They have become mere 'nodes of communication' without shape or coherence. The old 'core' city is submerged in a mass of unplanned and inappropriate sprawl, which begins to deteriorate almost as soon as it is erected. If this were really so it would seem to sound the death knell of responsible self-respecting local government such as we have known, and been proud of, for many centuries, especially in English-speaking countries.

I believe that this is too gloomy a view, although the plight of some American and Japanese cities would seem to lend some support to these contentions. Moreover the great cities of some of the less developed countries are in a still more parlous state. Their troubles nevertheless are of a somewhat different nature, mainly due to their poverty and to the dearth of competent administrators. But, given the initial low standards of health and literacy of the majority of their inhabitants, less is expected of them, and, apart from areas devastated by political upheaval, the cities in the less developed countries are not conspicuously deteriorating. In some ways they are definitely improving. In the long run the direction of trend may be more important than immediate performance. Nevertheless in spite of arguments to the contrary the cities as organisations with community consciousness and pride continue to exist. If they should disappear something very precious to mankind will have been lost.

My first objective in these essays (the earliest of which dates from 1970) has been to discuss the characteristic troubles of large cities in sufficient detail to form a basis for a judgement of the nature and seriousness of their troubles. Secondly I have sought to explore the possibility of policies which would make the cities once more into places to be proud of, good to live and work in, to love and admire. In this quest two things seem to me to be of first importance: first to inquire what different countries are attempting and experimenting with to improve their cities, so that others may learn from their experience. Secondly it is essential to examine and to evaluate the financial side of the condition of the cities. Without the will and the opportunity to raise and use sufficient finances it is clear that there can be no effective regeneration. However attractive the plans for renewal and development may be they will remain stillborn without adequate financial backing.

While rejecting the conclusion that the day of the cities is over it is clear that for successful reform there needs to be a substantial degree of administrative reorganisation. The city is not going to survive in its traditional form, even if its boundaries are extended to include some of the nineteenth and twentieth century suburbs. The expansion of cities beyond their established boundaries is no new phenomenon. In some areas its consequences were observed well back in the nineteenth century. In localities which were not densely settled it was possible for the cities to deal with the problem adequately (at least for the time being) by taking in surrounding rural areas or small towns. But this policy became increasingly difficult as boundaries crystalised. With the improved services which the cities were offering tax differentials appeared. The small towns and villages 'at risk' preferred less tax rather than more services (for which at first at least they did not have so much need as the city dwellers). The result was the appearance of the 'conurbation', much discussed in the 1930s. It might consist of many miles of built up area, some parts densely settled, others no more than ribbon development that was neither town nor country. The great weakness of these conurbations was that they had no cohesion, no administrative integration nor common services. They were unsatisfactory to everyone.

This type of conurbation still exists in many places. With the passage of years and the growth of populations it has become immensely bigger than anything that was thought of in the 1930s. Those who foresee the death of the city, but are very conscious of this phenomenon would like to call them 'regional cities'.[1] But 'region' is a term with too vague a connotation to be appropriate, and

[1] Derek Senior (ed.), *The Regional City* (Longmans, 1966).

it is unclear how it is intended that they might work. If it
is to mean anything precise the word 'region' is probably
better confined to a geographical area of a substantial
size, definable by particular characteristics, physical,
economic or ethnic. But we still need a word to define a
very large urban complex strung out probably along a
seaboard or other physical axis, in a manner such that
jurisdictional integration would be very difficult if not
impossible. To describe such a development the word
'megalopolis' has been suggested. There are as yet not
many such areas in the world. By far the most striking
example is the 'Tokaido Megapolis' in Japan, stretching
along the Pacific coast and Inland Sea from east of Tokyo
to west of Kobe, a distance of well over 300 miles. Not
only is it heavily settled throughout, but the nature of the
terrain almost wholly precludes communication except-
ing along the axis. Another candidate for the title would
be the Eastern Seaboard of the U.S.A. from west New
Jersey to north of Boston, but this is not so heavily settled
throughout its length. The San Francisco Bay Area
(which we shall discuss later) might also be a candidate.
But for the far more general case of the enlarged city unit
it is becoming increasingly common to use the term
'Metropolitan Area' (Metro for short). This is a
convenient term although not a very nice one (especially
as the Parisians call their subway 'The Metro') but
nevertheless I shall use it at need. In any case what we
have to think in terms of, and to develop a policy for, is a
new sort of entity, with appropriate organisation and
finance which would be sufficiently flexible to be able to
manage the sort of urban agglomerations we now have to
expect, of up to six or eight million or higher (the
Tokyo/Yokohama complex numbers fourteen million,
and that is only a part of the Tokaido Megalopolis), as
well as effectively reorganising overgrown cities of more
moderate size – say of one or two million.
     The problems of the great cities are all around us,
whether we live in New York or London, Detroit or
Manchester, Paris or Marseilles, Tokyo or Osaka,
Calcutta or Ibadan. Their solution will depend on the

interest and co-operation of the ordinary voter/citizen, as much as on the administrative and financial planners and executives. If the exercise is regarded as essentially a job for experts it will fail to realise to the full the opportunity which is being offered.

My own specific interest in the problems of the large cities arose from an invitation to contribute a paper on the financial side of Metro problems at a 'Study and Training Programme' in Toronto[2] in 1967 (of which more below). But I had already, since before the war, been interested in problems of local finance, especially in the U.K. This involved an analysis of the incomings and outgoings of some of the largest English cities, as well as those of some of the smaller urban and rural areas.[3] Thus the ground had already been prepared to some extent for my later studies.

My approach is essentially that of an economist with a special interest in finance. But finance depends a great deal on organisation and management, especially on the relations between the city and other forms and levels of local and higher governments. Hence organisational questions cannot be left out, although it would be outside my plan to attempt to carry them through to embrace political considerations. Nevertheless we cannot be unconscious of the importance of politics in particular policy decisions. Similarly other demographic, economic and social aspects cannot be neglected, although they do not occupy a central position here. This is especially true concerning the impact of urban policy on employment and the distribution of wealth between the citizens, both within the city and between cities. Since the arguments and conclusions of the Toronto discussions have already been ably summarised[4] it would be otiose to cover that ground again. But the

---

[2] Organised by Intermet, with the Bureau of Municipal Research.

[3] *Standards of Local Expenditure* and *The Problem of Valuation for Rates in Great Britain* (Cambridge University Press, 1944 and 1945), both with J. R. Hicks.

[4] S. R. Miles, *Metropolitan Problems* (Methuen, 1970).

Toronto meetings were a unique and seminal experience
in many ways, and so call for a brief description.

The occasion of the seminar was the centenary of the
foundation of the Dominion of Canada, and the tenth
anniversary of the establishment of the Toronto
Metropolitan Area. The discussions were consequently
closely oriented to the problems of large cities. The
procedure was that twelve 'consultants' were asked to
contribute papers on their own expertise on the most
important aspects of Metro activity: transport, utilities,
housing, education, public health and welfare on the
services side; development of government machinery,
the Metro administrative process, intergovernmental
relations, finance and planning, on the organisational
side. Forty cities across the world were personally
contacted and briefed in advance. Each was asked to
supply a Report on the physical features and climate of
the area, population growth, administrative organisation
(including finance and planning area, if it had one
extending beyond the jurisdiction of the city). Most of
the cities reported on the physical details reasonably
fully, as also the main organisational features. But
unfortunately there was very little to be gleaned from the
answers on finance. Obviously a great deal more
investigation was required on this side.

In the second place the selected cities (and one or two
other conurbations, such as the San Francisco Bay Area
and the Netherlands conurbation) were asked to send
delegations to the Toronto meeting we mentioned before.
Most of them did so.[5] Those which were actually
represented were: Athens, Bangkok, Belgrade, Budapest,
Buenos Aires, Calcutta, Detroit, Edmonton, Glasgow,
Hanover, Ibadan, Johannesburg, Karachi, Leningrad,
Lima, London, Madrid, Manila, Mexico City, Milan,
Montreal, Moscow, Nagoya, Naples, New York, Paris,
Philadelphia, Sydney, Vancouver – and of course the
Toronto Management was available throughout to
answer questions.

[5] Cairo sent its Report but was too preoccupied with the Six Days
War to send a delegation.

Some of the replies were sketchy, and the delegation might consist of one person (six were asked for). But many groups had obviously been keenly interested in the project, had taken a great deal of trouble with their Reports and sent excellent delegations. The consultants' papers were circulated in advance and three cities were invited to make a special report on the subject in which they were most interested. In addition any city could ask to see and if it wished to do so, write a report on any paper it pleased.[6] Nearly all the cities selected were of true Metro standing, both in size and in relation to their country's background. As will be apparent there was a very wide spread of political and constitutional background and also in the degree of development represented. Only a few capital cities were included. This was probably as well since the position of capital cities is inevitably somewhat different from others, so that they are not wholly typical of their countries. Generally they have less autonomy, but on the other hand the standard of the services which they supply is frequently high because they receive more assistance from national governments, who tend to regard them as the showpiece of the country.

Once assembled in Toronto •the delegations were divided into small seminar groups, electing their own chairman for the day. The groups were then organised functionally according to their special interests. The relevant consultant was always at hand, to further the discussion or help resolve difficulties. For three very solid days the little seminars discussed their problems with thoroughness and determination (at least that was my experience). This was the most exciting part of the programme. Discussion was very free and friendly, each delegate speaking from his own personal experience. Throughout there was not a sign of political or racial animosity, no lining up. They were all there to discuss their immediate practical problems, and to seek advice as to how they might be solved.

[6] I am particularly grateful for the criticisms of the Athens, Calcutta, Istanbul, Johannesburg and Sydney groups.

A striking similarity of the problems quickly emerged. This was probably only to be expected since the basic causes of their troubles were essentially the same, especially the urban population explosion of which they are all victims. Similarities were also apparent in respect of the commitments and services which the cities were expected to undertake and in their relations with other government entities, both at their own level and at higher levels. The sources of current finance which they might expect to command (although obviously not the volume) were also similar. Only in respect of investment finance were broad differences apparent. Since this is a vitally important aspect of urban regeneration and development, it is worth pausing to consider the point for a moment. To some extent the differences were a matter of scarcity or abundance of potential savings on which a city might expect to draw. Thus at that time Calcutta had an excellent Plan which it was anxious to implement but neither its poverty-stricken population nor the troubled state of West Bengal were in a position to help, so that it looked as if nothing could be done.[7] In other countries (for instance in Japan) the savings were there, but the cities had insufficient opportunities to draw on them in anything like the required volume. As will emerge later[8] this was partly a matter of the constitution and of traditions dating from the time before rapid growth began.

Aside from the particular causes of differences in the availability of investment funds in individual cities, this seems to be the direction where differences in the degree of central control (or vice versa local autonomy) show up most forcibly. This is an aspect of city finances on which it is particularly difficult to get an adequate account. A separate capital account is rarely kept adequately. Moreover many of the investments are joint projects of national (or state) and local government. The share of

[7] Finally the terrible troubles of the Bangladesh War convinced the authorities in Delhi that Calcutta must be considered a national problem, and additional central funds were made available.

[8] See below, Chapter 7.

higher level governments may well be substantial, but it is not easily identifiable. Further, the timing of the arrival of grants may be very irregular, thus upsetting the budgetary accounting of the city. India is a good example of this type of difficulty (see below, Chapter 10), where assistance may come from Parliament through the Planning Commission (under a multiplicity of arrangements) from the State or from a public undertaking such as the Life Insurance Corporation.

The delegations from Soviet-type countries at Toronto reported that for them investment funds presented absolutely no problem, so long as the central authorities approved a project. Otherwise implementation was flatly impossible. There are other cases where a particular Metro plan is the pet of the national government, as the plan for the Paris region was the pet of General de Gaulle. In such circumstances also it is certain that capital funds will not be lacking. It is relevant in this connection that in the U.K. since the abandonment of specific grants (especially for education) central control has tended to be exercised on the investment side, not so much by actual grant (or withholding of grant) because British local authorities normally have a number of sources on which to draw for asset creation, but rather by persuasion and occasionally by direction. The control of local capital accounts by whatever method has serious implications for urban reform since the modernisation of all large cities must invoke much capital investment.

Among the cities represented at Toronto there was wide agreement on the need for jurisdictional reorganisation, so as to secure uniformity of policy and planning over a larger area than that of the present city. Although experience of the actual functioning of a Metro area was, of those present, confined to Toronto and London, this seemed to be the sort of outcome most cities had in mind: an area which would include most of their day as well as their night populations, which would be an adequate base for land use planning in a wide sense and would include some measure at least of control (or means of common action) over resources shared with outer areas, such as water, or inter-area communications. It was interesting to discover in how many of the reporting cities Planning Areas, official or unofficial, had been designated over the previous two or three years. Since 1967 there have been further developments. In Chapter 3 we shall have a look at a number of actual experiments in establishing and operating Metro areas which then and since have been made in different parts of the world.

While the fundamental similarity of the problems of large cities everywhere needs to be emphasised, from another point of view each city is unique – in its combination of economic, social, racial, locational and climatic characteristics. Even slight differences in any of these can make a not negligible difference in optimum policy; thus although needs are similar the weighting to be ascribed to the various elements may be very different, and this will affect the volume and type of finance required. Thus two alternative approaches to the subject seem possible: either one can proceed entirely on a case study method, city by city, analysing the special problems and circumstances of each in turn. Alternatively one can proceed functionally to discuss what sort of services are being supplied, how far they are appropriate at different levels of size and wealth, and *mutatis mutandis*, what funds can be made available to support them.

I have always been attracted by this second line of approach as potentially leading to informed and useful generalisations which could contribute to general improvement, or at the least aid towards the avoidance of pitfalls. My experience at Toronto strengthened my conviction of the usefulness of this approach, and on the whole I have followed it in these essays. At the same time this method obviously needs to be followed up with some case studies if only to appreciate the relationship between the various outlays and resources with which cities have to work. A city is something more than a collection of people, buildings, streets, services and finances. A Metro is an entity which has continuing relations with other entities, both on its own level and above and below. Although they are in a sense also functionally organised I regard the essays on Japanese and on Indian cities as essentially falling into this class, of mixed functional and case study exercises.

It may be asked why I have devoted so much time and space to these two countries, to the neglect of others. The first reason is that I had the opportunity to make detailed investigations on the spot, and to talk to my heart's content to the Managements. Once again my experience at Toronto confirmed my view that to obtain any real insight into the problems of a city this is essential. Apart from that, the cities of Japan and India are of special interest for the world not only socially and economically but also politically. Although they cannot be described as autonomous, in both countries the elective assemblies and executives retain substantial powers of decision making in ways that are easily understandable to those brought up in the Anglo-American tradition. This is in some contrast – although the difference should not be exaggerated – to the Australian great cities which tend to be more subordinate to the states, and in much greater contrast to cities in many other parts of the world.

I would naturally not claim that these are the only examples which would illustrate my points. A great deal more research is called for into all such aspects of urban conditions. These essays are no more than an interim report of what might be done. But such tentative inquiries as I have made into other European cities which I have thought might be worth including, such as those of Sweden, Denmark, and Holland, proved less interesting from my point of view than I had hoped. Their budgetary procedures do not seem to be forward looking; they apparently make no effort to restrain the creation of tax havens, and they continue to perpetuate the distortions caused by war-time rent controls. Again, a fine city like Barcelona with a strong independent democratic tradition, is at present at least as much controlled by the national government as it would be in a Soviet-type country.

The basis of the troubles of all the cities, one way or another, is the population explosion. The population of the world is still growing very fast and a much larger proportion of it is becoming urbanised. In 1870 the world population is estimated to have been some 1300 million, of which no more than 1 per cent lived in cities. By 1964 the number of people had (very roughly) grown to 3200 m., and over 11 per cent of them were living in cities of over one million. The processes of growth and concentration have unquestionably accelerated since 1964, but the available figures in national censuses do not allow of a close quantification of the change. Both the growth of population and its concentration are world phenomena; but there are great and significant differences between countries, and even between cities in the same country. In the more advanced countries growth tends more and more to take place on the fringes, while at the same time the traditional core city may be losing population at a non-negligible rate. A double problem is thus set up, as is well illustrated by the present state of London, where the Inner London boroughs have declined from 3·3 m. in 1951 to 2·7 m. in 1971. In the less developed parts of the world populations are still increasing at a rate of between 2·3 per cent a year. This is the background to their urban concentration.

In the advanced countries (including Japan) the general rate of population increase, in contrast to the less developed countries, has slowed down to 1 per cent or less. (In West Germany the latest figures actually show a decline in the indigenous population, but this is masked by the presence of a large number of foreign workers.) In overall growth there is thus a very large difference between the advanced and the less developed countries. But there is much less difference between the *rates* of concentration between the two sorts of countries, although there may be a great deal of difference between the *types* of in and out movements. In the more advanced countries urban immigration is virtually the other side of the medal of the rural exodus, which inevitably occurs during the process of industrialisation. In a few countries this type of movement is almost completed, for instance in the U.K. and in parts of the U.S. The agricultural sectors in these countries can hardly sustain much more shrinkage. As a result of the end of this movement the average city growth is decelerating, although there are often special reasons which cause certain cities to continue to grow fast. Elsewhere in Europe, and even more in Japan and India, the rural exodus is by no means complete. It is largely for this reason that I have put Japan into a separate part.

In some ways differences in types and intentions of immigrants are more important from the point of view of urban policy than differences in numbers or percentages. Broadly speaking the urban immigrants in the more advanced countries are educated, or at least literate; they can fit easily into the expanding industrial and commercial sectors. The immigrants into Indian cities are very different; but they seem to conform to two types. On the one hand there is a relatively moderate sized group who are deliberately seeking employment and better wages than they could get in the country or in a small town. (This type seems to predominate also in Latin American countries, for instance Mexico.) Such immigrants fully realise that it may be some time before they get a satisfactory full time job; in the meantime they will take any odd opportunities that offer. For them migration is a calculated risk, and on the whole it works. Thus in Bombay unemployment is found to be lower among the immigrants than among the indigenous population (if they can be so designated, when most of the families will probably have come from elsewhere). The net reproduction rate of the immigrants is also lower, but this may be partly the result of their transitional situation. In Calcutta by contrast, there are few immigrants and population growth is almost wholly due to the indigenous families. (One is tempted to conclude that in Calcutta the calculated risks are too high to be attractive.) The second and more traditional type of Indian city immigrants are those who drift in from the country without a definite aim, or even much hope of employment. They come because they hope that urban conditions will somehow be better; they can hardly be worse for the landless peasant than village life. These hopes can very easily be frustrated.

There are naturally many exceptions and halfway houses to these generalisations, some of which we shall explore later. But there is a profound difference between the situation of a Metro expanding against the background of an almost stationary national population and which is already supplied with the basic necessaries of urban life (although for a smaller community) and a Metro in a less developed country where even the most basic necessaries of community life are non-existent. This is mainly the reason why I have segregated into a separate Part the special problems of poor countries with rapidly growing populations.

The special significance of these population movements lies in the ways in which they give rise to *congestion* – of people, of houses, of street circulation. And to congestion can be traced, directly or indirectly, most of the troubles of the cities: pollution of various sorts, inadequate housing, serious health hazards, unruly populations and heavy unemployment, especially of young persons. These troubles are present in different degrees in practically all countries. It is this circumstance which gives a unity to the quest for the diagnosis and cure of the large cities. It is indeed a world problem.

A final word should perhaps be added here concerning the sources from which the different chapters are drawn. (This is also noted, in more detail, at the head of each chapter.)

Part I is intended to be of general application, although mainly to the advanced countries.

Chapter 2 had its origin in some lectures which I gave in Italy in 1970. They were intended as a general introduction to urban problems to which at that time the Italians had devoted very little attention. A version was subsequently published (in Italian) in an Italian quarterly. The chapter ends with a plea for the establishment of larger units (Metros) so that the traditional city could cover its commuting zone, with all that that implies.

Chapter 3 takes up this idea by describing some of the experiments of international interest which have been planned or are already operating for such enlarged entities. Suggestions are put forward as to the form which such an organisation might take, and some of the problems which it would have to face. Details concerning British experience in this field come from an article in the *Three Banks Review*, December 1971, 'Metropolitan Areas, a New Problem for Local Government'. The information concerning the rest of the world was derived from a number of sources. Some of it has been published by the new journal *Local Finance*, of the International Centre for Local Credit, in The Hague.

The material on Japan, which occupies the next four chapters, is derived from some intensive field work which I had the opportunity to undertake in October/ November 1972. Japan's urban problems are such a special case that I finally decided to give them a Part (II) of the book to themselves. The transitional social and economic situation in which Japan finds herself today implies that in some ways she is very highly developed, while on the other hand little has been done (or even planned) on the welfare side to fit her for her new position as an advanced country.

Part III largely explains itself. Chapters 8, 9 and 12 were written for a Seminar at the World Bank in 1971, under the title of 'Management of Resources for Development'. They have not been previously published.

Chapter 10 on Indian urban problems was written for the *Second Nehru Memorial Volume* with the title 'Towards Socialist Transformation of Indian Economy', and published therein in 1972. It derives from field work carried out in various parts of India, mainly in 1969, and from many fruitful discussions at the Indian Institute of Public Administration.

Chapter 11 on city transport and circulation problems is concerned with one of the most difficult fields which confronts city modernisation in the Third World. It was written for an All India Conference on Roads and Transport held in Mysore State in 1972, and so has special reference to India.

Chapter 12 formed the last part of the World Bank assignment. Its main reference is to the less developed countries, but much of it is relevant to more advanced countries also.

2 How Does One Run a Large City?*

Of all the diverse troubles which beset the modern world
the economic and social shortcomings of the great cities
have a primary importance. They are the growing points
of a country in every sense. They should be the leaders,
in civilisation, in culture, in amenities, as well as in
personal incomes. But far too often exactly the opposite
is the case. Throughout the U.S.A., in particular, there is
a growing consciousness and preoccupation with the
'crisis' of the cities. It is indeed evident to anyone who
visits that country that there is a crisis; although
the problems are not limited to the great cities of more
than two million inhabitants. Some of the smaller cities,
such as Detroit and Newark (N.J.), are in a still worse
condition. Disgust at the inefficiency and corruption of
the (white) city council has brought into power the first
black governments in the Eastern states. Thus the
general city background of the U.S.A. may be described
as one of crisis. But the situation in the great cities is
more difficult to deal with, not only because of its
magnitude but also due to the basic fragmentation (and
often confusion) of boundaries and administrations.

It is a sad reflection that the richest country in the
world cannot assure its city dwellers reasonable
satisfaction of the basic needs of community life:

* Based on lectures given at the Institute of Economics of the
University of Siena in April 1970, subsequently published under the
title 'Problemi Economici e Financiari della Grandi Città, *Rivista di
Diretto Finanziario e Scienza della Finanze.*

protection and control of crime, tolerable living space,
circulation of transport, adequate education services,
basic sanitary needs – pure water and efficient waste
disposal. Not only are individual services often of poor
standard, but there is discernible a growing apprehension that the condition of the cities is inevitable. They
will never be able to assure a satisfying life for their
inhabitants. It is impossible for children to have a free
and happy existence in high rises. Civil disturbances are
perpetual (some American cities have experienced them
daily for over a month). Unemployment and a hopeless
future for the poor seem unavoidable. Worst of all,
especially in the U.S.A., such conditions exacerbate
racial tensions.

The problems of the great cities are not confined to rich
America. If we turn to one of the poorest of countries,
India, with an average per capita income of not more
than £25 p.a., we find very similar troubles, but
inevitably at a much more bedrock level. The large
Indian cities are indeed large, several of them exceeding
4 million. Essential services are not just inadequate, they
are completely non-existent.[1] Notwithstanding some
improvements over the last twenty years, disease and
malnutrition are still everywhere apparent; the coverage
of education is still fragmentary and only a small
percentage of the population is really literate. Unemployment is high both in the city centre and on the fringes.
There have been some attempts to establish low-price
shops, but these do not meet the case. In every corner,
both on the fringes and even in the heart of the city,
wherever there are a few square yards vacant, even
temporarily, the signs of over-population are apparent:
large families ill clothed in rags and with bare feet, living
in huts of cardboard cartons and sacking, eating little and
doing less. Over the whole of India the expectation of life
hardly exceeds 50; for the wretched dwellers in these
shanty settlements it is a good deal less, even for those
who manage to survive infancy.

[1] See below, Chapter 9.

Although the position in India is thus very grave, it is still by no means unique. Throughout the greater part of the world crime and disturbance in urban areas are common phenomena. Low rent accommodation is just not obtainable. There are shanty settlements in most urban areas (especially, for instance, in Latin America). Where there are no shanty settlements (as in Nepal), the reason probably is that the harshness of the climate makes them untenantable, and the alternative of immense over-crowding of large buildings takes their place. But in the less poor countries (for instance, Italy, South America and Mexico City) the city shanty-town dwellers are by no means destitute. They have at least radios and bicycles; what they principally lack is living accommodation at a reasonable price. But in nearly all the urban areas unemployment is high.[2] It is not possible for new jobs to turn up at a rate that parallels the rate of urban immigration. In many countries the effort to provide 'employment at any price' actually makes the situation worse by stimulating urban immigration.

Just as the problems and afflictions of metropolitan areas are similar the world over, so the means to improvement are also basically similar, notwithstanding great differences in the political and constitutional infrastructure, in the type of the relevant population and the general level of wealth. The basic causes of the crisis in the standard of city life are three: (1) the population explosion, (2) the advent of the motoring age, and (3) the revolution in domestic technology, which has substantially altered the way of living of the housewife. The first two of these are largely responsible for the congestion of people, houses and streets, which in turn principally gives rise to secondary evils, especially pollution, civil disturbance and health hazards.

These are all concentration troubles, but there are also some troubles of deconcentration, for instance, the introduction of new manufacturing methods which require one-storey buildings for continuous flow

[2] Probably least in Japan, where recent urban immigrants return to their home villages when unemployment threatens.

techniques, and thus demand much more space, of
necessity on the fringes, than that occupied by the old
town factories. The advent of the motoring age has also
caused troubles of decentralisation: out-migration of the
wealthy for country residence, paralleling, but never
balancing, in-migration of the poor. While a certain
amount of deconcentration at the centre is generally
desirable, the out-migration of better-off families and of
factories sets up problems which we shall discuss below.
The results of haphazard deconcentration emphasise the
desirability of a larger area and a more peaceful
organisation to replace the traditional city.

In order to fix ideas it is worth pausing for a moment to
look broadly at the statistics of urban population
movements. (These figures refer to the period 1951-64,
but there is every reason to suppose that the trend has
continued and even accelerated since then.) By and large,
urban populations have tended to grow much faster than
national populations. The fastest growing cities between
1951 and 1964 were in Latin America, where rates of 160
per cent were not uncommon (equivalent to an average
annual rate of 3·7 per cent). At least ten large cities in
different countries registered expansions of 100 per cent,
and Tehran and Mexico City, both already very large,
were only just below that figure. The average city growth
in the less developed countries was 42·5 per cent. In the
U.S.A. it was 32 per cent, but the Miami complex
registered 142 per cent, and other cities such as Los
Angeles and Houston were close on 70 per cent. In
Western Europe the rate of concentration, as of total
population growth, was generally lower, but Madrid
recorded more than 50 per cent, Rome 44 per cent, Paris
26 per cent, and Naples and the Ruhr/Essen complex
24 per cent. In the United Kingdom things moved much
more slowly. Population growth was very moderate and
the degree of concentration was, on the standards of
other countries, relatively light. The average growth of
the five largest British cities over the period was 6·3 per
cent, but Birmingham reached 10 per cent, and London
7 per cent in spite of much overspill into New Towns some

distance from the Metropolis. By contrast, Glasgow's growth rate was only 3 per cent and Manchester's 2·3 per cent.

These figures give a reasonably good idea of the order of magnitude of urban growth and of its incidence, but they obviously cannot be pressed. In such a rapidly moving scene the timing and accuracy of censuses make a great deal of difference. Moreover, we cannot always be certain that equivalent entities are being compared. To measure the growth of population of a city within its administrative boundaries can be grossly misleading: they may not have changed for a century. Yet to compare what are informally referred to as 'Metropolitan areas' or 'Greater . . .' gives no precise idea of what is being included.

Even apart from statistical uncertainties, percentage changes cannot tell the story adequately. What a city government has to face is actual numbers, not percentage changes. In a city that is already large they may be formidable. For instance, in the immediate postwar years Rome received a flood of returning Italians from the former African colonies, as well as a steady stream from the poor regions of the South. Similarly, a flood of returned colonists from North Africa poured into Paris. Taipei in Formosa, a city of over two million inhabitants, was flooded with refugees from Communist China. On the other hand, Australia, which is underpopulated, desires and deliberately subsidises immigration. The greater number of the 'New Australians' come from the poorer part of Europe: southern Italy, Greece, Czechoslovakia and Poland. All are attracted by city life. Hence the populations of the largest cities (Sydney, Melbourne and Adelaide) have already passed the two million mark, while the cities of the next rank (such as Perth and Brisbane) are growing even more rapidly. Hence, in spite of its small national population, a country like Australia finds itself already confronted with grave problems of metropolitan areas. Obviously, in all these situations, political as well as economic and social pressures have been at work.

In Rome immigration is thought now to have 'settled down' at about 50,000 a year. Even this is a large number to house and employ, especially in a city which has no industry and is not intended to have any. In the cities of the Third World the situation is a good deal worse. For instance, Bombay received about 122,000 immigrants a year. Even with a fairly good rate of industrialisation this is clearly too high a number to be digested without adding to unemployment and shanty settlements and all that these imply in congestion, pollution, health hazards, crime and unrest. The most spectacular rate of concentration has, however, been in the three great cities of Japan; Tokyo, Osaka and Nagoya. In Tokyo, for instance, up to 1965 there was an annual increase of 600,000. The *rate* of increase has since then somewhat declined, but the actual numbers are still enormous. Only the abnormally high rate of economic activity of Japan, giving minimal unemployment, has kept things going, but at great cost in human welfare.

Added to the difficulties of coping with a high rate of population growth, modern cities are beset with another problem: that of the extreme mobility of the population. This is due essentially to the ease of road transport. There are really two aspects to this mobility: (1) relatively long-term movements due to the propensity to change location of residence much more frequently than in the past, and (2) the daily commuter tide. The two aspects are usually, but not necessarily, closely linked. Modern mobility, coming on top of the population explosion, has finally destroyed the peace and homogeneity of the city. The deep roots from which local loyalties and civic pride spring no longer exist when nearly all the inhabitants were born somewhere else. In particular, commuters do not feel themselves to belong fully either to the area in which they live or to that in which they work. As in- and out-migration continue and the commuter tide swells, the structure of society, the age and income grouping, perhaps even the racial make-up of the population, all tend to change. In densely populated countries such as Holland and Belgium, and parts of England, the traditional distinction between urban and rural becomes largely obliterated in an amorphous mass of development. It is here that reorganisation is required.

The most frustrating type of urban immigration is that where the immigrants belong to a different ethnic group from the citizens. England has experienced something of this difficulty, with immigrants from Southern Asia, East Africa and to a lesser extent from the Caribbean; she has had to limit the rate of immigration to ensure that those who come can be absorbed. But the most difficult urban population movements have been in the U.S.A., where the cities of the North are flooded with negroes from the South who are accustomed to a much lower standard of social life and are poorly educated.

At the same time, urban emigration is becoming more significant, although it is of much smaller dimensions. To start with, the outward movement consisted mainly of middle class families, who found that their nineteenth century houses had become technically obsolete and could not be run without an army of domestic servants who were no longer available. They sought in the suburbs better air and greater quiet. Their new residences were likely to be outside the boundaries of the city, where land was cheaper. Thus arose the American 'tax havens' which have been such a trouble to city administrators. It would seem, however, that of recent years this movement has become relatively of less importance, due partly to the rising demand for better local services and partly to the increase of other types of emigration.

Before examining these other types of urban emigration, we should glance at the remaining fundamental causes of the crisis of the cities mentioned above. The motor car makes it easy to live in a chosen spot outside the city, up to the point where the labour of daily commuting, with its traffic congestion and parking difficulties, does not outweigh the escalation of noise and other evils in the city centre, making it an impossible place to live comfortably. Moreover, life on the fringes has further attractions. It is possible to find there small,

modern houses with central heating, readily adaptable
for a full range of modern domestic appliances without
which the modern housewife is 'tied to the kitchen sink'.
There are further attractions for the suburban family. A
recent development, especially in the U.S.A., is the
establishment of 'shopping plazas', 'hypermarkets', on
the fringes, where the weekly family purchases can very
conveniently be made and also longer-term needs, such
as for food, drugs and books, be satisfied under cover
(very important in the American climate). There will also
be cafés, radio and other entertainment, and above all
there is ample parking space. These complexes are much
more easily reached from the suburbs than from the city.
Finally, an increasing number of factories are moving
out into the country, where they have the advantage of
the space needed for modern techniques, as well as
parking facilities for the employees. Initially, this
locational change probably sets up a reverse commuter
tide – from the centre to the suburbs – but eventually it
must be expected that the workers will also tend to
change their residences, vacating the city centre.

These daily population movements (the most important of which are from the fringes to the centre) are a
source of much trouble to the cities, especially in respect
of traffic congestion and parking facilities. It is difficult to
extract any contribution from the commuters towards the
cost of services supplied to them. In many cities,
especially in Italy and in famous British cities such as
Stratford-on-Avon or Oxford, tourists also contribute
heavily to traffic congestion. In India and other less
developed countries, on the other hand, the main cause
of circulation congestion is the heterogeneity of the street
users.[3] Thousands of bicycles, bullock carts, rickshaws
and other slow-moving vehicles throng the streets, while
enormous lorries forge their way through, holding up the
passage of buses and private cars.

In addition to the regular commuters, the large cities
especially have a problem of 'contact population', those

[3] See below, Chapter 9.

who visit the city from time to time for particular purposes, such as professional services, cultural opportunities or entertainment. This also contributes to congestion, particularly parking. These additional demands for street space and urban services underline the need for structural adjustment.

The result of all this is that the city centre ('heart' or 'core') is no longer suitable for residence and tends to be evacuated. The question then arises whether the now obsolete buildings should be demolished, or, if the structures are solid and viable, fully reconditioned and fully adapted to modern use. Too often, before a decision is taken, the buildings are disastrously occupied by a vast crowd of immigrants. To the problems of the costs of restoration are added the reform of slums and the provision of alternative accommodation. If some of the newcomers establish themselves permanently in the interior of the city, the result will be a different age as well as income structure: a need on the one hand for more schools, and on the other for more medical and other social services, both for children and for the remaining population from an earlier time, who will now tend to be elderly. These changes constitute a new charge on the administration.

As a consequence, it is probable that the inner city will emerge as an area calling for more public expenditure but with a smaller tax base than the suburbs. Thus arises the 'peri-central tax deficit ghetto', to use the picturesque American phrase ('peri'-central because it is assumed that the central business district – C.B.D. – will remain more or less intact). The emergence of this condition is probably the most difficult to solve of all the troubles of the city. Should it try to tempt back some of the higher-level income families weary of the labour of daily commuting, by offering them good old houses suitably divided and completely modernised? (In fact there is a zone in central Sydney where this policy has been followed with great success. A street of charming early nineteenth century houses has been entirely reconditioned and has altered the whole tone of the neighbourhood. But it must be remembered that Australia is not troubled with *destitute* immigrants).

If, on the other hand, a policy of demolition is decided upon, it is necessary to clear a sufficient area for wholesale reconstruction. Isolated demolition is completely useless because it cannot change the character of an area. Historic cities, such as Rome (or Dublin or Oxford – or to a lesser extent London and Paris), present a special problem in this respect because they possess a number of beautiful and historic buildings, in different areas, whose destruction would be a real loss to posterity. A few years ago, in many countries the tide seemed to be running strongly in favour of demolition; in the most recent period the conservationists have been winning some striking victories. This change may throw the planning of urban regeneration back into the melting pot.

In so far as demolition is decided upon, the problem of the displaced families has to be faced. The policy of slum clearance breaks up a genuine centre of community life. Further, the small shops and other providers of services for the community are left without means of existence. For many of the evacuated families, moreover, it is essential to find alternative accommodation in the neighbourhood. Their occupations are likely to demand long or awkward hours (bus drivers, night watchmen, for instance) so that they must live within reasonable distance of their work. Experience amply demonstrates that it is useless to leave the required process of readjustment to 'natural forces'. The clearing of one slum area immediately leads to the creation of another, next door. At the same time, in so far as private enterprise can be persuaded to take part in the process of readaptation and to assume some of the costs, the better for the city finances. Sometimes a modest subsidy may persuade charitable foundations, or promoters of cultural facilities, to provide buildings. But it would be necessary for the city to see that designs and materials conformed with the general planned lay-out. One has seen many situations in which this has not been properly looked after, with disastrous and costly results.

The regeneration of the core city is likely to be more expensive than securing the orderly development of the fringes, but the two exercises need to be coordinated and planned together. The precise steps to be taken in respect of the development of the outer areas depends in large measure on the legal structure and on jurisdictions. In many countries, but especially in the U.S.A., the exercise is rendered very much more difficult by jurisdictional fragmentation (see next chapter); but we shall find that it occurs again in Japan in respect of prefectural boundaries. In the U.S.A. relatively wealthy suburbs are allergic to financing the special needs of the inner core which they do not share, be they residents or industrial tax-payers. This is markedly true in respect of education (especially primary education) and social services. In fact, the standard of those services inevitably falls in the inner city. As an answer, the suburban and rural communities have found a means of protecting themselves from this burden by adopting rules of low density settlement, which keep down the level of assessment for property tax. Whether such a policy is considered anti-social depends on the legal system of the country; in the U.S.A. it is not so regarded. But if this situation becomes established where the centre is poor and the outer areas are rich many difficulties arise, not least finance for the essential redevelopment of the core city.

II

It is evident that for the successful solution of Metropolitan problems it is essential to have some form of programme, as comprehensive as possible. The progressive deterioration in the condition of the cities is largely due to the fact that in the past there was too little thought for the needs of the future, or for the practical steps that would have to be taken.

The first exercise is to establish the area to be included in the programme. We may take it that the basic objective is to achieve an agreeable and safe atmosphere, clean,

healthy and pleasing for all who participate in the life of
the city. But this fundamental objective needs to be
broken down into the needs of different groups. For the
residents there must be provided the essential community services, including security, health and a broad range
of educational facilities, probably up to senior technical
standards, so that a full range of training is locally
available (in respect of universities, which will be
planned to serve a large 'catchment area' a small town
rather than a Metro area may well be a better location).
Further, there needs to be available provision for leisure
occupations, and general ease of access, especially means
of mass transport. Above all (and this is the most difficult
to achieve) there should be a sufficiency of low cost
accommodation to eliminate over-crowding or shanty
settlements.

The *commuters* are full daytime citizens, and it is
important that they should be made to feel so, for
potentially they can contribute much to the life of the
city. Their special need is for easy access (if possible by
public transport) to their place of work. Security is of
special interest to commuters (it has been demonstrated
in the U.S.A. that the demand for increased police
services is closely correlated with the increase in the
proportion of the labour force which lives outside the
city). Closely related to this is the question of how to
make the commuters pay for the services provided for
them (we must return later to this point).

In certain Metros the *contact* population has a special
significance. They visit the city only for particular
purposes, but for them these purposes are of great
importance. What they need above all are good parking
facilities at particular, defined points. Tourists, who
increasingly arrive in large coaches, should ideally be
accommodated initially some distance from the centre, to
which they can be conveyed by public transport if
necessary. This, in my view, was an important aspect of
the Rome Plan (prepared in 1962 but not implemented).
The idea was to develop a new commercial area to the
east of the historic city, where most of the autostrade

converge. These points would be linked by a new north/south highway, along which would gradually be developed a series of new high density settlements. By means of these, and a planned new circular road, it would be possible to remove most of the ordinary commercial and business traffic from areas of high historic interest and high income residence (including hotels). The plan is ingenious, but the costs would be enormous, and the difficulties of the necessary public land acquisition (given the powerful interests of the Church and other big landowners) might well be insuperable.

It is clearly desirable for successful planning that the satisfaction of these various demands should be allowed for in a homogeneous area, since they are all closely linked. But there is also another aspect to consider when selecting the administrative area for the Metro. For certain services, especially public utilities, technical and physical constraints have to be taken into account. Improved water supply (which depends on the catchment area), waste disposal, prevention of air pollution, electricity supply and transport – each has its own optimal area for administration and control. To satisfy all these desiderata would require a vast Metro area. The Zone of Paris extends for 50 miles or so from the centre. Hanover's planning area extends far into the country. Similarly, difficulties would be encountered – and have been encountered – in amalgamations even for common planning of such areas as the Dutch conurbation or the San Francisco Bay area.

In attempting to extend Metropolitan areas difficulties quickly accumulate. The first is the number of administrative entities which have to be persuaded to accept the programme. The relatively modest Hackensack Meadowlands project[4] of 28 square miles contained 14 'cities' and two counties; the Zone of Paris has 243 communes. Suspicion among them quickly arises on the fiscal front (after a long battle the head of the Zone of

[4] See below, pp. 65 ff.

Paris organisation resigned, defeated by the impossibility of extracting small contributions from the communes). These experiences suggest that it is better not to attempt to cover the whole contact zone but to be content with a smaller area. For this, the daily commuter range would seem to be appropriate; this will probably include some areas not yet heavily settled, which will give convenient room for replanning. An area of such dimensions should succeed in covering all the night and most of the day population. It is also desirable for the Metro management to have some say in the affairs of the immediately outside areas. Thus the Paris authorities succeeded in moving the Central Market (Halles) out of the city, also establishing two new universities on the periphery. Admittedly a Metro area which included only the commuter zone would be too small for the economical administration of such services as water supply, electricity and waste disposal. It should nevertheless be possible to make an arrangement for co-operative activity with the administrations concerned (such a policy has been successfully carried out by Toronto).

The number of local authorities which should appropriately be included in a Metro area differs greatly from country to country. There is always great difficulty in extending the boundaries of the inner city, which thus becomes one of the included entities (albeit with a somewhat special character). As regards the other entities some at least are likely to exhibit a strong 'national' feeling, depending largely on the legal structure. In the U.S.A., with the general enthusiasm for jurisdictional fragmentation, the average S.M.S.A. (Standard Metropolitan Statistical Area) contains 90 local authorities, but in some areas the number exceeds 1000. In the G.L.C. (Greater London Council) area, in addition to the unique historical 'city', there are 32 London Boroughs. But this relatively moderate number is the result of a very considerable policy of concentration (see below). What can eventually be done to rationalise the situation depends very largely on the level of administration which has been achieved and on the attitude of higher level governments, whether national or, in a federation, state or provincial.

The Toronto Metropolitan area (which corresponds very closely to the daily commuter zone, plus a little room to manoeuvre, as suggested above) has received much encouragement and friendly co-operation from the Province of Ontario. Initially, 13 jurisdictions were included, but after ten years of generally acceptable administration the Council wished to reduce the number to 4 in order to secure a more coherent policy. After much wrangling a compromise at 6 was promoted by Ontario; but this is probably not the last word. Similarly, when it became imperative to enlarge the area of the London County Council (established in the nineteenth century), the national government decided to include all closely built-up areas. Some of these had been part of the surrounding counties (Middlesex, Hertford, Essex and Surrey), who were very reluctant to lose a useful tax base. Some authorities even had to sacrifice their status as 'boroughs'. The desired rationalisation was only achieved in the face of strong and even passionate opposition.

One of the chief difficulties in the U.S.A. is that few of the states are disposed to take the initiative, and still fewer are prepared to co-operate actively in the consolidation of jurisdictions. Some of them have, indeed, passed legislation which would not prevent the process, but it is very rarely that they would be prepared to face strong local opposition. In many areas also, zoning regulations and statutes make it impossible to proceed. The most that can be hoped for is a union of a city and the county within which it lies. A successful example of this is Nashville, Tennesee, where a true Metro area has been established in the sense that a centralised administration has been set up by statute. The co-operation of the State Assembly was obtained by representing that consolidation was of purely local significance; in fact it was very important for the state. The initiative for this exercise came essentially from interests in the city. We shall examine this and other American experience more fully in the next chapter.

A reduction in the number of jurisdictions is desirable not only for the administrative economies which it facilitates (although they are quite important), but also because in larger areas there is some automatic spreading of tax burdens between rich and poor areas. Nevertheless, some disparity is likely to remain and it may be necessary in the common interest to make a further direct contribution. In London, as long ago as the last century the L.C.C. operated a 'Metropolitan Common Poor Fund', and since public assistance was the heaviest item of local expenditure this produced a certain degree of equalisation. In the U.S.A. the two most serious obstacles to urban reform are still the fragmentation of jurisdictions, and the persistence of inter-city disparities of wealth.

An alternative policy, which today has considerable support in the U.S.A., is the establishment of Special Commissions or Councils which can circumvent the worst evils of fragmentation, especially in the fields of education and road policy. The implementation of this policy encounters few obstacles, more especially because some local authorities see in the Special Commissions a reinsurance against any future pressure for outright consolidation, although they are prepared at least for area-wide planning on a partial, functional basis. A number of states have succeeded in consolidating School Districts by means of subsidy manipulation, but this is not possible for other services. In another part of the world, Melbourne (Victoria State) has succeeded in establishing a Metro Council for Water and Sewerage, which operates over the entire area; but it has no further common services.

Undoubtedly Special Commissions can secure good development in their particular fields, and achieve at least a temporary rationalisation in some directions. But they are no substitute for a comprehensive policy which will take all interests into account together. Sooner or later there will be a need for a confrontation of all the aspects of urban reform, and for their integration. Even the most effective policy of functional development may turn out to be a case of the good being the enemy of the best. The Toronto Metro gained an initial success by the reform of the chaotic transport situation, which was regarded as essential by everybody. But troubles began to appear over policy proposals for the extension of social services, especially low-income housing. If the Metro Council had not already established a good reputation, these might conceivably have been fatal to its future. This particular policy seems now to have been accepted, but (as hinted above) the Metro still feels the need of greater concentration to control the separatism of certain local interests. This, no doubt, is partly due to its method of election (see below).

A comprehensive plan calls for the establishment of some form of organisation which has reference to the whole metropolitan area, preferably a single Council for a designated area. Such an authority can take various forms: a strictly unitary council, or a 'federal' assembly, in which the various components retain their identity and can exercise a certain amount of legal and fiscal independence. The method of election to be adopted is closely related to this question. In a unitary council, clearly all the members will be elected directly to represent the entire area. In a federal council the members may be elected to represent their own particular area in the first place. This is the method which has been adopted in Toronto, but in Winnipeg (the second Canadian Metro) the Council is directly elected, as also is the G.L.C. The advantage of the direct method is probably a greater unity in the policy of the Council (apart from party differences); but as a consequence the individual entities may feel that their interests are being betrayed. Under a system of indirect election, on the other hand, there is a danger that the members may put the interests of their own localities above those of the whole Metro. The experiences of the Canadian Metros provide interesting examples of the interaction of these cross-currents.

It is clear that the decision concerning the type of Metropolitan authority which is to be established bristles with difficulties. In principle a unitary authority is likely to be the most efficient, but to administer a really large city a really high-calibre body of able and experienced civil servants is required. In many countries these simply do not exist. Further, it is possible that one (or more) of the entities which are to be absorbed is of an exceptional nature which does not fit in with the rest of the area. (An example is the Polish colony of St Boniface in Winnipeg.) Special arrangements may have to be made for such an area, but this gives rise to a danger of delaying the redevelopment of the whole. In London the government of the L.C.C. was strongly centralised and its 'Metropolitan Boroughs' were hardly more than shadows. But the 'London Boroughs' of the G.L.C. have been given rather more powers and duties (especially in regard to planning). This is in part a compensation for the semi-independent position which some of them (formerly 'county boroughs') have been forced to abandon. (In the six new British Metropolitan Counties which began to operate in April 1974, the Metropolitan Districts would seem to have been endowed with a substantially larger degree of independence.)

The first aspect in planning a Metropolitan area will probably be the infrastructure of the whole area. This is fundamentally an exercise in urban land use. It is essential to know, on the one hand the physical and technical characteristics of the area to be reformed and developed, and on the other the legal procedure for the acquisition of land and other assets. For this purpose, and also in the interests of the future development of taxation, it is virtually necessary to have an expert valuation of the whole area. The science of urban planning is still only in its infancy. In the U.K., at least, the town planners much prefer to plan an entirely new city than to replan an old one, notwithstanding that the second exercise may well be the more important.

Already in the initial stages it will be necessary to make use of the services of economists and statisticians, above all because the exercise is essentially dynamic. It is essential to make the best possible forecasts of future changes in population (including age structure) and of industrial plans. On the basis of these forecasts the distribution of areas for the allocation of residential, commercial, educational and leisure pursuits, and the implied traffic flows, can be provisionally determined. Naturally the progress of the plan will need careful watching to check the extent to which actual development is following or diverging from the forecast.

It would seem necessary to assemble a mixed team of town planners, including topographical, engineering, demographic, economic and educational experts to formulate the plan. In the first place, it may be useful to concentrate on a relatively short period (say 3–5 years) as an operative plan, but to work out also, for later use, a non-operative plan covering a period up to 20 years or so, which would provide a series of guide lines. (A good example of this procedure is the Plan for Boston and East Massachusetts, described in the next chapter.) The long-term plan will need to be adjusted periodically as the situation develops. A large and advanced city should be able to recruit from among its own staff an adequate group of this sort, but will have need of their continuing services in the different aspects of development. Other Metro areas, which find themselves less favourably placed, will probably find it useful in the first instance to engage a firm of professional consultants; but they would do well to arrange that selected members of their own staff should, from the first, cooperate actively with the specialists in order to learn the job.

It would take us too far afield to discuss the mechanics of Plan formation. It is of vital importance that the Metro administration and the consultants should feel that they are working together on their own plan, and that it is not simply a beautiful scheme imposed from outside. (In the next chapter we shall meet some examples of this mistake being made.) This implies continuity of contact during the whole exercise. Analogously, the consultants will need to be thoroughly familiar with the internal working of the Metro, although naturally not exercising any control over the administration. If the school system is separately organised it is particularly important to bring it into the picture, since the location of schools is intimately connected with other locational decisions, especially housing and streets. Finally, it is essential to obtain the cooperation of the important landlords in the city. Without this, important programmes of renewal may be frustrated, or at least greatly delayed, notwithstanding that there may exist apparently watertight legislation permitting compulsory purchase (use of eminent domain). In the last analysis the development and reorganisation of the city depend on the citizens themselves. Their interest in the complex problem, and their active participation, are vital. There are several possible means of stimulating public interest, such as seminars[5] and meetings, well reported, publicity in the local press of current problems, discussion on the radio and television.

III

We must face the crucial question in urban reform: how is it all to be paid for? In many ways this is the most difficult problem of all. It must be realised that sooner or later very heavy expenditure will be required. It does not make sense to plan only on one side of the balance sheet. Both for an adequate renewal of the core city and inner suburbs, as well as for orderly development of the fringes, there will need to be great outlay on infrastructure – not merely on housing – more especially if heavy immigration is taking place. The dimensions of the relative balance will differ from place to place. This depends first on the extent to which entirely new structures will be required. (To shift the commercial centre of Rome, as proposed, would be extremely costly,

[5] I took part in one such seminar, organised by the Indian Social Institute round the title 'The Challenge of Indian Poverty'. The papers and discussions were well reported in the press and in reviews, and very considerable local interest was aroused.

not only on capital account but also subsequently for maintenance.)

In the second place, deriving from the needs of the physical structure, great differences may be encountered in acquiring the land necessary for realigning streets and making the necessary demolitions and new structures for the purpose. This exercise is capable of encountering endless delays and legal processes; and delay is always costly. In the U.S.A., for instance, it may be difficult to determine the value of the rights and consequently the fiscal obligations of landowners adjacent to the 'improvement'. In the U.K. compulsory purchase must take place at 'a fair market price', and this, too, can cause delay, although in the last analysis the city can obtain the land it needs. The worst situation is when certain well-established interests succeed in rousing powerful political opposition to the Plan, serving their own benefit rather than that of the community. The balance sheet of the infrastructural reform may also differ very greatly from country to country, according to the cost of labour and materials. Figures collected by the O.E.C.D. show that construction costs are lower in the U.K. and in West Germany than in France.[6] Similar differences no doubt occur in the costs of street construction. Even in the most favourable circumstances, infrastructure costs will inevitably be high, and it will be desirable to have substantial recourse to loan finance. This poses three types of problem: (1) the ease or difficulty of obtaining investment finance, (2) the required rate of interest and (3) the effect of debt service on the financial position of the Metro.

At the Metro Conference in Toronto in 1967 it became clear that the problem of obtaining loan finance was the most intractable of all,[7] unless a higher level government was prepared to come forward with aid or provide a subsidy to cover the debt service. In the U.S.S.R., on the

[6] See J. R. Hicks, 'Saving, Investment and Taxation: an International Comparison', *Three Banks Review* (March 1968).

[7] Two striking illustrations of these difficulties are Japan and India, which we shall examine below.

other hand (according to the Report of the Soviet participant), if the Government has initiated or approved a project it will look after all the finance, but if this is not so nothing will be available. In France, since the Paris Plan was a special interest of General de Gaulle, investment finance was never lacking; but this depended on the continuance of the régime.

In the U.S.A., indeed, local bonds for the construction of roads and for school building (although rarely for other purposes) can normally be placed without much difficulty, although some state laws require a referendum before the loan can be launched. The subscribers are usually banks and insurance companies, and interest rates are high. A poor city, whose needs will be specially heavy for cheap finance, will have little chance of obtaining it. In Australia even the largest cities are almost wholly dependent on what they can acquire out of the quota allowed to their respective states by the Australian Loans Board. Their powers of raising local debt are strictly limited by statute.

In the U.K. the G.L.C. has the unique right of promoting a private Act of Parliament to cover its investment needs every year. This is usually accepted without difficulty. Other cities are subjected to borrowing rules, ultimately to the consent of the relevant central Ministry. In fact, enforcement is not very strict, since the cities have many sources of capital funds (including the use of internal reserves) so that they borrow relatively freely, both at home and in foreign countries, on short term, notwithstanding the height of interest rates. For longer-term loans control is more strict, but is enforced rather through the control of the type of asset to be acquired; the duration of the loan is normally linked to the expected life of the asset. The problem of the inferior position of some localities is largely overcome by the existence of a central Public Works Loans Board, which borrows centrally and transfers funds to local authorities, usually at a concessionary rate of interest.

A further problem concerning loan finance (which we have not space to pursue) concerns the question as to how far it should be sought to finance investment out of current resources rather than to resort to loan. It cannot be denied that recourse to loan finance increases the monetary cost of the development, relatively to the use of current finance, by the amount of the interest that has to be paid. On the other hand, the expected benefits from the investment must be carefully considered. Only a thorough cost/benefit analysis, properly discounted, can show which method is to be preferred in a particular case. One of the great advantages of loan finance (apart from the earlier realisation of the benefits of the investment) is that fluctuations in tax burdens, due to varying annual investment costs, can be fully avoided. By and large projects which are long lasting indicate that loan finance would be preferable. On the other hand, both more modest investments and those which call for regular periodic investment (such as a programme of school building) can be allowed for in the budget, and so need give rise to no fluctuating revenue demands.

Current account finance will be needed principally for the conduct of services and the maintenance of capital assets. For these purposes it is essential to have a firm fiscal base. It is desirable that this should contain as many autonomous sources as possible, so that the city can to a certain degree determine the size of its own budget. The Rome Plan concentrated on land use and population movements. It contained no estimates of costs and how they would be met. For an outlay of about £650 million it was hoped at least to complete slum clearance and the demolition phase. But this seems quite unrealistic. In addition there would be heavy maintenance costs, including those of the new structures. It was hoped that additional funds could be obtained from the tobacco monopoly and taxes on motoring, but this would be most improbable.

It is pretty clear that it is not possible to think up entirely new sources of local revenue. Experience reveals only two or three reliable tax sources for local authorities: a tax on land and buildings (or alternatively on land only, or on a few other categories of property); a tax on local incomes (including profits); and a sales tax. Of the three, a well-administered local income tax (as has been traditional in Sweden, but is now perhaps better represented by the more independent Finnish tax) is considerably the most lucrative and possesses the greatest elasticity of revenue. It is true that the revenue will fluctuate to some extent with the level of economic activity, but since the schedule of the local tax cannot be allowed much to exceed proportionality (lest it interfere with the national progressive tax), the variations will probably not be relevent. But the ambition of emulating the Swedish/Finnish 'Paradise'[8] (as it has been called) is likely to come up against two difficulties. National governments tend to be jealous of their rights over the taxation of income and profits, and are little disposed to share them with any other level of government. Secondly, it must also be reflected that if a national government does not make much of a success of income tax, a local government would be still more unlikely to succeed. This need not imply that it might not succeed with a simple pay roll tax, which could have the advantage of getting most of the commuters into the tax net. Otherwise they can only be got at through parking charges or a local sales tax.

Sales taxes (including taxes on factors, such as the Value Added Tax) are generally speaking more administratively suitable for a higher level of government than purely local. Nevertheless, North American experience shows that they can work well in a large city, especially if it has metropolitan responsibilities. At the same time, the delimitation of the area must always be an obstacle, more especially given the modern tendency to establish shopping centres outside the city. If a successful sales tax is achieved it has the double advantage of elasticity in respect of incomes and of catching the day population. On the other hand, it can be

[8] The happy financial position of the Swedish cities is partly due to the fact that they control important profitable undertakings, especially in timber.

very regressive on low-income families who cannot do
their shopping outside the city.

In principle, the implementation of a tax on land and
buildings should always be possible for a local
government. In fact some form of it is the base of local
taxation in most countries of the world.[9] The base may
either be the capital value of the property, as in North
America, or the annual (rental) value, as in the U.K. and a
number of other countries in the British Commonwealth.
Generally speaking, the capital value base is preferable.
It implies a valuation of the capital, or of the selling
price. The capital value base gives a more elastic revenue
than does the annual value base, since if valuations are
carried out correctly they will rise *pari passu* with land
prices. In this way, to a certain extent capital gains will
be taxed as they arise. This should operate as a brake on
land prices, although it would be impossible to eliminate
rising land values (which have many causes) by this
means alone. When the rental value base is used it is only
possible to raise the tax base when a new rent contract is
drawn up, and the incidence of this occurrence will be
quite fortuitous.

The difficulty with all taxes of this sort is that they
require regular revaluations. The valuation process is
costly, and calls for experts. In principle it is a great
advantage to a local authority if a higher-level
government can be induced to undertake the exercise, so
long as it has a genuine interest in local affairs. In the
U.K. valuation for the 'local rate' (occupation tax) was
transferred from local to central responsibility very soon
after the end of World War II, but, for want of national
interest in local affairs on the one hand and heavy
preoccupations of the Treasury on the other, the result
has not been a success. In other circumstances the result
might be quite different. In the U.S.A. some states have
taken over the function of valuation for the local property

[9] On all this there is an immense literature. For a consideration of
the problems attending the introduction of such a tax, see my
Development from Below (O.U.P., reprinted 1971) and *Development
Finance, Planning and Control* (O.U.P., 1965).

tax with very happy results. If there are no public sector
experts available for a first valuation for a property tax,
probably the best solution is to engage a team of valuers
from the private sector, who will have great experience in
real estate valuations for such purposes as sale and
amalgamation.[10] They can be pledged to assist in the
training of local valuers for future occasions; but
valuation is essentially a matter of experience as much as
of learning, and this inevitably takes time.[11]

In a sense it does not matter too much what base is
chosen for the local tax on land and buildings. It is far
more important that a viable base should be finely
chosen, that valuations should be objective and regular,
and tax collected promptly without corruption or
favouritism.

But no matter how efficient the local tax may be, it
cannot be expected that the revenue will cover more than
60–70 per cent of the Metro area's needs. Hence it will be
necessary to arrange for a substantial transfer of funds
from a higher-level government, probably as an aid to
current account expenditure, certainly for urban regeneration. Much depends on the range of services for which
the city has financial responsibility, especially in relation
to education, public health and public assistance. Hence
it is not possible to lay down a norm concerning the
desirable extent of financial aid, although in particular
circumstances a good deal can be said.

For our purposes we can broadly divide grants into
two classes: (1) those to which no strings attach, so that
the local authority can make what use it pleases of the
funds (block or unallocated); and (2) specific aid to be
spent only for particular purposes (in U.S. terminology,
'categorical' or 'matching' grants). Both types of grant
have their uses, and they can very well be combined into
a rational structure. The grant without strings (unallo-

[10] I have seen this course followed in Freetown, Sierra Leone, with
very good results.

[11] In 1958 Nairobi possessed a uniquely experienced officer who
could determine at sight the value of a development with
extraordinary accuracy.

cated) goes some way to cover the disparity between needs and resources which afflicts all lower-level governments. Unallocated grants easily lend themselves to a system of redistribution in favour of poor areas. Their effectiveness depends on the spending propensity of the local entity and on the citizens' desire for public goods and services.

A specific grant has (or should have) the nature of a carrot-and-stick. Normally it is arranged to cover a determinate part of the expected cost of a service or project, subject to the conditions laid down by the grant-giving authority. These conditions may be of varying types: for instance, an obligation on the local authority to 'match' them out of their own money to a defined proportion, or to undertake an investment complementary to that for which the grant is awarded. Thus the grant given by the Australian Commonwealth Government to the state of Queensland to build a railway connecting a new mining area with the coast was conditional on the state government providing the port installations. The grant-giving authority may also insist on selecting at least the top executive.

From the point of view of getting things done, a specific grant is the more useful variety; but it has its own limitations. It tends to distort the budgets of the grant-receiving authorities in favour of certain services (and hence against others). Thus their freedom of choice is restricted.[12] If the conditions imposed are severe, unless they are geared in a redistributive manner, specific grants discriminate against poor authorities. Only rich cities can afford to take full advantage of them. Without proceeding further it is obvious that the policy opportunities offered by a judiciously selected grant system can be of very great importance both for urban regeneration and for the general development of city life.

Almost as important as the type of grants is their timing. In order to plan their budgets sensibly, city

[12] For this reason the Shoup Mission's Report on Japanese Taxation, 1949, recommended that specific grants should not exceed 18 per cent of the total.

governments need to know in advance – say, for three
years – what will be coming to them by way of aid and on
what terms. Once the assistance is firmly committed,
planning the budget within their means is the
unquestioned responsibility of the grant-aided governments. They must learn to realise that nothing more will
be coming to them, except in circumstances of
unforeseeable local disaster. It is implied, however, that
in addition to their local taxes and other revenue sources
fully exploited, grant aid will be of sufficient dimensions
to enable the city to balance its current account budget.
A great responsibility is thus placed on the city budgetary process. Our final task must consequently be to
discuss briefly the significance of budgeting for urban
reform.

Budgetary sanction at the city level will differ
substantially according to the legal and constitutional
basis of local government. Broadly there would seem to
be two main methods. Either the city itself is responsible
for the budget size and structure, and after discussion
accepts it for implementation without further references.
Or, alternatively, after the budget is drawn up it must be
submitted to a superior officer (prefect or provincial
administrator, usually on the national government cadre)
for approval and perhaps modification. Within these two
broad categories there are naturally many varieties.
Where budget-making is a purely local process, there
may (and should) be a specific Finance Commission or
Committee to co-ordinate (and no doubt prune) the
estimates of different departments. At the top there has to
be one officer who is ultimately responsible for the
whole, be he called Chief Executive, Commissioner or
City Treasurer. Where the budget is subject to review by a
national government officer (or a state government officer
in a federation), there may be substantial differences in the
degree of censorship which is in fact exercised. The
essential point remains, however, that the budget is not
wholly the responsibility of the city. If the process of
review at the higher level should suddenly be tightened
up there is nothing that the city can do about it.

In spite of these differences in the machinery of budgetary control, the actual process of budgetary planning can be very broadly similar, and it is this, rather than the legal framework, which is our concern here. The initial steps will no doubt take place within the departments, in discussions between the relevant Committee or Commission and its technical officers. While each Department will naturally try to make itself as important as possible in order to draw a good share of the available funds, its planning must be subject to the general policy of the city government. This in turn will be subject not only to local political and economic pressures but also to the policy pressures of the national government, both directly, and also indirectly through the inducements offered by way of grant or subsidy. These forces also operate strongly where there is no prefectorial system, so that 'autonomous' city budgets are not by any means completely independent. In the U.K., where in spite of large grants local budgetary choice is not much distorted, substantial influence is nevertheless exerted by ministries on the investment side (especially school building and low-income housing). In the U.S.A. the grant system is less developed, but the 'annual pilgrimage of mayors to the State Capitol, to appeal to the Governor and Legislature', is a normal sight.[13]

The traditional city budget, like the traditional national budget, is a strictly annual account, drawn up subjectively by inputs: so much for wages and salaries, purchase of materials, contractual services and so on. In fact, this type of budget is an essential foundation for a proper system of financial planning and control. It is a record of accountability or stewardship, without which there can be no accurate check. But it is only the beginning of modern budgeting. It can be improved upon in the first place, while still keeping to a financial record by inputs, by rearranging the items, breaking them down, or amalgamating them where appropriate,

[13] A. K. Campbell (ed.), *The States and the Urban Crisis* (Englewood Cliffs, N.J., 1970) p. 52.

into a functional account. It should then be possible to determine, by means of what the Americans call 'cross walks', the cost of the whole of a particular service. For some services convenient 'units' can be identified (for instance the running costs of a hospital expressed as 'patient bed nights'). These can then be compared until standard costs are seen to emerge. Deviations from these will then provide material for relative checks.

Local budgetary reform can indeed be carried still further, although with some difficulty, by concentrating on outputs rather than on inputs ('performance budgeting'), and by grouping the individual items under large objectives (provision for transport, provision for leisure, and so on). This is known as 'programme budgeting'. It requires that the objectives should be frequently questioned and if necessary revised. These further developments relate directly to the science of Management as it has been developed in the U.S.A. Its applicability to the Public Sector has only recently been appreciated.

In respect of control, such innovations are no substitute for the traditional annual budget, representing the physical cycle of the year, the accounting period of business, and so on. But alone this is not enough. In only a very limited sense is the budget truly an annual exercise; it is only a cut-off of a continuous process. Naturally, all future developments cannot be foreseen, but it should be possible to estimate reasonably the volume of incomings and outgoings for a period of, say, three years. Such forecasts are necessary for the rational construction of the current account. For certain services it should be possible not merely to draw up a programme, but to construct a hypothetical balance for a longer future period: for example, for costs of education, street works and buildings. The more this can be achieved, the more reliable and rational will be the annual exercise. These long-period forecasts will no doubt require periodic adjustment, but they are not therefore less useful, more particularly because they will stimulate the citizens to think in terms of the long-period destiny of their city.

3 Experiments in Metropolitan Areas

From what we have already seen it would appear that the most practicable administrative and jurisdictional reform to enable a large city to meet the problems of the modern world would be to establish a 'Metro area' to include the settlements closely related to the city. The need is that there should be a common plan, or policy, which would enable the whole area to be developed (and redeveloped) into a more or less integrated, rational and equitable entity. The present chapter attempts a brief review of the efforts which have been made or planned for this purpose in different parts of the world. This review is by no means intended as a catalogue or complete list of such efforts. Its objective is to emphasise developments of particular international interest in the first place, and secondly to consider the obstacles which have been encountered in attempting to implement a policy of this nature.

Before proceeding, it will be useful to define a little more closely than we have done so far what is meant by a 'Metro'. Although a Metro may be a very large and populous area (the G.L.C. area is responsible for nearly eight million inhabitants, Tokyo Metropolitan Government for 11·4 million; both of these are official 'Metros'), it should still be essentially a unit of *local* government with a degree of autonomy, of decision making, on both the legislative and financial sides. This would distinguish it from a regional government (which cannot be regarded as local) on the one hand, and from an unorganised conurbation on the other.

How do we define a Metro? No formal definition has yet been put forward, but the following criteria seem to meet the case well. A Metro area consists of communities, connected with a central city by a continuous extension of the urban area (this would not necessarily include all ribbon development). In particular it includes communities where a majority of the population is supported by commuters to the central city or to areas included in its orbit. To satisfy this test 15–20 per cent of the labour force should be commuters. Generally speaking, the functional centre of a Metro is quite obvious and unique; but it may be double centred. When two important cities initially separate (say, London and Westminster) converge with much inter-city commuting, the result should then clearly be treated as a single Metro. There is, however, a more complicated problem (which in England had already emerged in the last quarter of the nineteenth century), when densely settled areas stretching out into suburbia and beyond collide with other cities following the same path, to constitute a vast industrial and residential complex, for instance South Lancashire, the West Riding and the Black Country.

In the 1930s we called these 'conurbations', but little attempt was made to consider their problems except within the confines of the individual boundaries. In the last thirty years the situation has become very much more complicated and it is now realised as a special problem (first formally in the U.K. by the Maud Commission on Local Government Reform, 1968). It seems to me that this phenomenon deserves a special name, as well as special treatment. I would suggest calling this complex an 'impacted area'. Britain is not alone in having to deal with impacted areas, but they first emerged here and probably are still most numerous in this island. Other conspicuous examples are the Ruhr/Essen region of Germany, and north-east France/Belgium around Lille. There are also a few (surprisingly few considering its size) in the U.S.A. Impacted areas are a special problem on their own, and are also a special contemporary interest in Britain due to the establishment of six Metropolitan Counties which started operations in April 1974. But these are only one aspect of the 'urban crisis' which is afflicting virtually all countries in the world.

Two aspects of the problem of metropolitan policy need, I think, to be distinguished. First, there is the problem of the development of the entire area so that as it grows it follows well thought-out lines of economic and social development. This is largely a matter of planning the new suburbia. (It has been said that in the 1970s and 80s the problems of suburbia may well be more important than those of the cities themselves.) Secondly, there is the specific problem of adapting the form of government so as to make it possible to look beyond the bounds of the component units for the benefit of the whole. What the optimum size for the new jurisdictions should be is still a matter for experimentation and the consideration of particular cases. An optimum area for some purposes – say, education or housing – may not be appropriate for other services, such as electricity or water, which work under particular technical constraints. It is unlikely that a haphazard Metro would prove a suitable governmental area, since its effective boundaries are forever shifting outwards (in almost all areas) as population grows. The Americans and Canadians have a statistical device for meeting this problem: the concept of the Standard Metropolitan Statistical Area (S.M.S.A.). (The name is different in Canada but the concept is the same.) The S.M.S.A.'s are redefined as need arises, so are useless for most administrative purposes except that of recording population density.

The first aspect of urban reform is essentially a socio-economic exercise calling for the united efforts of town planners, economists and social anthropologists to advise the government and the citizens. The plan calls for continuous examination and perhaps revision as it becomes more apparent how development is shaping. (It would be inconvenient, however, if major area revisions had to be made at very short intervals.) For the second aspect the problem is to select the jurisdiction which will be the most practical for local and semi-local problems, widely considered. It is desirable to select it so that

it can stand – with no more than minor boundary
adjustments – for a long term of years. The London
County Council area was fixed in 1889 and was only
redrawn and enlarged to become the Greater London
Council in 1964. Perhaps it was not wise to leave it so
long; with modern intensification of urban problems it is
hard to believe that such a long period should be allowed
to elapse without revision. But the origin of many of the
evils with which a modern city has to contend, especially
two of the worst, congestion and pollution, may be well
outside the bounds of any practicable area for local
jurisdiction, and there is little that an individual local
authority can do about it. This suggests that planning
areas should be worked out to include, so far as possible,
the sources of damage caused by others. Even more
importantly the planning area will need to ensure a
rational organisation of population expansion so that
adequate services (housing, education, circulation,
health, security and recreation) can quickly be made
available as areas are developed. One should probably
visualise (as they do very well in Paris) a series of zones
outside the city centre: the urban 'belt' (*couronne*), the
suburban belt and the semi-rural belt. Each of these
zones will have a different rate of expansion, and its own
problems calling for special study. Even within a single
belt, growth will be taking place at different rates due to
geographic, economic or locational differences. Some at
least of these should be forseeable. Within the whole
Metro area thus conceived, the Metro government,
Council, County or whatever it will be called, would be
set, covering the urbanised areas plus a little room to give
flexibility for immediate development – resiting of
streets, open spaces and so on – the actual size of the
Metro government area would (as suggested above) be
drawn essentially for practical administration conveni-
ence.

  If these are broadly the problems of modern
metropolitan areas, and if we may assume that the
solution lies in this direction, it is very relevant to
enquire how the world is tackling them. As suggested

above, it is highly desirable that it should be possible to
establish a Metro council of some sort – so we may set out
from that side of the problem. Its area should be of a
practicable size, not too large (especially to start with) for
efficient management with the personnel available, not
too small to realise the economies of scale administration. As laid down by the Royal Commission on Local
Government in Greater London (Cmnd. 1164 of 1960),
the objective would be to secure 'the active participation
by capable, public spirited people responsible to and in
touch with those who elect them as well as the efficient
performance of professional administrators'. There are
thus three elements: (1) active and sensible electors, (2)
willingness of high calibre citizens to stand for election,
and (3) capable professional administrators to serve the
Council. This may be taken as a good description of the
needs of a Metro council in a mixed economy. It is
interesting to find (as emerged in the Toronto
Conference) that the need for such a government, which
would have substantial local responsibilities and duties,
and which could exercise some powers of independent
decision-making, is recognised also in Soviet-type
countries as an important means of tackling modern
Metro problems. In these countries, presumably, there is
little difficulty in getting such a council established, the
problem would rather be of how freely it could in
practice work. In mixed economies the first hurdle is
likely to be (as we shall discuss) getting the council
established; but we would expect it then to make most of
its own decisions.

London was probably the first city in the world to
develop modern Metro symptoms. The London County
Council was a bold pioneer experiment which lasted
with a good deal of success for nearly eighty years. It was
natural that London government should be organised as
a County (in the English sense rather than the American,
where the counties are very small jurisdictions), since
contemporaneously the whole country was being
mapped out into counties. Apart from a limited number
of large towns which were excised from their jurisdiction

(the County Boroughs), the counties were two-tier authorities containing districts of various sorts arranged in a hierarchical pattern. After ten years of administration London was also given a second tier in the form of 28 Metropolitan Boroughs, but with more limited powers than (at any rate the larger) districts in the rest of the counties. As part of the combined London operation 130 minor authorities and jurisdictions were abolished.

This set-up of a federal, or quasi-federal, two-tier organisation embodying also a general rationalisation of minor jurisdictions seems to have established the pattern for modern metro councils, although these did not begin to appear for some 60 years, and then in North America. In the meantime, the other great British cities continued as before, expanding when they could by absorbing suburban and rural areas on their boundaries. This process was in general strongly opposed by the counties, which objected to the loss of good tax base. It was often also resented by the inhabitants, who preferred the lower taxes of the county to the improved services of the city. But there was no change in the form of city government, which remained strictly unitary. It was not until the 1960s that the extension of the concept of Metro government to some (in fact, two) of the most impacted areas of industrial England was formally suggested by the Royal Commission under Lord Redcliffe-Maud.[1] Under the Conservative government their number was increased to six.[2]

The doyen of modern Metro government is Toronto, established in 1954 to service a population of some 1·7 million. In terms of political theory the Toronto Metro is a 'federation by aggregation' made up of the 13 jurisdictions lying close around Toronto city. In this it differs from the London situation, where the second tier was an artificial creation, largely imposed from above. As is common in federations by aggregation, the individual towns retained a good deal of power in the counsels of

[1] In 1963 a local government Commission had suggested a two-tier Metro for Tyneside, but the idea was not put into effect.

[2] As from April 1974.

the Metro, much more so than do the London units. This divisive tendency in Toronto was, as we saw above, fostered by the adoption of a system of indirect election for the Metro Council. This does not seem seriously to have reduced the efficiency of the Metro government, but it undoubtedly gave trouble, so that it was agreed (after ten years' experience) that a certain amount of amalgamations of units would be desirable.

The second Canadian Metro to be started was in Winnipeg, Manitoba, in 1960. This city has particular difficulties of racial and cultural disparities; these aroused the desire to copy the Toronto experiment, by amalgamating the nineteen municipalities within its orbit into a single Council – a federation, indeed, but drawn more tightly than Toronto and with direct election. After four years' experience some amalgamations were felt to be necessary and the number of units was reduced to thirteen. The comparative ease with which Metros are established in Canada is largely due to the co-operation of their respective Provinces. Ontario has further encouraged the Metro principle in the Niagara peninsula.[3]

In other parts of the world the establishment of Metro councils on the Anglo-Canadian model has been hampered by two opposite causes. Either the national government has been so powerful in relation to local government that the local decision-making power, which needs to be strong in a Metro, may on the contrary be very limited; or, contrariwise, the units are so fragmented and withdrawn within their jurisdictions that they can be brought to co-operate only with the greatest difficulty. Thus in the Netherlands less than 10 per cent of city revenue is fully under local control, and the Chief Executive (Burgomaster) is appointed by the Crown, so that although most parts of Holland are closely inhabited no Metro authority has been established. (Rotterdam is a

[3] See Report of the Commission for the Niagara Region, 1966. Ontario apparently plans to extend the principle to other areas in the Province.

special case, to which we must return later; see below, p. 62.)

In the massive 'District of the Region of Paris', although more than 300 communes still exist, there has been a rationalisation of eight multipurpose authorities at a higher level. Nevertheless, the Paris Organisation is essentially the creation – and largely the creature – of the national government. Indeed, as we have seen, it was especially the child of de Gaulle, who saw to it that it never lacked for investment funds, whatever the state of the market. In point of fact the Paris Zone Council has quite limited powers and duties, mainly concerned with land use, communications and recreation. For these purposes the communes are supposed to make contributions to the Council, an obligation they do not readily accept.

The Japanese experience in Metro organisation is of great interest. With its dense urban population crowded into a seaboard area, from which the terrain makes it difficult to escape, it is inevitable that the urban and metro problems should be matters of urgent concern. Although only one formal Metro has been established (Tokyo Metropolitan Area – T.M.G.) there has been much discussion in other areas, both inside and outside the Tokaido Megalopolis. To T.M.G. is physically attached, but jurisdictionally separated, the city of Yokohama (2·2 million inhabitants) which lies in another Prefecture. Two other giant towns, Osaka and Nagoya (which also form part of the megalopolis) could well qualify for Metro status if it were not for the difficulty of prefectural boundaries. A substantial number of other large cities (at least four are well over one million) which lie outside the megalopolis could also be candidates for wider responsibilities. There have been various attempts (especially on the part of Osaka) at voluntary co-operation where prefectorial boundaries stand in the way of closer integration. (These matters are analysed in considerable detail in the following chapters, so that we need not delay over them here.) But in view of other countries' Metro experiments, two points are worth

noting here. First, T.M.G. is wholly a national
government creation, and has been given the status of a
Prefecture on its own. Thus it is somewhat more
independent than the other large cities. Secondly, in all
other cases the prefectural boundaries are still regarded
as inviolable. These were established at the time of the
Meiji revolution, and although the Mission sent by the
American Occupation Forces after the war distrusted the
power of the Prefects, they were unable to interfere with
boundaries. Thus the establishment of any further Metro
areas in Japan would require very direct action by the
national government, which seems unlikely to be
forthcoming.

A number of interesting efforts to tackle Metro area
problems are those currently being made in the U.S.A. As
is normal in a federation, local government is a state
responsibility; most of the states are indifferent or even
hostile to the plight of the cities and this constitutes a
first hurdle to be overcome if any sort of Metro council is
to be formed. Local government units are everywhere
extremely fragmented, with separate rights enshrined
even for a 'city' of a few hundred households. In some
states, moreover, it is possible for a local government unit
to entrench itself against any attempt to force it into a
Metro council by securing a perpetual Charter, which is
upheld by the courts. Indeed, in some states it is the
hostility of the judiciary which has prevented further
consolidation. State laws requiring a two-thirds majority,
and perhaps a referendum, before any change in status
can be made have also been a serious obstacle. In the
mid-nineteenth century it seems to have been relatively
easy for American cities to expand their jurisdictions by
absorbing their suburbs. This practice seems no longer to
be possible. The only method of imparting some
rationality into Metro area government seems now to be
through agreed amalgamation and the establishment of a
joint government. Only a very few areas have been able
to proceed this far, and that so recently that it cannot yet
be said how successfully the new American Metros will
work. But the fact that it has now been shown that with

persistence an American Metro Council can be established is none the less significant. It may or may not be significant that, up to 1970, the successful areas were mainly in the south.

The simplest method of creating some sort of Metro government in the U.S.A. is by the 'consolidation' of the city and the county where it lies. (The word 'consolidation' is often perferred because it seems to denote a less 'dangerous' change than the establishment of a Metro Council.) The first move of this sort was the union of the chief town and its county (Baton Rouge) in Louisiana in 1947. The union was not, however, thorough; the two communities continued under separate Commissions, although with interlocking 'directorates'. The experiment seems to have been of little practical importance.

The next consolidation is more interesting because it comes nearer than any other to the Anglo-Canadian model; it was that of Dade County/Miami in 1957. There followed after much heart-burning and tribulation, in 1962, the union of Nashville and Davis County in Tennessee. The state seems to have been exceptionally co-operative. It was involved in the plan for about ten years, and in 1953 it actually amended its Constitution so as generally to facilitate consolidations. For the change to have a widespread success, however, greater initiative on the part of local government than has so far been forthcoming would be necessary. The Tennessee judiciary was also helpful, so that the expected mass of litigation did not in fact materialise.

In 1967 Jacksonville and Duval County in Florida decided to throw their fortunes together, after an exceptionally bad experience of local administration in both city and county. The state was anything but helpful. Finally, in 1969, the consolidation movement spread to the north, where the heavily industrialised area of Indianapolis and Marion county managed to agree to come together without the necessity of a referendum. Their new Council is known as UNIGOV, but in fact the union seems to be not very complete, since the two units continue to function independently, even retaining their pre-Metro officers. Although these American examples of getting together are but few, they have been watched with great interest by the rest of the country. If they work out well there may be a greatly accelerated development in the course of the next few years.

The desirability of setting up a 'federal two-tier' Metro council on Anglo-Canadian lines has been much discussed in the U.S.A. but so far the only approach appears to be the Dade County/Miami council mentioned above. The 27 constituent units are retained as a lower tier for matters of local concern; but they are not represented individually on the full Commission. This consolidation was only achieved in the face of considerable opposition by the state of Florida. Florida has retaliated by not allowing the Metro to enjoy the full finances previously accruing to the city and to the county, so that its development has been financially hamstrung from the first.

Observing the extreme difficulties in the U.S.A., at both the state and local levels, of getting round local separatism and building local authorities into viable Metro councils, various ways of bypassing fragmentation have been tried. By far the most popular both with states and with the local authorities has been the setting up of special (single purpose) District Councils for particular services. The economic argument for this policy is that it should be possible to select areas of optimal size for each service, on which basis rapid and efficient development can take place. In respect of certain services, as we have seen, there is a strong case for such a policy, for instance, fuel and power, water supply, conservation and some transport. Only by operating these services over a large area is it possible to control water pollution, especially because some of the worst offenders are local authorities situated upstream. Much the same holds good, although with somewhat less force, for air pollution produced by factories and vehicle exhausts. In the U.S.A. in recent years the Special District policy has become extremely popular. States are in favour of it because it is easy to arrange and raises no awkward political problems. No local government upheaval is caused, no jobs become redundant. For suburban areas the establishment of a few Special Districts is a strong reinsurance against absorption. While Special Districts could be established for social services (education has long had its own school boards, and in fact they have been considerably consolidated), the present enthusiasm is for districts producing goods (hardware) rather than services. These are activities whose efficient functioning is of most interest to the middle-class businessmen who are important in the local scene.

More recently a new use for the Special District plan has been found by some (very well-off and homogeneous) communities in California who are anxious to enjoy more congenial and efficient services than those normally supplied in the area.[4] Realising that their neighbourhoods are too small to attain scale economies in a number of important services, they 'contract' with large specialised producers to provide a certain volume of (say) gas or electricity on terms that can easily be favourable to both parties. These 'contract cities' thus secure for themselves the best of both worlds, irrespective of what happens to anyone else. Local option and service efficiency are combined, and they are safe from consolidation with less 'desirable' communities. Not many countries would be able to provide the space for such settlements, even if they were generally acceptable. Yet the idea of contract supply, which enables small areas to enjoy the economies of scale production, is ingenious. It would seem to be more generally applicable in ways that would not necessarily be politically divisive. It is a question of weighing up the efficiency of some (admittedly important) services against a rational and democratic background of a wide community.

Another country which is making great use of the single purpose district as a means of improving the

[4] See R. L. Bish, *The Public Economy of Metropolitan Areas* (Markham, Chicago, 1971).

efficiency of local services is India,[5] although her reasons
are somewhat different. Neither the Union government
nor the Planning Commission has much faith in the
ability of urban authorities to reform themselves, or even
to spend grants and subsidies efficiently. Consequently,
where national funds are concerned, they much prefer to
channel assistance through an *ad hoc* body. Other
potential lenders, such as the Life Insurance Corporation, take much the same view. The Indian *ad hoc* bodies
have a wider scope than their American counterparts and
so are in greater danger of breaking into and reducing the
range of normal local government responsibilities and
powers. The result of the use of Special Districts in India
has been that the relations of local governments and
higher level governments become more and more
'functional' and vertical rather than horizontal and local.
This is especially true in respect of the national
government through the Planning Commission. A new
sort of fragmentation, between services, is taking place.
This may be dangerous from the point of view of local
government reform. On the other hand, an improvement
in important services may well be a greater boon, in the
short run at least, than a more comprehensive system of
local government.

The use of Special Districts in the U.S.A. is not
dissimilar. The inefficiency of geographical fragmentation for certain services may be reduced, but functional
fragmentation is substituted for locational fragmentation. The various special bodies tend to conduct their
work in watertight compartments, interested only in the
development of their own services. It is difficult for local
government officials to keep an eye on their finances or to
integrate them with general budgetary policy. States also
have tended to ignore the necessity for supervising either
the performance or the finances of the special bodies. In
addition to these difficulties there are two particular
dangers if single-purpose authorities are over-used.
Every reduction in local government responsibilities

[5] See below, p. 210.

lessens the interest of the work and tends to deter potential councillors of high calibre from seeking election. Secondly, comprehensive planning of the Metro area is virtually impossible if a wide spread of services are following their own investment programmes without reference to the location or timing of others.

In view of the great difficulties experienced in many countries of getting local authorities together in a Metro community, but feeling an urgent need for interlocal planning and service operation, in several parts of the world it has been attempted to secure voluntary co-operation among a group of local authorities with a common interest. No doubt there have been many such attempts which have gone unrecorded, but some, at least, have gained considerable notice and are worth brief mention. I will select three,[6] one in the Netherlands, one in Italy and one in California.

(1) Urban areas in the Netherlands frequently run into one another, so that it would seem a simple matter to organise voluntary union. This has only proved possible to a very limited extent. The configuration of the urban area (essentially a large-scale piece of ribbon development) may cause difficulties. Nevertheless, under special legislation Rotterdam has managed to bring together the 23 local authorities in the area concerned with the outlets of the Rhine (and hence sharing many local problems) into the Rijnmond Council, which largely replaces the Provincial Authority. Rijnmond has been given considerable powers of direction concerning such matters as the building of docks and the location of industry, housing and recreational facilities. It can also give directions concerning the construction of roads, waterways and bridges and the control of pollution. If necessary these directions could be turned into instructions; but so far this has not occurred. It is apparent that Rijnmond's powers fall considerably short of those of a comprehensive Metro, but they could be extended by voluntary transfers by the municipalities. While it has undoubtedly

[6] See Miles, 'Metropolitan Problems'.

improved the standard of local government in the Rotterdam area, it has not on the whole been a very effective body.

(2) The city of Milan lies at the heart of a very rapidly industrialising area in north Italy. In every direction factories are springing up, turning farming hamlets into towns and swallowing up good alluvial land. Although Milan is a large city (already over one million in 1936), most of this development is taking place outside the area of the main city, and almost totally without planning. In 1959 an Intermunicipal Plan (I.P.M.) was established by decree for an area of 1,444 sq. kilometres. It contains 136 municipalities, each with its own council. They vary in size from nearly 100,000 inhabitants (Monza) to 400,000. Development has been taking place very rapidly. Between 1957 and 1961 the population of I.P.M. expanded by 825,000. Since then the rate has accelerated. I.P.M. is described as a 'free association' of municipalities in the area. But in spite of much hard work, mainly undertaken by the city of Milan itself, virtually nothing has been accomplished. It is considered locally that voluntary co-operation has more or less completely broken down.

(3) The San Francisco Bay Area is an unofficial designation of the Association of Bay Area Governments (A.B.A.G.). It was organised in 1961 and covers an area of 6980 sq. miles. Of these, 3714 sq. miles are sufficiently heavily built up to qualify as census S.M.S.A.s (San Francisco, Oakland and San Jose). But the whole coastline is effectively urbanised in a species of ribbon development. The population of the Bay Area has been growing rapidly – between 1930 and 1960 it increased from 1·6 million to 3·6 million. Nevertheless, a glance at the map shows that vast stretches of the hinterland are still entirely rural. Jurisdiction is divided among 850 local authorities: there are 91 cities, 9 counties and 8 single purpose multi-county Special Districts; there are also 500 Special Districts of more limited scope and 250 school districts. Above these, but also having a finger in the pie, are the state of California and the Federal

government. Considering that in London close on eight million people are administered by the Greater London Council and its 33 lower-tier London Boroughs, the Bay Area seems to be somewhat overprovided with local authorities, even by American standards.

There has been a certain amount of co-operation between A.B.A.G. authorities, and it is claimed that planning has been much improved as a result of the existence of the organisation. Three counties sponsored a joint rapid-transit system, but the finance of its implementation encountered very heavy weather. There appears to have been no move at all in the direction of consolidation, without which there is no certainty that plans can be implemented.

These examples demonstrate pretty clearly that voluntary co-operation between local authorities is only a weak and difficult method of getting together. Some sort of pressure, or perhaps grant sanctions, from a higher government is necessary unless there is real local enthusiasm and leadership, as there was in the few U.S. areas that broke through all the barriers to form joint Councils. But in the U.S.A., at any rate, there is more to it than that. Although A.B.A.G.'s achievements to date have been small, it has led the way in attempting to think of, and to plan for, the area as a whole. It was not the first in the field of organising groups of councils. New York and Detroit, for instance, had established similar organisations in the 1950s.

The A.B.A.G. experiment is typical of a new and rapidly growing enthusiasm on the part of the American states for promoting local government co-operation under the aegis of new departments. These are known variously as State Departments of Community Affairs, or of Local Affairs, or of Urban Development. In the last few years state after state has started these organisations. They normally consist of a body of officials, representative of the relevant local authorities. Some of them, in fact, seem mainly designed to preserve the *status quo*; but others are keenly aware of the crisis of the cities. Their special concern is with civil disturbance on the one side, and with pollution on the other. Enthusiasm for area planning has been much fanned as a result of the Federal Housing and Urban Development Act, 1965. 'H.U.D.' distributes substantial grants for planning (although none for plan implementation). Indeed, the whole movement should be more accurately described as nationally – rather than state – inspired. The plans which have been or are in the course of being made with H.U.D. assistance are legion. All of them command large resources of specialised workers and equipment. All of them produce stacks of literature, to an extent which (at least initially) staggers those who are supposed to implement them. By way of illustration of what is afoot, we may glance briefly at two of the most interesting of such large sponsored schemes: the New York Urban Development Corporation, and the Hackensack Meadowlands Development Commission of New Jersey.[7]

The Urban Development Corporation of New York was created in 1968 with a nine-member Board. The Chairman had already won a national reputation for his reorganisation work in Boston and New Haven. N.Y.U.D.C. was authorised to raise one billion dollars in revenue bonds. It was anticipated that at least five billions' worth of physical assets would be created. The Corporation was given powers over housing construction, urban renewal and commercial and industrial development. It had authority to override local objections to urban renewal and to disregard zoning regulations. The original intention was to back up the Corporation with two other organisations: one a private enterprise corporation to redevelop blighted areas commercially, the other a Guarantee Fund for the costs incurred in development. In fact neither of these organisations seems to have got off the ground, and throughout the participation of private enterprise has been disappointing.

The N.Y.U.D.C. seems never to have had the courage to use its overriding powers fully. It would certainly

[7] See 'The States and the Urban Crisis' (The American Assembly, Columbia University, 1970).

meet with very great opposition from local government authorities if it were to attempt to do so. In fact it now looks very much as if the Corporation would settle down as an agency for establishing New Towns, something after the British model. For instance, it has announced its intention to develop a new community of 60,000 inhabitants in the northern part of New York State. Exactly in accordance with British experience, it is easier and more congenial to plan a New Town rather than patch up an old one. A virgin site similar to the one of which it is planned to situate Milton Keynes (a very doubtfully wanted city of 250,000 in Buckinghamshire, England) is the town planner's paradise. One can deduce two serious weaknesses of N.Y.U.D.C. First, it was the creature of the State, and never won the co-operation of local government. In fact there was very weak opposition to the Bill creating it while it was being debated. Probably the local authorities felt that they would be able to master its activities. Secondly, it was not dovetailed into the activities of a number of other Development Agencies working in the same area.

No one travelling southwards by train from New York can fail to be deeply shocked by a tract of derelict marshland used as a general dumping ground, not more than five miles west of Manhattan. It is euphemistically named Hackensack Meadowlands. The area was left untouched when all around became heavily urbanised because of the technical difficulty of building on soft boggy land. But modern constructional techniques can readily overcome this obstacle. It is estimated that for an outlay of some $500 million, assets worth many billions could be created. After years of strife and lobbying the New Jersey government succeeded (in January 1969) in getting a bill passed to establish the Hackensack Meadowlands Development Commission, with a mandate to reclaim and develop 28 sq. miles containing 128 local authorities (of which 14 were 'cities'). It was given extensive powers to oversee reclamation and redevelopment building, including housing, construction and roads. It was enjoined to work with the Mayors of the 14 cities. These, however, were given veto rights over particular projects; but the Commission retained overriding powers over any vetoes. A Master Plan is to be prepared, but it is envisaged that this will take years to accomplish. Thus the H.M. Commission is a colossal 'direct action' programme.

This type of approach to Metro problems has two weaknesses, both of which quickly showed themselves. First, it comes into direct conflict with existing authorities, who do not feel the Plan to be in any way 'theirs'. Secondly, the inquiries suggested more action than anyone could handle. Programmes and projects multiplied with bewildering rapidity. Meanwhile, the existing cities and local authorities continued in their old ways, so that the situation further deteriorated. This created a danger of putting the Commission's Reports out of date as soon as they were made. In truth, the sort of research that the Commission was undertaking – and all that it could undertake – only touched the outer crust of the real problems. So long as the 'ground rules' in respect of local monopolies, boundaries, zoning and so on remained unaltered, the roots of the problem could not be reached. States have powers to alter these ground rules; but in view of the attitude of most States to Metro reform this is not likely to happen.

N.Y.U.D.C. and H.M.C. misfired because they could not be integrated with or develop out of the existing local government establishment. A more promising and practical approach was meanwhile being worked out in the Boston area of Massachusetts. The significant difference between the Boston plans and the two large-scale programmes which we have been examining is that it is essentially planning by the people, for the people. Prominent local citizens, chairmen of improvement societies, heads of local government commissions and so on, have all been brought into the work. Participation by the public is earnestly sought and it would seem that the response is good. Perhaps it is only Boston, with its unique traditions, civic pride and fortified by the presence of two of the most famous universities in the U.S.A. (if not in the world), that could do it. It deserves to succeed.

The East Massachusetts Planning Project is a comprehensive land use and development programme covering 152 cities and towns. In 1965 the Metropolitan Area Planning Council was established and immediately brought into the picture, care being taken to demarcate the exact role of each co-operating Agency. The project thus became a two-level planning exercise, (1) for the area designated as Metropolitan Boston (containing 110 cities and towns) and (2) for the surrounding areas of the East Massachusetts region, up to the State borders. It is drawn up in the form of alternative policies, between which the citizens are to choose. It works at two levels, one a long-term planning scheme, up to 1991, the other recommendations for priority implementation within a six year period. Nine special Commissions of Enquiry have been set up,[8] and these record many interviews with specialists in their subjects. The M.A.P.C. Executive Committee numbers 24, but there are over 130 members of the organisation. They are drawn from all over the area and from all walks of life.

From the first the Boston projects had some federal financial assistance, and this was increased after the establishment of H.U.D. But they were able also to draw substantially on local funds. Federal assistance for planning appears to be rather easily available, but it does nothing to assist implementation. In Boston, which has already carried out a substantial renewal programme in the core city, there seems more prospect of a carry through than in many cities.

Metro planning on the grand scale such as we have been discussing is only possible with American money.

[8] (1) Economic Base and Population Study; (2) Open Space and Recreation; (3) Projected Distribution of Families by Income level; (4) Affluence and Mobility (the Motor Car in the Region); (5) Hospital and Health Facilities in E. Mass.; (6) Education Facilities and Land Use in E. Mass.; (7) Residential Renewal in Boston Metro Area; (8) Employment and Manpower Requirements in the Core 1950–1990; (9) Development Opportunities in Metropolitan Boston.

Assistance from international Foundations may, however, also be available for planning outside the States.
One example is the very fine (and very necessary) Plan
which has been made by the Ford Foundation for urban
regeneration in Calcutta, with aid from the Government
of India. As we have seen, a beginning has been made of
implementation. Another fine Plan of international
standing was made for Rome in 1961. The main urgency
for this was the hope of reducing traffic congestion,
which had almost brought movement to a standstill in
the middle of the city. It is a bold piece of work. It plans
fundamentally to move the business and commercial
centre of the city further east, where the autostrade from
almost all quarters would debouch onto a newly
developed area, and be connected by a ring road, thus
greatly reducing through traffic in the city. Some of the
ring has now been completed in spite of a considerable
amount of mismanagement and doubtful financial
transactions. The main plan has been accepted by the
city, but no steps have been taken to implement it. There
is always something to wait for. The finances suggested
by the planners would today be hopelessly inadequate,
and in any case the city finances are perpetually in the
red. Both the Calcutta and the Rome plans are good
pieces of work prepared for situations where they are
urgently needed. The basic trouble is that they are too big
for the resources which could be made available.

It is quite apparent now that the need for urban
improvement is widely recognised through the world.
Dating from about 1968, cities in many countries have
designated planning areas and have started to make
plans: of the 40 cities reporting to the Toronto
Conference, 14 had already done so. Most of the
designated areas covered a much larger stretch of country
than had actually been developed. The two exceptions
were London, where the G.L.C. plans only its own area,
and Toronto, where the external planning area was small
relatively to the size of the Metro. It is interesting that
these are the two cities which had really got down to the
practical details. It appears that the cities which had

designated large planning areas were becoming very conscious of the need for orderly fringe development, but had little hope of establishing a formal Metro council, if indeed they had considered the matter seriously.

Finally, the British situation calls for brief discussion. It is unique in that a comprehensive reform of the local government structure is in course of being carried through and should be in full working order from 1 April 1974.[9] The changes that are being made have emerged from a long series of enquiries by Commissions and Committees,[10] the proposals of the late Labour government and the decisions of the succeeding Heath government. The changes are strictly organisational. Fundamental questions, such as the relations between the public and the private sectors in such matters as the conduct of the social services, or again, between the national government and the local authorities, are either not mentioned or touched upon very lightly. The position in respect of finance for local services, especially of autonomous sources, has so far been left in a very unsatisfactory condition.

The previous structure of local government authorities in England and Wales comprised: (1) the Greater London Council with 32 second-tier London Boroughs and the City of London in the narrow sense, (2) 83 County Boroughs largely independent of the counties within which they lie, (3) 58 Administrative Counties comprising 1,258 second-tier Districts, and (4) some 7,500 Parish Councils with limited (but not altogether negligible) powers and finances. Scotland has four cities and 31 counties comprising 395 towns ('burghs') and Districts.

This structure has been streamlined into a structure of 44 Administrative Counties comprising 406 Districts, plus 6 'Metropolitan' Counties (all in England) compris-

[9] The new Councils were elected in advance, and are being initiated by the old ones. Many of the councillors are continuing.

[10] For further details on British experience, see my 'Metropolitan Areas, a New Problem for Local Government', *Three Banks Revue* (Dec. 1971).

ing 34 Metro Districts. (The G.L.C. organisation is untouched.) Scotland is to have eight Regions comprising 49 Districts. There is provision for Parish or Community Councils in all areas where there is a demand for them; but it is envisaged that these would be considerably larger than those now operating. The most interesting change, from our present point of view, is the provision for six new Metro Counties: for Merseyside, Greater Manchester, South Yorkshire, West Yorkshire, the West Midlands and Tyneside. Between them they cover most of the impacted areas of England. In several ways the task of reform should be easier in Britain than in most countries. In the first place, a considerable amount of jurisdictional consolidation has already taken place. Due to the hierarchical system of local government, it is now possible to reduce the number of authorities as much as is needed. It is indeed noticeable that a number of counties and towns which for decades have strenuously resisted the efforts of Boundary Commissions to force them together, now seem prepared to combine. Perhaps they hope for a freer hand in conducting their affairs if they are part of a fairly large unit. It has been stated that a population of 40,000 would be considered a suitable minimum for a County District.

The urban population explosion is also very much less menacing in the U.K. than elsewhere. The overall population growth rate of the country is one of the lowest in the world. Immigration to British cities is also (as we have seen) very moderate. The main reason for this is that the shrinkage of the agricultural sector and the accompanying exodus from the villages took place well in advance of other countries. A little more can be squeezed out, but not much. Partly resulting from this factor, rural incomes in Britain are only marginally below urban incomes, whereas in most countries they are 50 per cent or less. Thus this cause of incentive to migrate to the towns is less pressing. At the same time, the standard of rural services (at least in the south and Midlands) is so little below that of urban services that a usually potent cause of immigration operates weakly. This is reflected in the apparent drying up of what

seemed a few years ago to be a mass immigration to the
south-east. Good services in rural areas are costly, so that
tax levels tend to be not much lower in rural than in
urban areas. This at least takes the edge off the propensity
of the wealthy to seek country tax havens as they do in
the U.S.A. Thus in both directions the flows are relatively
small. Finally, the administration of large areas has been
much facilitated by the mobility of Councillors and
officers. The non-availability of railway communication
is much less of an obstacle than it used to be.

Another factor which should ease the path of urban
regeneration in Britain is the progress which has already
been made in dealing with some of the worst evils of city
life, especially pollution. The Thames has been so
successfully purified that the fish have come back. The
worst fog centres, such as London, Manchester and
Sheffield, have been much improved by the decline of
domestic crude coal burning: legislation imposing
'smokeless zones' seems to be acting powerfully. These
improvements, however, are far from complete or
sufficient all over the country. Bad air-pollution from
factories and power stations is only too apparent. Local
authorities are most strictly enjoined not to discharge
untreated sewage into the nearest water, and on the
whole they acquiesce. But by no means all the sewage
works are large enough or technically modern enough to
deal adequately with the ever-increasing problem. Solid
waste disposal also has to catch up with modern habits of
living in flats and the problems of disposal of the in-
destructible plastic packages in which food is now sold.

In one respect the British situation is at least as difficult
as is to be found in other countries: in the mobility of the
population and especially in the twice-daily procession
of commuters. This is perhaps now the biggest cause of
congestion, carrying with it much air pollution from
vehicle exhausts. The other aspect of congestion
requiring immediate attention is, as everywhere,
housing. Given the slow-growing British population this
should not be a major problem, but in fact the long years
of deterioration of houses subject to rent control, and the

obsolescence of many other houses which although
sound are not fitted for modern ways of living, have
turned it into a very urgent matter. Although U.K.
amenity standards are high relative to those of most other
countries, in some of the older industrial areas
waterborne sewerage, indoor toilets or adequate means of
heating water are by no means universal.

Thus a heavy programme of investment faces British as
well as all other urban authorities. Luckily, most of them
have had a good deal of planning experience, some of it
going right back to the 1930s. There are, however, a
number of services on which they could then take
decisions which have now been removed from local
jurisdiction. Electricity, gas, some transport and almost
the whole of the health and hospital services are now
under central control. There is a strong probability that
water, sewerage and waste disposal will also be
transferred to some sort of *ad hoc* authorities. Other
services may well follow. This narrowing of the range of
local responsibility means that less has to be looked after,
but it increases the difficulty of integrated area planning.

The new structure of British local government
deserves a word because it is an effort to deal
comprehensively with a universal problem. The reformed local government system which comes into
operation in 1974 is to consist of a universal structure of
counties and of districts within them. Six (plus London)
will be Metropolitan Counties, 38 will be non-
Metropolitan. The new Metropolitan Counties should
cover all the worst 'impacted' areas. There is one rather
important difference between Metro and non-Metro
counties – in the former, education, libraries and
personal social services are a District responsibility,
elsewhere they are under the County. In both types of
county, planning, including acquisition of land for
planning purposes, development and re-development,
are concurrent responsibilities, just as they are in
London. It seems right that all authorities should have
planning in the forefront of their minds, even although
(as London experience suggests) this can easily lead to a

conflict of interests. The new Metro counties will have to shoulder the responsibility of bringing their whole areas up to G.L.C. standards of integration. It is a heavy, but a challenging opportunity. Metro council planning will presumably be tied to their own areas, as in London. Although it seems as if their areas will be drawn fairly tightly, there should in all of them be considerable stretches of country which are as yet by no means fully developed. In these, development will be under their control. But they will have no external 'planning areas' such as we have seen to be drawn for Metro areas in other countries. When the time arrives for expansion into non-Metro counties this is a question that will have to be looked into.

It would be unrealistic to expect that local government costs will not rise, quite apart from the additional 'setting up' costs that the new system will entail. How is all this to be financed? Even had no reorganisation been suggested, an urgent need already exists to expand the base of local autonomous revenue in order to reduce the heavy dependence of local authorities on grants. (Specifically, for instance, to reduce the central/local ratio of finance from the present around 63 per cent to 50 per cent or under.) Finance was not included in the terms of reference of the Royal Commission, but nevertheless they very wisely devoted a chapter to it. In the course of this they made two very relevant recommendations: first, that the forty-year-old scandal of agricultural de-rating should be ended, and secondly that the reform and expansion of local resources should be considered as a programme, not tax by tax (which merely gives the Treasury the opportunity to emphasise the objections to every plausible innovation). Unfortunately, the Government's suggestions (Cmnd. 4741) *The Future Shape of Local Government Finance,* which were published as a basis for discussion, are the weakest aspect of the whole reform programme. In fact, the sources are discussed (and practically all condemned) piecemeal, and the idea of agricultural re-rating is turned down.

On the publication of the Royal Commission Report

the leading professional societies involved (the Royal Institute of Public Administration and the Institute of Municipal Treasurers and Accountants) lost no time in making detailed investigations into possible additional taxes for local authorities.[11] There are two parts to this discussion: (1) new (or more probably transferred) taxes for local use, and (2) ways in which the local rate might be improved while remaining the backbone of local finance.

On the first aspect discussion centred on three main possibilities: (1) a local income, poll or pay-roll tax, (2) a local sales tax, and (3) the transfer of some part of the motoring taxes (fuel, vehicle licences and driving licences). It had been shown in the 1956 R.I.P.A. Report on *New Sources of Local Revenue* that a local income tax, or *a fortiori* a pay-roll tax, would be perfectly feasible; there are several ways in which it could be administered. Swedish local authorities have always benefited from this source, and confirm that their city finances are in quite a happy state. Quite recently the West German local authorities won from the national government a share in the central income tax. In Britain it is estimated that a local income tax would require no more than a 3 per cent rise in income tax yield to secure the desired reduction in grants, and *a fortiori* a poll or pay-roll tax (which would have a broader base) would bring about the same effect with a smaller rise in tax rates. All of these would spread the burden now falling on householders through the rate. (Although the rate is a tax on the value of occupied property, not on the number or wealth of the occupants, it is frequently, but erroneously, regarded as a tax on the house occupier because it is he who is assessed for the rate.)

Without doubt the best and most immediate way of improving the independence of local finance would be to transfer to local authorities as much as is necessary of the motoring taxes. The largest part of the revenue would naturally be secured from the fuel tax; but British vehicle

---

[11] See U. K. Hicks, 'New Sources of Local Revenue, an Assessment', *Local Government Finance* (May 1969) and A. H. Marshall, 'New Revenue for Local Government', *Fabian Research Series 295* (1971).

licences, and more especially driving licences, are low on many international comparisons and could well be raised. The administrative difficulties of a local sales tax on motor fuel would not be serious. There are about 40,000 outlets for petrol, but Local Authorities already have records of these for the purpose of issuing annual storage licences and permits for additional installations. No single authority would have an unreasonable number of garages to deal with. The increase in the size of local authorities, and the fact that future boundaries will mainly pass through rural areas, should help to reduce avoidance through mobility. The same would be true for a sales tax if it proved feasible.

Thus it cannot reasonably be claimed that the grant ratio in Britain could not fairly easily be reduced to 50 per cent, even if nothing were done to improve the rate. But the rate is in sad need of reform, although hardly in the manner suggested by the Government. What is required is an expansion, not a contraction of rate revenue. This should not fall on commercial or industrial hereditaments. In times of bad trade it is by no means a negligible tax on overheads. In respect of the rate, there are three broad issues to be considered: first, the scope for extending its coverage, secondly the problem of valuation, and thirdly the relative impact of rates on domestic, commercial and industrial premises. The answer to the first is clearly agricultural re-rating. There is no reason why local authorities should go on paying farmers a subsidy of £100 m. a year. If farmers require further help after entering the Common Market (which is by no means certain), it would be better allocated under central control. Even Metro areas would benefit by this change, although obviously not so much as more rural counties. The first valuation would undoubtedly be a substantial exercise; but there would be no need to rush it, so that there would be opportunity to train valuers. In the first instance they could be borrowed from the private sector. There is no reason why later valuations should be difficult.

It must be acknowledged that the first experience of the transfer of valuation for rates to central control, from which so much was hoped, has been a sad failure. One quinquennial valuation was completely slipped, two others have been shoddy and inaccurate. Experience of both local and central valuation strongly suggests that a new method has to be tried in Britain. There is a possibility that the answer could be found in a permanent independent Commission representative of both central and local interests. Its business would be to keep rating and valuation continually under review and to carry out regular and thorough revaluations. This would remove one important reason why rate revenue has not been more satisfactory in recent years.

The main type of rate reform suggested by the Government in Cmnd. 4741 is a further de-rating of the domestic ratepayer, at the expense of commerce and industry. This is a device which has been tried before, with very poor results.[12] It was the considered opinion of the (Allen) Committee on the 'Impact of Rates on Households' that only in exceptional circumstances were rates either a heavy or a very regressive burden. Such special conditions could much more effectively be tackled on the expenditure side. This finding is supported by American research workers (in comparisons with the American Property Tax). Since the Allen Committee reported, the inconvenience of rates has been much eased by arrangements for payment by much smaller, frequent instalments.

There is one other aspect of financial arrangements which especially concerns Metro counties. Successful urban regeneration and expansion will require a large volume of investment. The Government states that it is anxious to make it easier for local authorities to borrow. It is to be hoped that this does not imply an intention to make artificially low interest rates generally available for local government investment whatever the purpose. But the Metro counties are a special case. The G.L.C. possesses the privilege of promoting an annual Bill in Parliament to cover its investment needs. Although in

---

[12] See U. K. Hicks, 'The Valuation Tangle', *Public Administration* (summer, 1954).

fact its Bill is seldom debated, it does give Parliament an opportunity of keeping a watch on the G.L.C.'s capital formation. While clearly it would not be possible for each of the new Metro councils to be given a similar privilege, it would be interesting to explore whether arrangements might not be made for them to promote a joint Bill, either directly, or by a separate Agency on the lines of the Australian Loans Board.

Many details remain to be settled and ends tied up before the new British system of local government can get into its stride; but at last the opportunity is presented for a real modernisation of British local government and its finances. It will be a disaster if the administration falls back on the line of least resistance, merely tinkering with the rate and increasing grants. This is not a party matter. All parties have repeatedly affirmed their belief in strong, lively and independent local authorities. The reduction of the number of local jurisdictions, area revisions and particularly the new plan for Metropolitan Counties now make it possible to modernise the system effectively.

The costs of local government services are rising all over the world. In many countries – as in Britain – there will be heavy 'setting up' costs of new organisations, as well as the inevitable rise in costs of existing services. How is all this to be financed? In most countries an urgent need exists to expand the base of local autonomous revenue. Specifically, (in Britain) it would be a great improvement to reduce the central/local ratio of current finance from its present level. This would substantially increase the freedom of decision-making for local authorities. (In Britain the situation is not quite so serious as the present ratio suggests, because the highest grant-aided areas are rural, due to the fact that there is no local tax on farm land and buildings. It should also be noted that all British local authorities enjoy, in an important sense, complete budgetary freedom within their sphere of activities. There is no Prefect or other revising authority to interfere with their budgeting.)

The backbone of local taxation in almost every country is a tax on the land and buildings in the jurisdiction. It takes principally two forms: (1) On occupancy,[13] and consequently related to rent or annual value (the chief example of this is the British local 'rate'; it is also used in a number of British Commonwealth countries); (2) on ownership, and consequently related to capital value or selling price.[14] This is used in the U.S.A. and Canada, and – with variations – in many other countries. Whatever its form, the local tax on land and buildings is nearly always unpopular. This is especially true in the U.S.A., where the rate tends to be high because the revenue is largely used for financing education. The administration is usually poor, valuation in particular being carried out in a slipshod and irregular manner. Thus the local tax on land and buildings, whatever its nature, is less productive than it should be: it fails to keep pace with rising land prices as it should do (in this respect, a tax on capital values makes a better showing than one on annual values). Nevertheless, there is no doubt that a tax on land and buildings is actually (and still more potentially) a very powerful element in autonomous local tax structures. Moreover, it is especially appropriate for large cities because of their high and rapidly rising land values (to this, of course, there are exceptions where the city is declining).

Even given every plausible increase in local taxes, in most countries there would still be need for grants (subsidies) to local authorities (especially to Metros) from higher level governments. In a unitary country these would naturally come from the national revenue. In a federation the greater part of them would probably come from the states. But is it noticeable that in the U.S.A. in particular, federal aid to local government is

[13] Local Authorities in England have recently obtained permission to rate empty property at 50 per cent of the normal rate.

[14] Some areas tax only the site, or 'unimproved' value. This increases the difficulty of valuation.

increasing very rapidly.[15] Even in Sweden, where the
financial resources of the cities are relatively abundant,
the national government is taking a substantial and
growing share in local finance. Just what form central aid
can best take depends on the constitution of the country
concerned and on its ideology. Some countries value
more highly a policy of increasing efficiency and growth
in the most promising areas; others put more weight on
reducing disparities in wealth and opportunity between
one region and another. To attempt to pursue this
fascinating theme further is beyond our present purpose.

There is one other aspect of financial provision that
especially concerns Metros. More than any other type of
authority they are in urgent need of capital funds for
urban regeneration and expansion. Some part of this
investment finance might come from current budget
surpluses; but given the rigidity of local taxes this is not
likely to be large. A source of investment finance which is
much used by British authorities is the (circumspect)
application of internal reserves which are being
accumulated for such purposes as pensions and sinking
funds. It may be that higher-level governments will be
prepared to give a specific grant to meet the service
charges on loans for a particular purpose. In Britain great
use of this device has been made for the finance of
low-income housing. In Holland also there is a Joint
Municipal Fund, locally managed but increasingly
supported by the national government. This is intended
for current needs. For capital works actual loan finance
will probably be required.

In respect of Metro borrowing two questions arise, the
first concerned with the power (authority) to borrow, the
second with the choice of the means to be used. In this
field also the situation may vary greatly according to the
constitution and circumstances. It is a subject on which it
is particularly difficult to get precise details. In some
federations the national government or the states do the

[15] By recent legislation the National Road Fund in the U.S. may
now be applied to assist Road Boards with buses and other
equipment.

borrowing and parcel out the proceeds among the local
authorities (this is the situation in Australia, India and
Nigeria). In Australia external borrowing is looked after
by the Loans Council, on which the state and
Commonwealth governments are all represented. Little
but contractor credit for municipal projects remains
outside the system. Nigeria also makes large use of
contractor credit, but more for industry than for
municipal purposes. There are also possibilities of loans
from international agencies, particularly the World Bank.
Indian Metros also have hopes of borrowing from the
World Bank for specific projects.[16] Virtually all their
internal loans come ultimately from the Reserve Bank of
India, and are made to the states in the first instance. But
the (nationalised) Life Insurance Corporation is also
becoming a large lender to the cities for investment in
such things as public utilities, infrastructure and
housing. On the European continent, especially in
Germany, funds come principally from savings banks.
This is part of a long tradition. In addition the
Bundesbank may itself come to the rescue, as it did for
the completion of the Frankfurt subway. A number of
countries have established specialised institutions for
local credit.

In the U.S.A. the decision to borrow is within the
powers of the cities themselves, but a number of the
states require a two-thirds majority by referendum for the
transaction to take place. Once this majority has been
obtained it is normal to make a specific bond issue for the
project. Most of the scrip is usually taken up by local
banks and businesses. Stock exchange loans can also be
floated, and for Canadian cities a bond issue on the New
York stock exchange is resorted to not infrequently. In
Britain the G.L.C. has the unique privilege of promoting
a private Bill in Parliament to cover its needs (which are
always very large). The combined needs of the six new
Metros will also be large, since together they cover a
population which cannot be far short of London's eight

---

[16] For further details, see below, pp. 201–13.

million. Moreover, London (or the G.L.C. area) is losing
population and the provincial Metros are expanding. It
may prove desirable to make some special provision for
them also.

The general rule for British local authorities who wish
to borrow is that they must first obtain permission from
the ministry responsible. At one time the large British
cities regularly borrowed on the London stock exchange;
but since it became national policy to control the capital
market by means of queuing, in the interests of the
balance of payments, this source of funds has virtually
dried up. An alternative for long-term loans is the Public
Works Loans Board. This is a national organisation
which borrows (indirectly) on the London market and
re-lends to local authorities at rates determined by the
national government. According to current public policy
these may be either concessionary, when an expansion of
local investment is desired, or in accordance with rates
ruling in the market. (The former has tended to be the
policy of the Labour Party and the latter of the
Conservatives.) For short-term borrowing – other than
temporary cover, which is supplied by the banks – cities
have in the past made considerable use of local mortgage
bonds. These were popular with the local public and
certainly enhanced local pride. For a time this method of
borrowing was removed by the Labour government,
which wanted to keep all local borrowing in its own
hands. More recently it has not only been restored, but in
practice local authorities can now borrow rather freely on
short bonds or mortgages. This they do not only from the
general public in England, but also on the Continent.
These funds are mainly intended for investment in local
service infrastructure, and from the nature of the capital
formation they are not likely to be self-financing.
Considering the high interest rates which have been
ruling, there is some danger that a heavy debt service
problem may be accumulating, almost unnoticed.

The above somewhat sketchy account of methods of
raising investment finance open to Metros in different
parts of the world can do no more than indicate the

magnitude of the problem. It calls urgently for thorough investigation.[17] Without adequate capital formation the crying need of the great cities for modernisation can never be met.

[17] For a useful account of conditions in the U.S., see L. Moak, 'The Administration of Local Government Debt', *1970 Municipal Finance Officers Association*.

Part II – Japan

4 The Background*

In Japan the situation of the great cities is uniquely difficult for a number of reasons. In the first place they have exceptionally large populations, even exceeding the Indian cities. Tokyo, the largest city in the world, has 11·4 million inhabitants. Seven Japanese cities each have more than one million inhabitants, apart from a daily influx of commuters. (In Osaka the net day population is 3·85 million compared with a night population of 2·98 million, a net influx of 29·4 per cent.[1]) The most intractable Japanese problems are concentrated in the three giant cities of Tokyo, Osaka and Nagoya, and it is mainly with these that I shall be concerned. The Tokyo figure mentioned above referred to the Metropolitan area, as of September 1970 (the census month). It is doubtless larger now. Completely contiguous with it but politically separated by a prefectural boundary is Yokohama, with a 2·2 million population. Osaka has as yet no formal Metro organisation but in addition to its own population of nearly three million there are 5·3 million in the surrounding areas, who on tests both of propinquity and work belong to the city. Also within a short and almost continuously built up area lies Kobe with 1·29 million

* My special thanks are due to Professor T. Fujii of the University of Nagoya who distributed my questionnaire to the authorities of Tokyo, Osaka and Nagoya and subsequently arranged most fruitful interviews with them. I am most grateful for the excellent and detailed Reports which each city prepared for me, and for the goodwill and patience of the officers in dealing with my many queries.

[1] Commuters may be double counted, especially in Japan where there are few cross communications or ring roads. A worker living in one suburb but working in another must first be an in-commuter on his own line, then change over to another and become an out-commuter.

inhabitants. Nagoya (as of September 1972) had a population of 2,064,000, with in-commuters of over 204,000 and out-commuters of about 70,000. These three giant cities, together with Kobe and Yokohama, and even further built up areas, form the 'Tokaido Metropolis' of almost continuous urbanisation predominantly concentrated along the Pacific coast.

Although the number of their inhabitants is large, the areas of the cities are relatively small, with consequentially high densities. This does not fully appear if one takes the Metropolitan area of Tokyo, for its 11·4 million inhabitants are spread over 2140 sq. km, so that the density is greater, but not so much greater, than that of the Greater London area, with 7·5 million over 1562 sq. km. If however one looks at the inner city of Tokyo (the former city area) which is little more than a quarter of the Metropolitan area (577 sq. km) one finds that it houses three-quarters of the total (8·6 million). There is no 'inner London' for which one can make a similar comparison, but there is surely in London no such concentration as this. The population of *inner* Tokyo is greater than that of New York (7·8 million spread over 830 sq. km) or of Moscow (7·1 million over 875 sq. km). But the concentration of population in Tokyo, as will be seen, is greater than either.

The concentration of population in Osaka is at least as great. Here it is best to look at the proposed Metropolitan area, including the periphery, which as we have seen houses more than eight million people. All these can be brought in, with an extension of area to no more than 1455 sq. km, only two-thirds of the area of Greater Tokyo.

In Nagoya the situation is much easier. Its two million inhabitants live in an area of 325 sq. km – more than half of the area of Central Tokyo for one-quarter of the population. The remaining large cities have still lower densities. Thus the problem towns are those which are crowded together on the Pacific coast, with Kobe just at the eastern corner of the Inland Sea which separates the island of Shikoku from the big island of Honshu.

Outside this area the only town with over one million inhabitants is Kitakushu, an oil town and rapidly growing industrial complex, on the westernmost island. There are also at least two very important shipbuilding cities, Hiroshima and Nagasaki, which have by now fully recovered (at least economically) from their atom-bombing.

These figures in themselves indicate the overcrowding and congestion to which the inhabitants of Japanese cities are exposed. Pollution of air and water is almost inevitable. Many of the inhabitants are recent immigrants from rural areas. Their living conditions, no less than the daily insurge of commuters, point to the dire need for more housing. Densities of this order imply that there can be little room for open spaces within the cities, so that relaxation is difficult. The road to improvement would be very hard going even if there had been a consistent and well thought-out policy and ample funds. Unfortunately neither of these is present. In spite of heroic efforts of a few, and great legislative activity both at the national and local levels, progress so far is pitifully small. In order to ascertain how the situation has become so bad in a country where the G.N.P. has been rising at a steady 10 per cent per annum for more than a decade, it is desirable to note on the one hand the peculiar physical data of the whole region, and on the other the succession of pressures to which city policy has been subjected.

The basic physical situation, which must always be kept in mind, is that in relation to the size of the country with its 100 million inhabitants, the land sufficiently level for general use (whether for residential, manufacturing or commercial development, even apart from agriculture) is extremely limited. It consists virtually of three enclaves carved out of the steep hills by rivers. Each of these contains one of the giant cities (from east to west, Tokyo, Nagoya and Osaka). Generally speaking the hills which surround the enclaves are too steep for anything but hill rice and tree crops (oranges and tea) all of which can be terraced. Building land is so scarce that in places it is necessary to bulldoze a mountain out of the way first. The result of this land scarcity is naturally that land prices are very high.

The building-material situation is also very difficult. Due to the frequency of serious earthquakes it is only really safe to build either very solidly and expensively in concrete (thus most economically in large blocks), or alternatively to erect small, light and flimsy houses. These are still largely made of wood, a commodity in which Japan is rich. These little houses are difficult to keep reasonably warm or cool by modern standards, and are a continual fire hazard themselves. While the housing shortage continues the wooden houses cannot be abandoned, and many more are still being built although they are recognised to be quite outmoded.

Like every other country during its industrialisation period Japan is undergoing a revolutionary exodus from rural to urban areas. This locational revolution is still in full swing, although perhaps at a slightly moderated pace. Simultaneously a demographical revolution is taking place. In the inter-war period the population of Japan grew very fast. (The supposed need for space was an important contributory factor in the Manchukuo adventure.) For a number of reasons after the second war the rate of increase slackened drastically, down to the level of the advanced countries. The main reasons for this extraordinary change seem to have been first the large number of war deaths, secondly alarm at the rate of population increase leading to the legalisation of abortion, and later, the difficulty of rearing children in the appalling housing conditions of the post-war cities. Small families are now almost universal. Added to this (although only to a minor extent consequential upon it) is a startling improvement in the physique of the whole nation, but especially of the rising generation. Food is more varied and in more ample supply, largely due to the increased imports which high export incomes permit.

These demographic changes have had the effect of making the Japanese 'population beehive' almost ovoid. No longer is there any 'splay' in the youngest age groups; while at the other end of life the death rate is now lower than in most advanced countries. This latter change is clearly only temporary, due to the fact that there are as yet few really old people. Economically the most important effect of the demographic change is the concentration of the population in the working age groups (15 to 65) whose percentage is well in excess of that of any other country. On the one hand this ensures an ample supply of manpower to satisfy conditions of high activity without having to import cheap foreign labour as some European countries have found convenient;[2] on the other hand the effect on the structure of consumer demand is to give special weight to the requirements of the 20/30 age group, particularly in respect of housing. They and their young families are eager to escape from traditional ways of living and to set up on their own, on the basis of the small nuclear family. Since their parents remain in the rural areas the traditional extended family organisation is being abandoned.

The stresses and strains falling on urban development in Japan are thus very heavy, so the fact that there have been frequent shifts in policy objectives is perhaps not surprising. The Japanese nation emerged from defeat (a new experience for them) puzzled and confused; but for the time being at least receptive to the new ideas which the American occupying force was urging upon them. The major cities have been devastated by bombing far beyond any European experience. In most of Tokyo it was only possible to exist in dug-outs or bomb-crater ruins.

The American administration lost no time in putting in reforms on the organisational side, both rural and urban. The broad objective of these was to reduce the power of the traditional élite, the land owners and prefectorial Governors, in order to create and strengthen a democratic outlook. The slogan was 'local autonomy'. The Japanese have cause to be very grateful for the land reform carried

---

[2] Nevertheless Japanese firms do 'sublet' processes such as the manufacture of parts for radio to countries with lower costs, e.g. Taiwan.

through with the authority of the occupying force.[3] The
large estates were broken up with the result that
productivity increased dramatically. A beneficial effect of
American policy on the cities is not so clear. In order to
make local government more democratic (after the
American model) three changes were promoted. First, to
reduce what was regarded as the stranglehold of the
Prefectures as agents of the central government, the office
of Governor was made elective. This system was
extended also to the office of Chief Executive, and lower
ranks. Secondly the establishment of larger local
government areas was advised, including some regional
development. The new areas were intended to promote
dispersal from the Pacific seaboard, where concentration
of war (and even pre-war) output had caused great
congestion. It was also hoped to secure greater
equalisation between rich and poor regions. An
important element of this policy was the development of
the northern island Hokaido as a source of temperate-
zone food production. After an initial period of hesitancy
this policy has largely succeeded, and the milk and meat
products from Hokaido have become an important
contribution to improved diet. The policy has been less
successful in Shikoko, the southern island, which
remains largely devoted to simple agriculture and
fishing.

Finally it was planned to deal with the problems of the
heavily developed area by establishing regional organisations for each of the three giant cities. The idea of these
was to promote comprehensive planning, uninhabited by
prefectural boundaries. So far only the Tokyo Metropolitan government has emerged from this policy. With the
status of a Prefecture the Mayor of Tokyo doubles the
role of prefectural governor. But the T.M.G. area is only
of moderate size and no attempt was made to override the
boundary with Kanagawa province where Yokohama
lies. The composition of T.M.G. has some resemblance to
that of the G.L.C., and probably owes something to that

[3] R. P. Dore, *Land Reform in Japan* (O.U.P., 1959).

precedent. The 23 Wards correspond to the inner London boroughs; but the remaining (outer) entities have not been reorganised.

The new local government organisation set up in 1947 reflected in general the ideas of the Mission headed by Professor Carl Shoup of Columbia University,[4] so far as acceptance for them by the Japanese government could be achieved. The 46 Prefectures were confirmed without even boundary changes (apart from T.M.G.). Secondly a handful of major cities were 'designated' with some not negligible responsibilities for managing their own finances. All other local entities were left under the Prefectures; but there were substantial amalgamations of the smallest authorities to enable them to discharge additional duties which might be thrust upon them.

The amalgamation process continued through the early fifties, achieving something like a threefold increase in average size. The principle was that all local entities should be self-supporting (apart from joint projects with the national government, for which tied subsidies would be available). It was expressly laid down that services 'close to the people' should be the responsibility of the minor authorities. In practice the prefectures have shouldered most of the responsibilities for new services, thus contrary to intention gradually extending their functions and influence. In spite of the introduction of the elective principle powerful Governors seem to be re-elected repeatedly, and the Chief Executives tend to be their men. This was probably inevitable, since the prefectural tradition is very deep, and the powers accorded to the local authorities have not been matched with a parallel expansion of autonomous revenue.

In pursuance of the regional plan for the largest cities, an area was suggested for Osaka which would have included Kobe, Kyoto and the industrial complex along the southwest shore of Lake Biwa, possibly also Nara. The implementation of this idea would have raised immense social and political problems, and it is unlikely

[4] Report on Japanese taxation by the Shoup Mission G.H.Q. Supreme Commander for the Allied Powers, Tokyo 1949.

to be pursued. There exists a smaller area consisting of the towns and villages north and east of Osaka city which are socially and economically quite definitely part of its conurbation. Osaka would be happy to include the 5·5 million people concerned in a Metro area; but politically there is little prospect of this being possible. A Conference of the cities of the Osaka conurbated area has however been established. By developing habits of joint working on such matters as land use planning, communications and pollution control the path to closer integration may be becoming clearer. Moreover there are plans for joining with Kobe in the next door Prefecture in a very large scale port and shipbuilding development, for which the coast around Kobe is very suitable.

More recently there seems to have been a considerable reversal of the post-war policy of dispersal. The power of the national government, exercised through the prefectures, has largely been restored at the expense of local autonomy, although this is regretted in some quarters. This seems to be due to a series of events. First, the rural exodus and the invasion of the cities sharply accelerated in the post-war decade. Today the urban population is nearly three times that of the rural, with 45 per cent of all Japanese living in the three great cities. To meet this situation national policy concentrated on a target of 'growth before all'. The easiest way to promote this programme was to build on the foundation of the war-expanded heavy industries especially those which were iron and steel using, including shipbuilding. Apart from shipbuilding (which depended on the deep harbours of Hiroshima and Nagasaki) all the heavies were concentrated on the Pacific seaboard, round Tokyo and Yokohama, thus promoting the very opposite of dispersal.

From the point of view of growth the policy was a brilliant success. From about 1955 output mushroomed and unemployment was avoided. (So many of the urban immigrants had only recently left their home villages that if employment was not immediately available it was easy for them to return to the country.) In addition to the heavy industries light industries were also encouraged. Most of these (cameras, binoculars, radio and television) are labour intensive so that they were particularly appropriate. Large firms, often foreign owned, sprang up especially round Osaka. At the same time small factories, employing ten or less workers, were occupied alongside in producing industrial components as well as on the traditional small scale production of silk, dolls and ceramics. These little 'factories' sprang up in densely settled areas throughout the cities. It is currently estimated that 2000 new 'factories' turn up in Tokyo every year.

Thus due to the expansion of prosperity (especially since 1955) something like the old power which the national government formerly exercised through the prefectures has come back, notwithstanding that the cities have popularly elected Assemblies and an elected Mayor. (The prefectural governors also continue to be elected.) The Tokyo Assembly numbers 126; but it only meets four times a year.[5] The Governor convenes the Assembly and the Chief Executive hands down legislation which is to be passed by it. (Amendments can be made if they do not call for additional finance.) In view of these arrangements it is not surprising that the business of governing and most of the decision making is the work of civil servants. Nevertheless, up to a point, citizen participation is encouraged. The Chief Executive reports half yearly on finance and the state of the budget. Citizen societies exist, and complaints are heard. This seems all to be at an informal level, without the involvement of Assembly men or the Committees of which they are members. So far as formal relations with the national government are concerned an annual financial programme is prepared for the local entities, to be distributed through the Prefectures. This includes an outline of the financial assistance (both current and capital) which is likely to be available from the state. This is especially important for Tokyo where there is

[5] As contrasted with the fortnightly meetings of the Councils of London and New York.

widespread support for a policy of building it up not
only as the national capital of Japan but as a trading
centre for the whole of East Asia.

We must now attempt to assess what sort of cities have
resulted from the 'growth explosion' and its concentration in the great urban areas. In the rush for growth there
has been neither time nor funds available for other
considerations. It is a commonplace that the crisis of the
cities across the world is due to their inability to keep
pace with the population upsurge by providing adequate
basic services: housing, sewerage and water supply, pure
air, health and welfare. But it is safe to say that in no
country in the world have the cities had to face such a
heavy burden as in Japan. There is no question but that
the Japanese public is extremely dissatisfied with its
urban environment, especially in Tokyo. It is worth
looking first at the situation there (although it is echoed
in the other large cities) both because Tokyo is by far the
worst, and because it affects a larger number of people.

T.M.G. publishes a chart of citizens' complaints. The
most recent edition (February 1970) records that the
following services were condemned by 50 per cent of the
citizens: traffic control, playground provision, child
safety and housing conditions. More than 40 per cent
demanded improvement in the fire service, in parks and
parking, in the provision of open spaces, better disaster
shelters and above all control of pollution. 30 per cent
demanded abatement of noise and vibration, specific
earthquake protection and street safety at night. From
what we have already seen of the circumstances of
Japanese cities there is an easy and obvious explanation
to all of these complaints.

It is interesting to observe that the citizens' priorities
for improvement have changed over the years. This may
reflect on the one hand a modicum of improvement in a
service, or on the other the emergence of a still worse
menace. Thus the demand for better housing was most
insistent in 1966 while the revolt against pollution had
hardly started then, but in 1970 pollution was regarded
as the worst evil. Demands for better sewerage were

highest in 1968, but never exceeded one third of the criticisms of pollution, notwithstanding that poor sewerage is a most important cause of much pollution. Demands for better education were extremely modest throughout the period (1966 to 1970). We may perhaps deduce that the Japanese are reasonably satisfied with their education system (which is indeed outstanding), but intermittently they were very dissatisfied with the school buildings.

It is evident that nearly all the causes of dissatisfaction are traceable to congestion, due mainly to the city population and industrial growth since 1955. Having discussed the general situation it will be useful to examine in some detail the most serious problems which Japanese urban administrations face today. These appear to be (1) street provision, traffic circulation and parking, (2) housing, (3) pure water supply and sewerage and (4) air pollution in its various forms.

5 Transport and Housing

The Japanese are excellent road builders, as is evidenced by the entirely new elevated railway which runs at 150 miles an hour from west of Kobe to Tokyo, by a number of express ways into cities and by some magnificent roads to temples and shrines on the tops of mountains. This is all the business of the state, and only indirectly affects the cities, but the national transport policy does add to their difficulties. Policy appears to be to promote rapid transit for passengers on the railways, leaving heavy trucks to go by road. Since even the best of the intercity roads are at most two-lane each way this policy causes great delay. Commuters are forced to use the already fantastically overcrowded suburban railways more than they would desire, although many still prefer to go by car whatever the delay. There was a twentyfold increase in cars on the roads between 1950 and 1965, and there are many more now. By contrast there has only been a 25 per cent increase in public transport over the country as a whole; 20 per cent in Tokyo, 27 per cent in Osaka and 52 per cent in Nagoya (which always seems to manage its affairs better).

The volume of commuters is swollen by the failure to build sufficient reasonably-priced houses within the cities. In Tokyo and Osaka commuting has also been promoted by the existence of special express ways, constructed for the Olympic Games and Expo sites. Many of the best roads are of no commercial significance, being wholly touristic, although it is true that they form a most important weekend escape route for the citizens of cities too crowded to afford the luxury of open spaces. Little attention seems to have been given to economic considerations in planning road works. (For instance the important commercial route between Kyota and Nara seems to have had no adjustment since the advent of the motor car and heavy truck.)

The cities have thus had put upon them an enormous volume of traffic for which they were utterly unprepared, either as regards circulation and control or in respect of parking facilities. Many of the streets are very narrow and twisty, with very small blocks (and thus now with very frequent traffic lights). The division of responsibility for street realignment and improvement between the different levels of government is not clear, so that little has been done, except in a few cities, such as Nagoya, where as a result of extensive bomb damage it has been possible to lay out at least a skeleton of wide modern streets. Osaka on the other hand is particularly unlucky because formerly most of the traffic went by water, on the numerous canals and streams which intersected the city. Street communication was by narrow lanes between them. Many of the waterways have now been filled in; but it has not proved possible to rationalise the streets.

The basic trouble of all the large Japanese cities is however insufficiency of street surface in relation to built up areas. Thus the Tokyo ratio is 12 per cent and that of Osaka 11 per cent (in western cities it is normally of the order of 25–30 per cent). The results of road policy (or lack of consistent policy) are first, waste of time and strain of the daily journey to work, which may require three hours each way in great discomfort; secondly, the inevitable traffic blocks cause additional pollution by keeping car engines running longer than should be necessary; and thirdly, there is a very high accident rate, especially of children, as drivers at last released from the interminable blocks race along the small cluttered-up streets with scant attention to crossings. (It must be borne in mind also that a large percentage of Japanese drivers are new and inexperienced.)

The second aspect of congestion which impinges directly on the urban environment is *housing*. Here again the position of Tokyo is worse than elsewhere. The short-lived drive for dispersal only affected Tokyo in that

it led to the establishment of T.M.G.; but as we have seen
this merely provided a little more room to grow in. The
build up of Tokyo had started with the preparations for
World War II. Most of the war production, both hardware
and administration, was concentrated there. Osaka, the
centre of the old capital district of Kansai, began to lose
both factories and the head offices of firms which moved to
Tokyo. Tokyo's pre-eminence was reinforced in the post-
war years when it became necessary to find employment
for the millions of immigrants. The concept of Tokyo as
a great world capital also added to the congestion.

At the end of the war the Ministry of Reconstruction
estimated that there was a nationwide shortage of 4·2
million houses. In Tokyo 820,000 houses were wholly or
partially destroyed, and an area of 156 sq. km was
desolated. The present residential situation[1] is that 3
million houses, one eighth of the national total, lie in
Tokyo; but the annual production of new houses of all
types is not more than 150,000. (This does not include
the division of existing houses which is increasingly
taking place.) The rate of production of living space does
not keep pace with demand. After the first frenzied
emergency measures (which were singularly ineffective,
no doubt largely for want of experience) a definite
housing policy was promulgated. The new houses would
be well built, the old wooden houses would disappear
and a substantial green belt would enable the inhabitants
of Tokyo still to catch glimpses of Mt Fuji. But these
good intentions were foiled by the new immigration tide
which started from about 1955. There are no real shanty
settlements in Tokyo as there are in Indian cities but no
space is left uncovered. Little wooden houses, or rather
huts, spring up everywhere, hardly a foot away from each
other and often built over the gardens of pre-war houses.
Many are of the flimsiest construction, so that every noise
in the vicinity is audible, and being so close together they
carry an exceptionally great fire risk. The green belt has

---

[1] *Tokyo's Housing Problem* (Tokyo Metropolitan Government,
booklet no. 5, 1972), p. 136.

been virtually nibbled away; but in any case the
perpetual smog would prevent anyone seeing Mt Fuji
from ground level.

As was to be expected land shortage quickly showed
up as a major bottle-neck and construction costs also rose
rapidly.[2] An index of land prices (1955 = 100) had by
1970 risen to an average of 1832 in the six large cities. It
is significant that the greatest rise in land prices was for
industrial construction (1969 = 1869 on 1955) but
residential areas were not much less (1525 on the same
base). Commercial sites on the other hand had risen only
to 915 by 1969. The (national) average cost of building a
typical wooden house had risen to 303 in the same
period, far ahead of the wholesale price index (116). At
the same time the national income per capita had by 1969
risen to 587 on the same basis. A population whose
incomes were rapidly rising could afford – and was
demanding – better accommodation. The difficulty was
to find where it could be built, and at a price to rent or
buy which did not eat up a third or more of family
incomes.

In the early post-war years the national government
was almost wholly responsible for housing policy. This
was true as much in Tokyo as in the less independent
cities. In 1955 a housing plan was launched to relieve a
housing shortage of 2·7 million in ten years. Later this
was abridged to build more smaller houses within five
years. In 1964 hopes were held out that by 1970 it would
be possible to realise 'a house for every family'. This
hope was extended to every province. In 1970 a new plan
was promulgated hoping (although perhaps not expecting) 'to relieve 3·6 million families of their bad housing
by actualising a room for each person'. In every plan great
reliance was placed on private effort and in every case
this was more successful than the government agencies
in getting houses built. The government had established
three agencies to accelerate the supply: (1) the Housing
Loan Corporation, which supplies funds on slightly

[2] Ibid., p. 152.

more favourable terms than the market (5·5 per cent for 18 years, wooden houses, or 35 years for fireproof, individual houses). Loans are also increasingly given for houses to rent if they are of good size and of fireproof construction, but the value of the loans in every case falls far short of the building costs. (2) T.M.G. also supplies loans for individuals and for the Tokyo Housing Corporation, on rather more generous terms. (3) Finally the government Japanese Housing Corporation builds houses in a number of places, with a strong branch in Tokyo. The sites which it controls tend to be rather remote so that although the rents are somewhat lower than those charged by other agencies the demand is somewhat less strong.

In all cases the number of applicants far exceeds the houses on offer. The Tokyo branch of J.H.C. recorded in 1969 the following situation:

TABLE 5.1   Completed Houses by J.H.C. Tokyo, 1969

Size	Number offered	Number of applicants
One 'bed'	609	19,200
Two 'bed'	5,335	79,403
Three or more 'bed'	6,813	79,902

Note: Japanese accommodation is commonly measured by the number of 'mats' in a room, i.e. thin rice-straw mattresses for sleeping.

The types of houses offered were 'Danchi' (very inferior) urban small houses and urban multi-storey flats.

Both the supply of and the demand for housing has substantially changed since the war. The greatest increase in demand (as will be apparent from what has been said above concerning family organisation) is for the very small apartment or single room for single males or young married couples. In pre-war days such people could usually obtain private houses (60 per cent of them did so). A few (4·2 per cent) went into employer-provided houses, and 14 per cent rented accommodation. The remaining 19 per cent had to be content with 'tenement' houses (not fully self-contained and probably without private sanitation), or accepting a room in their employer's house. In 1966–68 only 4·8 per cent obtained private houses: 19·4 per cent were lucky enough to have good houses provided by their firm: 0·6 and 0·3 per cent obtained houses provided by J.H.C. and T.H.C. respectively. 13·1 per cent were able to rent houses, but the remaining 59·2 per cent were forced to use tenement houses.[4]

There are several points of interest in these shifts of demand and supply: first, the extent to which firms have found it essential to provide modern accommodation for their mature staff (most of the occupants of these houses are over 45); secondly the great increase in the need to make use of the worst tenement type of accommodation. The poor performance of the public agencies is also apparent. Several reasons can be adduced for this. In the first place there has been some confusion between the type of accommodation to be supplied by national and local agencies. J.H.C. insists on a minimum income level for its applicants, T.M.G. operating directly has a low maximum, while T.H.C. works somewhere between the two. But in spite of these differing policies between them the public agencies do not cover several important income ranges. Secondly public authorities have had great difficulty in getting hold of suitable building land. (The same is true of private developers, but they are prepared to pay more for it.) The public authorities possess limited rights of Eminent Domain, but they do not extend far enough to be much use, and not much use appears to be made óf them. The result has been a great increase in high rise building (30 per cent of the new houses since 1968 have been of this type) intermingled with little wooden one-storey huts, with little regard for planning either in the centre or on the fringes.

The authors of the T.M.G. Report on housing speak of the 'darkening picture of Tokyo housing'. Fortunately the situation is less gloomy in Osaka and Nagoya, and

[4] Ibid., p. 107.

elsewhere. No doubt this is partly because other cities have not suffered from a build-up as a national centre, and consequent pre-emption of what might have been residential sites for offices and factories. But it would seem that a more single minded policy might also have helped.

Osaka lost 351,000 of its 630,000 houses by war damage. 190,000 were built by the city between the end of the war and 1955; by 1960 the pre-war situation had again been attained; by 1965 there were 750,000 units. Public funds had produced 20–25 per cent of the annual addition. Although private enterprise was reponsible for the lion's share numerically, the quality of private building was poor so that the houses are expected to deteriorate rapidly. A local agency to improve the quality of the city's houses was established in 1951 and in 1961 it became the Osaka Community Housing Corporation. In 1961 also four local laws were promulgated relating respectively to district improvement, land adjustment,[5] urban redevelopment and fireproofing of buildings. (The fire hazard in Osaka seems to be particularly high, probably due to the closely packed houses, with no space for wind breaks.)

Together these measures constituted a fairly comprehensive attack on the housing situation; but as usual the major bottleneck was the shortage of suitable building land. Osaka was slightly better off than Tokyo in that it had some vacant sites where factories had moved out. So far as it could do so (on current account) the city authorities bought them up and prepared them for redevelopment, either by public agencies or by private developers.

A major objective in Osaka was to build low-rent accommodation for low-income families, so that they could live near their jobs. Osaka built its first high rise in 1967 to accommodate 120 households (the building of

[5] 'Land adjustment' is effectively the voluntary exchange or giving up of land by private owners in order to produce useable sites for redevelopment. It has played a considerable role in Tokyo as well as in Osaka.

wooden houses by the city had ceased in 1964). Under
the first of the laws listed above 15 Districts were
designated for improvement, not only in respect of
housing but also for related public works such as school
building and landscaping. Another municipal enterprise
is to assist small firms to provide housing for their
employees; loans are available at 6·5 per cent for 19
years. There is a special subsidy for fireproof buildings
and guidance is offered to builders for this purpose. The
Osaka Housing Corporation is itself providing attractive
modern three-room flats (plus kitchen, bath and good
balcony) for medium-income families. These are
expected fully to cover their costs. The Osaka authorities
have undoubtedly made a most worthy effort to deal with
their housing problem and to improve the environment.[6]

Compared with Tokyo and Osaka, Nagoya has a
relatively easy task; its area is larger and its population
smaller than the other two cities. Moreover it has been
able to make good use of the areas cleared for it by
bombing. There are now a number of wide streets and
some small parks and playgrounds. As usual the main
bottleneck is still land. (Nagoya considers that the state
should take a more active part in securing building land
for cities.) In the meantime Nagoya is pressing on with
purchases of sites vacated by factories moving out of the
city centre. Under a strong Mayor and a co-operative
Prefecture Nagoya has formulated very definite objectives for its housing policy, in a five year plan. By and
large its aims are similar to those of Osaka, with perhaps
a greater emphasis on welfare. Nagoya wishes 'to reorient
thought in connection with the use of city owned
property'.[7]

It is planned to build nearly 24,000 new units of which
15,000 will be for low-income families. Old wooden
houses in the centre are being torn down and replaced by
high rise apartments. In this way already 8500 units have

[6] For further details see 'The City of Osaka and its Administration',
a series of booklets dealing in turn with all its activities.

[7] Interviews and mimeographed information supplied by the
secretariat.

taken the place of the 3000 previously available. Ultimately it is planned to provide a room a head. Although the rooms are still very small, their size is gradually being increased in the newer buildings. Some community facilities are being provided on the basis of a group of 100 units; sufficient schools are also planned for. One point which Nagoya particularly emphasises is that it aims completely to separate industrial from residential areas. (This is very different from the ambivalent attitude of Tokyo.) Nagoya is achieving this objective by developing a large industrial complex to the south of the city along the shore, where the land is marshy and unsuitable for residential purposes. The first five-year plan targets were for 57,000 units (new or remodelled) to be built by public authorities and agencies, and 88,000 by private developers. By 1972 direct city construction had fulfilled its quota and private enterprise was not far behind. Nagoya now plans to increase the output of private sector housing by giving loans at the rate of 75 per cent of cost for groups of 2000 units.

Heartening as are the efforts of some Japanese cities to deal with their housing problems, very much remains to be done. This will become increasingly apparent when we move on to the discussion of pollution. In view both of the high cost of land within the cities and the unpleasant even dangerous atmosphere of the city environment, Tokyo, Osaka and Nagoya are all experimenting with New Towns. This is more strictly a prefectural than a municipal exercise: but co-operation between the two layers of government is normally close. These New Towns are conceived as well balanced communities catering for a spread of income levels, housing tastes and cultural opportunities. But they are pure dormitories (bed towns to the Japanese). It is expected that 70–80 per cent of the families will include daily commuters to the city. It is specifically planned *not* to set up factories or in any way to make the New Towns independent self-contained communities on the lines of British New Towns.

The most advanced of the Japanese New Towns is Senri, 15 km north of Osaka. This will serve as an illustration of the sort of thing at which the Japanese cities are aiming.[8] Senri is situated in wooded hilly country on land adjacent to the 1970 Expo site, from which it derives the advantage of two express railways and two highways. The J.H.C. and the prefectural Housing Organisation have been the most active builders. With the aim of creating a balanced community five different types of houses are offered. A little under a quarter are 'public operated' low income houses; at the other end of the scale one sixth are detatched private homes; about one seventh are company houses. But the typical home is in a medium rise apartment block. Land use has been carefully planned with 24 per cent reserved for parks and green spaces. Roads occupy 22 per cent of the area (thus far above the level of the existing cities) and 23 per cent of the land is for residential use, with a rather higher proportion of flats than houses. All are provided with basic modern amenities including individual water supply and sewerage.

The social and administrative organisation has also been carefully planned. The town is divided into three zones, each with a zone centre, bus terminal, express railway station, a Municipal Branch Office, banks and shopping areas. The zones are subdivided into neighbourhood units (three to five to a zone). These in turn are divided into sections, groups and finally small units of fifty to a hundred households clustered around a children's playground. The maximum planned population has been set at 150,000.

There are long waiting lists for every type of accommodation in Senri. There is no doubt that life there is much more agreeable than in the middle of Osaka. As much as possible of the bamboo thickets and shrubs which formerly covered the Senri hills has been

[8] Visited on 10 November 1972. It is perhaps significant that Tokyo, in a 'glossy' advertising its New Town of Tama (still largely at the drawing board stage) includes a picture of Senri as an indication of things to come.

preserved and there are pleasant walks through the woods. Some of the public buildings are architecturally attractive, but there is not much to be said for the endless rows of blocks of grey medium-rise flats, which seem to be the hallmark of Japanese new building.

Not all the Japanese bed towns are as well planned or as well executed as Senri. There are complaints that the flats are too small: two or even one room, so that they are only practicable for a very small family; this entails a move as the family increases. The flats have been built small to fit the maximum number of households. (New towns are very greedy for space.) Many families would be prepared to pay for better accommodation if it were available. Another trouble is that funds are not always available to execute the whole of an elaborate plan, so that plots are sold off at random to private builders; planning then goes by the board. Roads and railways are already heavily overcrowded. In the background moreover there is always the consideration that if too large a percentage of the population move out into the new towns, only a tiny area of the best land will remain available for cultivation.

6 Pollution and Health Hazards

We come at last to what the inhabitants of Tokyo now regard as the greatest menace: *Pollution* in all its forms. We have to distinguish between water pollution and land subsidence on the one hand and air pollution on the other. Nowhere in the world is air pollution worse than in the Japanese cities, not even in New York and Los Angeles. As usual the situation is at its worst in Tokyo; but it is also very serious in Osaka. Water pollution is also very prevalent but in principle in Japanese conditions (with a good rainfall) it is easier to control. In fact measures dating from the middle sixties have already effected some improvement. Once again the situation is worst in Tokyo. In Osaka it is to some extent mitigated by the smaller size of the conurbation, and by the fact that it has a really big river flowing through it (issuing from Lake Biwa, the largest inland lake in the country). Although this water is to some extent already polluted when it enters Osaka, it does give the place a good scouring. Moreover Osaka has a much firmer policy of segregating residential and industrial property than Tokyo. Hence the big fight against pollution is in Tokyo.[1]

To start with it should be noted that in Japan pollution control is essentially a city responsibility. Since Tokyo itself is equivalent to a prefecture the entire burden falls on T.M.G. The other cities receive some (minor) assistance from the prefectures. In Tokyo the Wards and local entities carry out some minor works, but mainly with funds supplied by T.M.G. (The national government seems to have a suspicion that Tokyo spends too much on

[1] See Report (no. 4) issued by T.M.G., 'Tokyo Fights Pollution'.

Pollution control.) Tokyo also suffers from the fact that it has no means of compelling the local authorities further up its water courses to improve their habits of exporting pollution. (Another city might be able to get some help in this from its prefecture.) Tokyo has endeavoured to get agreements with the polluting exporters; but their prefectorial governments are not prepared to enforce them.

Although in Tokyo air pollution is probably the more serious issue, it will be convenient to start with water pollution as it is the larger subject. In respect of water pollution two aspects in particular need to be discussed: (1) improving the quantity of the available water and (2) improving its quality. An allied problem is that of land subsidence, which in Japan at least, is largely due to withdrawing more water than can be replaced by natural means, thus causing the subsurface layers of soil to become impacted and so tend to shrink. This problem is by no means confined to Japan. For instance it is becoming a menace in some American cities. The two worst victims in the world, Venice and Mexico City, have special causes in addition to the normal situation, but this does not appear to be true in Japan.[2] The basic cause of water pollution is waste disposal, so that it is convenient to discuss at the same time different forms of waste (including solid waste) and their disposal. Indeed one of the most promising methods of solid waste disposal is to liquefy it so far as possible, so that the two processes are closely related.

In many countries the first step to improve the quality of water is to increase its quantity. This is not always easy (for instance in India). But in Japan with its expected rainfall of some 60 inches this should not be difficult. Yet Tokyo has not got a good water supply, and there is no separate system of storm water disposal, so that when bad storms (not infrequently) occur the normal supply is in danger. Tokyo derives its water mainly from

[2] It appears that London and the whole south-east corner of England are also sinking, but very slowly and from natural causes. The trouble in both Venice and Mexico City is that their base is soft and boggy. This is not true in Japan.

three small rivers or streams, the Tama, Sumida and Edo. The upper Tama (which is the base of Tokyo's best New Town) has not yet been polluted although it is at great risk from development. It is still the great recreation centre for Tokyo for all water sports and picnics. The lower reaches are already polluted. Sumida means 'clear' which unfortunately is the last thing it is now. Millions of yen have to be spent annually on dredging, to keep up any sort of flow in the rivers. The Edo (the stream which gave Tokyo its historic name) is embedded in the heart of the old city. All the streams are shallow, with a poor flow, so that they easily silt up. The Tama is slightly better than the others because it has a gravel bottom. The natural supply of usable water is also reduced by factories pumping into Tokyo Bay water which could have been purified. Moreover (as we shall see in a moment) they are actually stealing water from the public supply, thus escaping legal charges.

As regards the quality of the water the trouble largely originates in sheer congestion – of houses and other buildings. The intakes into the streams are so close together that the water has virtually no chance of recovery, especially of its oxygen content. The worst trouble however is due to the near total neglect of a modern water-borne sewerage system. In the 'growth before all' mentality of post-war Japan no attention was given to such matters. According to the latest published figures (1969) in Tokyo city only 34·6 per cent of the population had the advantage of a sewerage system. In fact only 22·1 per cent of the T.M.G. area had been sewered (in the Ward area the coverage was better, 47·7 per cent by population and 40·8 per cent by area) and work is actively in progress. Although this is far from being satisfactory, over the country as a whole the average was no better than 21 per cent.

Water pollution in Tokyo is indeed now very serious. All the water courses are polluted in their lower reaches. T.M.G. has established twenty-one water sampling points.[3] In 1969 the degree of pollution was slight only

[3] 'Tokyo Fights Pollution'.

at two of these points. At sixteen the level of BOD
(Biochemical Oxygen Demand) was 5 ppm or more (the
level at which fish cannot live) while the mean value of
dissolved oxygen (DO) was less than 5 ppm. The sources
of pollution were almost wholly domestic waste and
factory effluent. Ten out of the sixteen sampling points
suffered from both causes: in most of the remainder the
trouble was overwhelmingly untreated domestic sewage.
The special evil of domestic waste is that if forms sludge
on the beds of streams, in which living forms thrive and
consume oxygen. This is especially bad in the Sumida
where the annual dredging exercise costs Y806,000.

Parallel with the decline in the supply of good water
the demand for it is steadily increasing. It is universal
experience that as incomes rise people use more water;
the Japanese public is no exception to this. Moreover the
annual 2000 increase in factories also creates a new
demand for water although many of them are very small
(16 per cent of all factories employ less than 20 workers).
But also the 83,000 factories already established are growing larger and demanding more water. The new residential developments up the Tama river short-circuit some
of the supplies which might otherwise come to central
Tokyo. Residential and industrial developments in the
neighbouring prefectures increase both the demand for
water and the difficulty of pollution control. The inner
city has itself also become a bigger demander of water
as it increasingly takes on the form of a 'management
centre'. The big new blocks of offices and flats need to
provide water-using facilities: central heating, refrigera-
tors, air conditioning, all of which are heavy water users.

On the side of water supply it remains to discuss
briefly the problem of land subsidence. This has evidently been taking place in the Tokyo area for more than 150
years; but has only come to notice fairly recently. The
Press first drew attention to it in 1932 and it is evidently
accelerating. A series of scientific enquiries have endeavoured to identify the causes. To some extent they
were undoubtedly right that a number of physical
phenomena not easily amenable to control were part

causes. The main explanation was only revealed when it was noticed that the rate of subsidence was closely correlated with the level of economic activity. In periods of slump and unemployment practically no subsidence occurred; the higher the level of activity the more rapid the rate of subsidence became. In fact the factories were 'stealing' the community's water by digging wells on their own premises and pumping up whatever they needed, free of charge.

Land subsidence of the order in which it has recently been occurring in Tokyo may have very serious consequences. Especially in a low lying area such as surrounds Tokyo Bay there is a danger of obstruction of the natural drainage, and so of stopping the flow of sewage. Moreover with high tides and strong winds there are serious dangers of flooding. In Tokyo a 'zero meter' area (sea level or below) has been identified. At high tide 117 sq. km is affected. The damage from subsidence depends importantly on the base on which a building is erected: one end of a bridge may break while the other is intact, a building may subside at a faster rate than the road, thus damaging underground mains. Tokyo has worked hard on subsidence problems and there are some results to show. Eight feet high protecting levees have been built in zero meter areas. A water control ordinance was passed in 1956 in an attempt to stop factories from stealing water; but it has only been effectively enforced since 1966, and even now it needs more diligent enforcement. But there has been a marked improvement. Full recovery of the soil level may never be achieved, and in any case it would be very expensive; subsidence is still progressing steadily. Presently we shall discuss methods of increasing the water supply, but a word must first be said concerning waste disposal.

One of the main troubles with the water supply (which is implicit in what has already been said) is the quantity of garbage thrown into the water, thus causing increasingly silting and sludge formation. Parallel to water use the volume of garbage rises as incomes rise, both on domestic and on commercial account. In Tokyo it is estimated that the volume is four times what it was in 1955. It is still very much less than in Western countries. On the basis of T.M.G. = 100 the relatively wealthy Ward area registered 947, compared with New York 2122, Greater London 1038 and Hamburg 1242.[4] As incomes rise not only the quantity but the composition of garbage changes. Between 1964 and 1969 in Tokyo the quantity of paper (the largest item) increased 71 per cent. That of plastics expanded threefold (but is still relatively small). There was also a large increase in food waste, and a rapid rise in industrial waste. There are no restrictions on the emission by factories of ammonia, hydrogen fluoride, cyanide and twenty-eight varieties of gas or aerosol pronounced by law to be noxious. As there are no penalties for these emissions control is impossible.

The cure or even the mitigation of Tokyo's water pollution calls for an extensive and complicated programme. Tokyo's sanitation budget grew from Y19,256 million ($53 million) in 1965 to Y35,020 million ($97 million) in 1970. Of this 56 per cent was the cost of garbage disposal, 23 per cent was for hygiene and 14 per cent for the construction of facilities. The towns and villages in the area also carried out some works for which they were subsidised by T.M.G. Since 1965 a stop-gap remedy of dumping sludge and garbage into Tokyo Bay for a land reclamation scheme has been in use; but there are limits to the volume that can be deposited without badly polluting the bay itself. The final disposal of garbage is everywhere a prefectural responsibility, in order that they can operate over a large area. But this does not help Tokyo. In fact only national action would serve. At present only 49 per cent of Tokyo's garbage is incinerated. There are plans for a number of new plants; but to be efficient they must be large, which makes them unwelcome neighbours in any residential district.

[4] The figures for non-Japanese cities pretend to no great accuracy, but are inserted for comparison. The highest figure for Japan is 1350 for Nagoya, probably a combination of slightly higher incomes and more efficient collection.

In the longer run in respect of water supply it is clear that a great many more sewers and treatment plants will be necessary on the one hand, and on the other a drastic reduction in the number of sewage intakes into streams is essential. It is estimated that in order to get the fish back 50 per cent of the existing intakes need to be abolished. An increasing volume of pure water also needs to be pumped into the streams, both to improve their flow and to help in restoring land subsidence. There is no clear indication of serious consideration as to where the water is to come from. Presumably Tokyo could follow Osaka's example in constructing a number of small multipurpose dams up in the hills, at no great expense.

Difficult as it will be to purify Tokyo's water her problems in respect of air pollution are in a sense more urgent. They are also less easily solvable even in principle. Just as in London and other cities, Tokyo's type of air pollution has changed its character over the last ten years. Formerly (as in London) it was mainly due to the burning of crude coal domestically. This has given way to the use of other fuels. In this respect Tokyo has not been so fortunate as London where solid fuel has been readily available so that with the use of 'smokeless zone' regulations it has been possible virtually to abolish the fogs for which London was once famous (as well as in Manchester, Sheffield and similar bad areas). Tokyo has had little solid fuel available, so has had to concentrate on oil, and unfortunately on sources where the sulphur dioxide content (the source of smog) is particularly high. Due to the winters being colder than those of the U.K. the amount of central heating required is also greater. Thus the smog gets steadily worse.

The explosion of the car population (twentyfold increase between 1950 and 1965 – so much more rapid than in London) implies that the full blast of carbon monoxide from car exhausts falls on the narrow unreformed streets. It is estimated that 90 per cent of Tokyo's air pollution comes from this source. It is an ever shifting community source, so particularly difficult to control. The sulphur dioxide largely derives from factory chimneys many of them in other Prefectures which may have no adequate legislation concerning the minimum compulsory height of chimneys.

The effect of carbon monoxide is quickly dissipated as the distance from the source extends. Wide streets with ample marges are a good protection. In this respect also Tokyo is the victim of its own congestion. Prefectural governors have no power to control motor vehicles. Insistence on better maintenance and the use of less-polluting engines would bring about a substantial improvement; but, as it is, Tokyo can do little beyond petitioning the national government to promulgate more stringent regulations.

Sulphur dioxide on the other hand spreads widely, especially in hot weather, when life in Tokyo is only tolerable out of doors. It has been identified as a chief ingredient of dangerous photo-chemical smog. This condition was first diagnosed in Los Angeles in the 1950s where it was caused by the action of the ultra-violet rays of sunlight on nitrogenous oxides, hydrocarbons from cars and to a lesser extent sulphur dioxide. In Japan sulphur dioxide concentrates are higher than in Los Angeles. There is a special danger when humidity is 50° or more that airborne particulate matter, consisting of olefine hydrocarbon and sulphur dioxide, forms a compound which may lead to the production of sulphuric acid, causing irritation and injury to eyes, throat and chest.

A shattering incident occurred in Tokyo in July 1970 when there were simultaneous alarming complaints of smarting eyes and sore throats from thirteen Wards and eight local authorities. From that time T.M.G. began to study seriously the effects of photo-chemical smog not only on humans but also on animals and vegetation. Osaka had a similar experience a little later, and it is clear that both cities are at risk from this menace to an even greater extent than Los Angeles or New York. It is now widely recognised that the oxidants rising high in the air from car exhausts and the sulphur dioxide from factories are the basic contributors to this state of affairs. This underlines the conclusion that only a comprehensive attack on air pollution at the national level can relieve the situation. Before we examine the steps which are being taken in this direction, a word must be said on another aspect of air pollution which is especially subject to complaint in Japan: noise and vibration.

It is not difficult to divine why noise and vibration (measured in decibels) should be a special trouble in Japan. In Western cities car noise has been greatly reduced by the suppression of horns and by regulations concerning 'mufflers' (to use the appropriate American term) even if they are not always obeyed. In Japan these improvements have not yet been enforced. Secondly, especially in Tokyo, the mixing of residential and factory areas exposes many homes to factory noise, perhaps all round the clock. Although many of the factories are small, they may still be very noisy, since the buildings tend to be flimsy. Thirdly there is a never ending din of construction activity, especially electric drills: houses, factories (those 2000 a year) and road works, all due to the phenomenal growth rate. These works are not even inside a building. There has indeed been some removal of factories away from the inner areas; but this mainly concerns the larger firms. Many of the smaller works cannot afford without subsidisation either to instal less-polluting equipment or to move. What makes things worse is that the great majority of Japanese houses are lightly built. Not only are they not impervious to street noises but it is possible to hear everything the neighbours are doing or saying. Noise is bad at any season but it is worst in summer because of the necessity of outside living, since small wooden houses cannot be kept cool.

Tokyo has a long history of attempts at environmental control through laws dealing with air pollution, water pollution and quality control, and noise, starting with the 1949 Factory Hazard Control Ordinance. Invariably shortly after the laws were passed they became obsolete. Thus there were noise control laws in 1954 and 1968; smoke abatement in 1955, 1962 and 1967, underground water regulation in 1956, 1958 and 1962. 1967 saw a

basic Law for Environmental Control, and was followed
by a consolidating Act the very next year. And so the
battle goes on, with (as we have seen) small gains in some
directions. A more fundamental reform would require
the removal of the basic causes, especially congestion,
and uniform controls in different prefectures. It is likely
that these would have to be nationally enforced.

Tokyo is engaged in fighting pollution on several
fronts. Since the whole cost falls on T.M.G. finances, the
burden is naturally very considerable. A summary table
(below) indicates the relative costs of different items. For
most services there have been substantial increases since
about 1967/8; this is especially true of direct operational
costs. The largest items here are assistance to factories for
relocation or for the installation of less-polluting equipment. The cost of acquiring factory sites is also relevant
here (it is listed under indirect costs) since it implies that
factories are moving out of the areas of greatest density.
These sites will no doubt be redeveloped for housing,

TABLE 6.1 Outlays for Pollution Control in Tokyo

	Main costs/Y million		
	1965	*1968*	*1970*
Direct Operation	188	309	1398
(of which factory relocation and assistance)	(134)	(152)	(654)
Indirect Costs			
Purchase of factory sites	2000	6602	8500
Domestic water supply and sewerage	22,965	38,587	54,750
River cleansing	49	31	40
River drainage	311	292	302
Noise (cost of new school buildings)	214	355	816
Subsidence (tidal wave precautions and disaster protection)	7218	7603	8729
Industrial water supply	2400	1650	3600

SOURCE: 'Tokyo Fights Pollution'.

probably in high rises, so that there may be little reduction
in density.

Of the indirect costs sewerage improvement is the
largest item; and this has doubled. On the other hand
river cleansing and drainage costs appear to be stagnat-
ing (but definitions are not clear); that of industrial water
works (listed under land subsidence) is also considerable
and increasing. Direct action in respect of land subsidence is clearly not yet sufficient. On the whole one
might venture the conclusion that Tokyo's priorities are
well chosen, but that there needs to be a great deal more
steam behind the whole programme.

7 The Finance of Local Services

It emerges from our discussion of the needs of Japanese cities that a great expansion of infrastructure and services will be required before they can be restored as pleasant and healthy places in which to live and work. We now have to examine the finances which are available to carry this heavy burden. But before we do so it may be helpful to review briefly the duties ascribed to local government and the division of the responsibility between Prefectures, cities and private enterprise for such services. Broadly we can identify four categories of outlay, roughly in order of their fiscal importance taking the country as a whole: (1) education, (2) public works, (3) social security, health and hospitals, (4) socially oriented enterprise, such as housing, water and transport.

(1) *Education* in Japan (as in most countries) is the most costly of all social services but, as is usual, the finance is shared between all levels of government. 1968 is the last year for which comprehensive figures are available but they seem to be still representative. Education then accounted for 28 per cent of local outlay; but only 25 per cent of this was financed from the local budget. Upper secondary and special schools are a prefectural responsibility. Primary and lower secondary schools are managed by municipalities, although the salaries of teachers are financed by the Prefectures (with a 50 per cent subsidy from the national government). 90 per cent of total prefectural outlay for education goes on salaries. For municipalities the costliest item is school buildings.

With the fall in the birth rate the school population is now declining. The change has been apparent among primary pupils from 1958, and among secondary pupils since the early sixties. This change hardly affects the large cities, due to the immigration of young workers and their families. Moreover it is incumbent on the city education authorities to spend more on buildings and on school meals than other authorities. Many of the schools are still housed in wooden buildings and it is estimated that about 45 per cent are short of space; there is evidently a big work to be done here. Still, as we have seen, complaints concerning the education system are few compared with those directed to other services.

Possibly due to the limitations which have developed in the public education system, there has been a great increase in privately owned schools and colleges since the war. At the upper secondary level it is estimated that about 25 per cent of the schools are privately organised and financed. This must go some way to ease the burden on local finances.

(2) The average of the budgets for local *public works* (as distinct from those classed as 'enterprises') break down into three main categories: roads 37 per cent, town planning 25 per cent, housing 14 per cent. As we have seen both Prefectures and municipalities have a hand in all these services. The small figure for housing reflects the extent to which reliance for house building is placed on private enterprise. When it is recalled that the number of motor vehicles on the streets increased twentyfold between 1950 and 1965, and that Tokyo's ratio of road space to built up areas is only 12 (and Osaka's 11) compared with about 25–30 in advanced countries, it is apparent that there is a crying need for more outlay in this direction. This is equally true in respect of modern sewerage, where the average for the country is only 21 per cent and Tokyo no more than 34 per cent. On average over the country some 50 per cent of human waste receives no treatment of any sort.

(3) *Social security* is a considerable element in local outlay. It covers both social insurance and social welfare services. The former includes health, unemployment insurance and 'welfare' pensions; the latter covers child

and geriatric services, public assistance and national pensions. Faithful to the principle of 'local autonomy'[1] almost all the services which are 'close to the lives of the people' are looked after by local authorities or their agents, and in the great cities they are mainly the responsibility of the municipal governments. Osaka in particular has long followed an active health policy. An Institute of Hygiene was established in 1906 and has maintained a high reputation for research.[2] In addition to the 'citizens' hospitals' scheme (started in 1940) it is planned to build additional hospitals in the very dense south-east area of the city and also in the rapidly developing north-east districts. The aim is to provide 58 beds per 10,000 population, although in 1965 they were 6700 beds short of the target. Osaka also operates children's hospitals and children's and general health centres which aim to eliminate disease as well as to give advice. They have been very successful in the reduction of infectious diseases. (A good many of these institutions are classed as public enterprises rather than as health services.)

(4) Most of the remaining local government activities are regarded as *public enterprises*. This category includes water supply, industrial water service, transport, electricity and gas. Their finances are kept in separate accounts, which use commercial methods, and in varying degrees they are eligible for loan finance. Most of the enterprises went into the red in the early sixties. In 1966 a Public Enterprise Law was introduced, making financial assistance available where it was clearly impossible for the authority to break even. Apart from particular causes this was frequently due to the diseconomies of small scale, making it impossible to raise charges sufficiently to cover costs. The greater part of the water supply undertakings are in municipal hands, although in sixteen Prefectures the prefectorial government has taken them over. They

[1] See Chapter 4, p. 91.

[2] Osaka had seven 'citizens' hospitals' aiming to provide a wide range of treatment at reasonable cost. Together they had 1455 beds and dealt with 3000 out-patients a day.

are in the red mainly because construction costs are steadily rising and it is increasingly necessary to seek more distant sources. Although it is permitted to raise charges for this service, there is generally a substantial time-lag before it becomes effective. In respect of industrial water there has been a remarkable growth of enterprises. In 1969 there were 73 undertakings (of which 34 were operated by Prefectures). This expansion is of course the reflection of the spread of industrialisation. Most of them are in the red because the national government sets the charges at a level at which deficits cannot be avoided. In respect of concessionary charges Tokyo at least is endeavouring to coax firms out of the practice of sinking their own wells.

Of all the public enterprises *mass transport* has the worst financial difficulties. Taking the country as a whole only 25 per cent of passengers use public transport: in Tokyo the percentage is 20, in Osaka 27. On the other hand Nagoya with its wide streets and efficient buses captures 52 per cent. All cities which operate subways do so at heavy loss. There seems to be no real effort to charge economic fares; instead there are vociferous demands that the enterprises should be formally subsidised by the national government. This bears out experience in various parts of the world that a subway system is an expensive and not very efficient substitute for an adequate street policy.

There are 43 public electricity supply undertakings of which the greater number (31) are operated by Prefectures. This is obviously sensible since Prefectures control larger areas than cities. In respect of gas supply there are 72 public enterprises of which 24 per cent are in the red. Finally, considering hospitals as a public enterprise, we must note that there are nearly a thousand operated by public agencies. 53 per cent of those owned by municipalities are in deficit, but for this a positive social policy may be responsible.

From this brief sketch of local activities and responsibilities two points seem specially to emerge. The first concerns the dichotomy of provision in many services between Prefectures and municipalities and the potential overlapping which this implies. Given the large expansion and diversification in local services since the war it was unavoidable that the Prefectures should be brought much more into the picture than the Shoup Mission envisaged or intended. Secondly, it cannot escape notice that local services are still inadequate for their long-term objective of urban rehabilitation. This is particularly true of public enterprises. We must hence enquire how far these inadequacies reflect the shortage of financial resources or other causes.

The fiscal relationship between national and local government in Japan is in several respects very similar to that in the U.K., but there is the substantial difference that they receive almost all their aid and subsidies through their Prefectures, and not from the national government. The central Ministries closest to the local government authorities are the Ministry of Local Autonomy and (to a lesser extent) the Ministry of Home Affairs. In the financial year 1968 (which as in the U.K. runs from April to March) national taxes amounted to Y 5324 billion, more than two-thirds of total tax collection. But this includes grants and subsidies to lower level authorities. Of the total expenditure of the cities about 60 per cent was in fact financed by higher level governments.[3]

In respect of the local budgetary process on the other hand there are substantial differences between the U.K. and Japan. In Japan the construction of the Budget, its implementation and control, depends very heavily on the Chief Executive. Although this is now an elective office the Chief Executive seems normally to be very close to the prefectural Governor and his administration. The other key local officer is the Chief Accountant, who seems to be in a similar position. The Chief Executive prepares the Budget and submits it to the Assembly. It is within the power of this body to amend it so long as no additional charge is involved (since the decision as to the

---

[3] See *Outline of Japanese Taxes* (annual publication of the Tax Bureau of the Ministry of Finance, 1972).

total is the prerogative of the Chief Executive). The C.A. is not permitted to grant any disbursements without the authorisation of the C.E. The C.A. reports on the accounts to the C.E. who first submits them to the Auditing Commissioners, after which they go back to the Assembly for final approval. As we have seen (above, p. 95) the C.E. submits a semi-annual Report to the Assembly on the state of the city's finances and the progress of the Budget. Most local authorities now have difficulty in financing their statutory obligations; and to aid the weaker ones a larger proportion of shared taxes (which we shall examine below) is being allocated to them. This change does not go far towards meeting the demand for more autonomous revenue.

Japan is still a lightly taxed country by Western standards (especially in respect of the taxation of business profits). Before the war the ratio of revenue to G.N.P. is said not to have reached 2 per cent. With war and reconstruction needs the ratio rapidly advanced, reaching 28·5 per cent in 1949. This was felt to be intolerably high so that it was gradually brought down; in 1968 it amounted to no more than 18·8 per cent. This reduction did not imply deficit finance since expenditure on development ceased to increase and in some directions actually declined (for instance in public sector housing) so that budgets continued to be balanced.

The taxes available to local government are classified into three groups: (1) legally prescribed, (2) specially authorised (by the Ministry of Local Autonomy) and (3) special purpose. So far as Prefectures are concerned the prescribed taxes include: inhabitants tax, enterprise (business) tax, real property acquisition tax, tobacco consumption tax, amusements, meals and hotels, automobiles and hunting licences. The other categories include tax on the acquisition of motor vehicles, light oil deliveries, water supply and on the profits of land transfers. In practice the only heads of any fiscal importance are the inhabitants and enterprise taxes. (This will become evident when we examine the accounts of T.M.G., see below, p. 129.) Local authorities on the other hand have, in the first class, rights over municipal inhabitants tax; tax on fixed assets (property), including light motor vehicles; tobacco consumption; consumption of electricity and gas; mineral products and timber delivery. Their special taxes include tax on city planning, spa bath resorts, water supply, profits on land sales and municipal health insurance. 78 per cent of the revenue is derived from the first two items.

The Local Tax Law of 1950 comes near to prescribing the permitted rates of taxes. These are of three types: specified, standard and restrictive. Rates of the first type are uniform throughout the country, in order not to distort the distribution of commodities. Rates in the third category may be varied locally, up to a prescribed ceiling. When the Law was introduced local authority revenues amounted to Y 181 million while the Prefectures had less than Y 126 million. But the prefectural collections have gradually increased, and since 1964 have exceeded the local revenues. This is of course a reflection of the greater activities now undertaken by the prefectural governments.

Most of the taxes are of familiar type; but two call for brief explanation. The *inhabitants tax* is levied on both natural and legal 'persons'. (The prefectural tax is collected together with the city tax.) On natural persons there is a low poll tax, combined with an income and wealth tax with a mild progression. The rates of tax on legal persons depend on a complicated formula. Taxpayers file returns in advance. The prefectural *enterprise (business) tax* is considered to be a charge for services rendered on industrial and business premises. There are three schedules: (1) general business, (2) primitive handicrafts industry, and (3) tax on professions. The basic rate is 5 per cent, with a 1 per cent concession for handicraft firms. Companies report their liability and the tax is collected by the tax office, if more than one Prefecture is concerned the revenue is apportioned according to the relative amounts of income accruing, the number of installations and offices and the number of employees, in the relevant Prefectures.

The remaining sources of city revenue on current account are the *local allocation tax* and the *local transfer tax*. These are in nature shared revenue, not autonomous taxes. They are broadly equivalent to block grants, save that the sums transferred depend on national revenue collections. The contents of the L.A.T. is 52 per cent of the revenue derived from national income, corporate business and liquor taxes. It is distributed (through the Prefectures) according to a complicated formula embodying interlocal variation in favour of poor areas. The contents of the L.T.T. are a local road tax, a petrol tax (for Prefectures and designated cities) and a special tonnage tax for port authorities. The revenue is collected by the national government and transferred by formula. In respect of both the L.A.T. and L.T.T. the Prefectures seem to play a very important part in determining the interlocal distribution.

Turning to capital account, loan finance is essentially intended for enterprises (trading services) which keep commercial type accounts. A local authority wishing to borrow must first get the approval of its own Assembly and then of the national government. The national treasury may also issue funds directly for earmarked (non-utility) investment, such as in school buildings and other civil works, which are included in the national Plan. The smaller the city the more important are direct government loans likely to be to it, no doubt because it is realised that small places might have difficulty in raising outside loans. The maturity of loans appears normally to be about 10–15 years. Interest rates have been rising: in 1972 Tokyo was paying 7·5 per cent, but most rates are still low by European standards. Borrowing methods clearly imply tight control by the national government.

Having broadly surveyed the general fiscal situation of urban authorities we must now endeavour to ascertain what funds our three cities have actually had at their disposal and how, out of all this, they are distributing them between uses.

In spite of a great deal of information kindly supplied by the three cities in answer to a detailed questionnaire, it is no easy task to find reliable answers to these questions in respect of any of the cities, still less is it possible to make a detailed comparison between the three. Although in principle the accounts are kept in a broadly similar way, classifications and nomenclatures exhibit many differences. Each city has a very substantial general Fund; but its boundaries are not the same everywhere and it is always accompanied by a large number of separate funds (mainly for 'enterprises' which are not integrated with the general Fund or with each other). Current and capital items seem to be distinguished fairly carefully in the city accounts (but not so well in the prefectural accounts). But they appear itemised under each separate activity. As a result it is necessary to collect the items referring to any one activity from a number of places if anything like a complete figure is to be obtained. There is no complete account either of current or capital items. In respect of each expenditure item the mixture of sources from which it is financed is identified as if they were earmarked for the purpose, but I do not think that this is strictly intended.

There is indeed a total budget account, but, as will be apparent, it is no more than an aggregate of individual items, essentially at the micro level, with both current and capital items on each side. It could not function as a useful instrument for decision making. Indeed there seems to be very little interest in such things as cost/benefit analysis. Nor is there any discernible attempt to introduce programme or performance considerations. In what follows I have endeavoured to identify (1) an expenditure account, covering the main lines, for the most recent years available (since Tokyo is its own Prefecture its accounts are naturally very much fuller than those of the other two cities; in particular the revenue accounts of Osaka and Nagoya have to be supplemented by a separate account of transferred taxes and subsidies). (2) The revenue side on which at least as regards individual sources, there is a good deal more regularity. This is especially true of the borrowing account because it is more strictly controlled. A complementary account for Tokyo would show the outlay of T.M.G., the Wards and other authorities within the Metro area, together with their subsidisation by T.M.G., but information to prepare it is insufficient. Although the accounts must be regarded as illustrative rather than as definitive, I believe that at least they serve to show the order of interest of the three cities in different directions. This may provide some guide to an evaluation of their power of independent decision making. Due to fairly large aggregates of unspecified items (under such headings as 'others' or 'expenses') no very reliable conclusions can be drawn in any detail. To do so would require a very considerable field research project, which should also include the accounts of the remaining large cities.

TABLE 7.1   Current Expenditure

	Million Y		
	Tokyo (TMG)	*Osaka City*	*Nagoya City*
Education	169·2	39·0	19·6
Protection			
Fire (+police in Tokyo)	125·1	7·8	4·9
Environment (including pollution)	6·1	n.a.	0·8
Social Services and Welfare	53·3	45·0	14·6
Health	30·9	32·8	4·4
Labour	12·1	1·9	1·7
Waste disposal	44·6	n.a.	n.a.
Economic services	49·1	n.a.	3·7
Utilities			
Housing and construction	19·9	34·7	22·8
Roads, parks, etc.	13·8	29·5	17·6
Plan implementation	3·3	n.a.	16·9
Port	2·6	1·3	n.a.
Hospitals	16·7	4·2	4·5
Water – domestic	64·4	17·0	11·6
Water – industrial	2·8	1·5	n.a.
Sewerage, sanitation	35·0	11·2	10·4
Total of the above selected items	648·9	225·9	123·0
Total current outlay	1,107,764	349,175	269,999

The best that can be done on capital account is to supplement the current account with what little can be gleaned of strictly capital outlay; but apart from the incompleteness of the figures there are great difficulties of classification. Thus T.M.G. appears to spend only a modest sum on pollution control (see above, Table 6.1) but there is a capital outlay of Y 22·9 billion on flood control, 24·8 for waste disposal and 18·9 for sewerage, all of which clearly have an impact on pollution. The largest item on capital account in T.M.G. was Y 88·3 billion on road construction; but housing at 81·8 was also large (a good deal of this consisted of works in connection with Tama New Town) and capital works connected with Plan implementation are recorded as Y 20 billion. There appears to have been very little constructional work in respect of water supply, but the port received Y 9·8 billion. There was only very modest outlay on hospital works (Y 3·1 b.). Capital outlay for education in Tokyo (Y 15·5 b.) was not direct, but took the form of transfers and subsidies to schools and colleges owned by local entities or private interests.

Although Osaka has not yet achieved Metro status it has some responsibility for 22 Wards, 30 'cities' and 2 'towns'. Since 1965 it has been following a very active policy of development, as the following figures from its 1972 city accounts reveal:

TABLE 7.2   Osaka City Capital Outlay on Selected Items

	Million Y	
	1965	*1972*
Public welfare	8·5	45·0
Sanitation	10·4	32·8
Civil engineering	37·4	90·6
Education	11·1	39·0
Housing	5·6	34·7

(This is a far greater expansion than can be
explained by inflation.)

It is perhaps not surprising that such a forward policy
has run Osaka into financial trouble. Deficits on its own
revenue collections have also been accumulating since
1967 when a deficit of Y 4·6 million was experienced. By
great efforts to increase city taxes total collections grew
from Y 46·9 m. in 1965 to Y 118·6 m. in 1972. But
whereas city taxes in 1960 represented 61 per cent of total
revenue, they amounted to no more than 38 per cent in
1972 (see Table 7.3 for breakdown). This means that
Osaka has increasingly had to rely on aid from higher
level governments, and on borrowing, implying additional control. Part of the trouble seems to have arisen

TABLE 7.3   Autonomous Tax Collections

| | Percentages for 1972 | | |
	T.M.G.	Osaka	Nagoya
Inhabitants: total	27·1	42·0	48·1
Individuals	(11·2)	n.a.	n.a.
Corporations	(15·9)	n.a.	n.a.
Enterprise: total	35·4	P	P
Individuals	(1·5)		
Corporations	(33·8)		
Real estate acquisition	2·2		
Tobacco consumption	2·1		
Recreational facilities	0·8		
Meals and hotels	5·0	P	P
Automobiles	4·4	P	P
Fixed assets (property)	15·2	39·0	33·6
Automobile acquisition	1·4		
Light oil (Kerosene) dealing	2·6		
City planning	3·7		
Others	0·1	19·0	6·0
	100	100	100

(P = prefectural taxes)

because Osaka's revenue suffered a heavier drop in the depression of the early 1960's than that of the other two cities. The financial situation seems now to be recovering, and a positive balance has appeared in the latest accounts. But this has only been achieved by the postponement of various works which the city considers important.

When we turn to the incomings side the going is a little easier, because as we have seen the permitted taxes are fairly closely defined. Tokyo (T.M.G.) due to its prefectural standing has a considerably wider range of taxes available than the other two. But in practice the only additional source of which it makes substantial use is the Enterprise Tax. Table 7.3 gives the most recent figures for autonomous tax collections for the three cities expressed as percentages in order to bring out the relative exploitation of different sources.

Osaka's relatively large minor taxes are stated to be city planning tax and tax on the consumption of tobacco. The tax collections of Tokyo appear to be about three times those of Osaka, which in turn are double those of Nagoya.

In order to complete the tax incomings of the two smaller cities (see Table 7.4) it is necessary to add the taxes and subsidies made available to them by higher level governments:

TABLE 7.4   Transferred Taxes and Subsidies, 1972

	Million Y	
	Osaka	Nagoya
Local allocation tax (shared revenue)	17·0	4·3
Local transfer tax	3·2	2·2
Grants in aid	—	5·6
Subsidies		
National	57·8	26·0
Prefectural	6·7	2·3
Others	6·3	—

On the incomings side of the budget it remains to take a
look at the loan position. As we should expect the loan
debt of all three cities is modest relatively to their other
commitments. In spite of her fairly large-scale borrowing
T.M.G.'s annual debt service amounts to little more than
her expenditure on education.

TABLE 7.5   City Public Debt by Source

	Billion Y		
	Tokyo Sept. 1972	Osaka May 1971	Nagoya End 1971
Higher level governments	294·2	226·5	108·0
Public issues	244·2 ⎫		62·7
(managed by the banks)	⎪	269·7	
Banks and insurance	⎬		
companies	325·7 ⎭		37·5
Foreign agencies			
(U.S., W. Germany)	9·9	14·8	—
Others	169·8	3·6	11·2
Total	1043·7	510·4	219·5

Note: Up to *c.* 1967 Y thousand = £1; later = *c.* £1.50

It would appear that Tokyo has good opportunities for
borrowing outside the government, and that banks and
insurance companies are happy to lend to her. Osaka has
also done fairly well on public issues, but has clearly
been grateful for the help accorded by agencies of the
national government. This aid is stated to have come
mainly from the Ministry of Finance, but to include also
small amounts from the Postal Services and national and
prefectural treasuries. Nagoya's loan funds are mainly
from the national government, with small amounts from
Aichi Prefecture. One would guess that it is less easy for
her to borrow outside, in spite of her relatively good
financial position.

As we reach the end of our excursions into the
organisation, activities and financial position of Japanese
cities we must pause to enquire what conclusions (either

of general or of specific interest) can be drawn
concerning the possibility of restoring these cities to a
position in which they are again pleasant and healthy
places in which to live and work. The Americans, who
had done so much to turn the Japanese cities into a
shambles, worked on broadly two aims: (1) to reduce
drastically the powers of the old élite – the large landowners, the Prefectures and their governors, working as
agents of an all powerful national government; (2) as a
defence against the return of the old system, to establish a
régime of elective local self-government on the American
model.

In spite of the creation of what was considered as the
necessary machinery for these purposes their aims have
only partially succeeded. The power of the prefectural
governors has been somewhat reduced (not conspicuously on account of the office now being elective). But on
the other hand, due to the fragmentation of local areas
outside the large cities and to the inelastic nature of their
finances, it has been inevitable that the lion's share of the
many new local services which have been introduced in
Japan (as in other countries) since the war should be
assumed by the Prefectures. The power of the
Prefectures and their governors has thus increased
substantially beyond what was intended by the Shoup
Mission. (The development of larger local government
areas is a common post-war feature of many Western
countries also, not least the U.K.) Autonomous local
government was an idea entirely foreign to Japanese
history and thinking; it takes much more than 25 years
for such a concept to be transplanted to the extent of
growing roots of its own. After all the Americans had
been practising it since the Pilgrim Fathers. Some of the
Japanese (mainly intellectuals) understood and admired
the principle and have been working hard to implement
it. Their number is probably on the increase, but the
'growth before all' mentality dies hard.

In evaluating the progress that has been made by
Japanese cities their deplorable condition at the end of
the war must always be borne in mind. The

unprecedented and exceptional volume of immigration which they have had to face has greatly added to their difficulties (urban immigration has been a worldwide phenomenon,[4] but probably nowhere has it been so great as in Tokyo). Discussion concerning the organisation of large cities into Metropolitan areas is proceeding in a number of countries, and already a fair amount of experience has been gathered. Tokyo is very much a case in point, so that we should also attempt to form a judgement as to the success of T.M.G., and as to whether the idea could usefully be extended to some other Japanese cities.

T.M.G. has scarcely been in existence long enough to form a very sure basis for evaluation. But it does seem that the larger area is potentially a great improvement in respect of planning and autonomous decision making. It has also helped the development of services which need a large area for efficient management, such as water supply, sewerage and pollution control. Very important also is the greater command over revenue sources which prefectural status confers. This does not imply that T.M.G. has an easy task in front of it; there is too much to do at once. The strain on the Mayor/Governor of having to wear at once two such headache-producing hats suggests that new methods of management and additional managers to support them would considerably ease the situation and free the Mayor/Governor for more general oversight. Some adjustment of prefectural boundaries (if not the complete absorption of Yokohama) would greatly assist area planning. Within the Metro area itself the many little towns and villages outside the Ward area would be easier to manage, and would probably contribute more to the area as a whole if they were somewhat streamlined and so less fragmented. It is evident that the standard of services outside the Ward area is considerably lower than inside. A measure of redistribution from the richer areas (as in London) would

[4] See U. K. Hicks 'Metropolitan Areas, a New Problem' and 'The Organisation and Finance of Large Cities', *Local Finance* (The International Centre for Local Credit, The Hague).

help. But apart from such a possibility Tokyo urgently needs more funds to develop the whole Metro area as it should be developed, as a unity. Shortage of funds is not a peculiarity of Tokyo; it afflicts all great cities. If national governments really want their cities to be reformed and modernised they must come forward much more generously.

On paper the tax structures of the Japanese cities look ample. (This is especially true of Tokyo with its prefectural status.) But in practice nearly all the revenue is derived from a very narrow range of sources; most of the lesser taxes are hardly used at all. It would be interesting to know how their costs of collection compare with the revenues they produce. It is not inconceivable that a streamlining of tax structures might result in a net gain. Funds and personnel set free by such an exercise might then be applied to build up the inhabitants tax and fixed assets tax. The former at present seems to be little more than a glorified poll tax. Perhaps it could be developed more in the direction of a true local income tax. The fixed assets tax seems to be both weaker and less flexible than the property taxes of many countries. In view of the enormous rise in land prices which has been taking place in Japan it would surely be useful to develop it into a powerful real estate tax. There would be new and awkward problems of valuation, which under the present system are largely bypassed; but this is not an insuperable objection.

The changes which would put Tokyo on its feet as regards finances seem to be by no means impossible; many of them would not be very costly. If this conclusion is just, there would seem to be a real case for gradually extending the Metro organisation to some other large conurbations.

Even with more autonomous revenue the Japanese cities would still need help from higher level governments, ultimately from the national government. If they could achieve better revenue collections and central assistance were kept at least in its present ratio to local sources (at the moment it is very similar to the position in the U.K.) the cities would be considerably better off. It would be a distinct improvement if the aid they receive could be built up into an integrated and rational grants system. Local authorities would then be able to forecast (at least for a short term of years) what was coming to them. They could then draw up their plans and budgets on a realistic and fairly detailed basis. Cities, and especially Metro areas, need more – not less – assistance than other local authority areas if they are to do their job properly. The return on investment (per million Y invested) would probably be much higher than if the same funds had been sunk in rural areas.

Asset formation is the biggest need of all for the cities, in all probability: general infrastructure, street improvement, housing, school building, water, sewerage and waste disposal equipment. As we went through the various services, it was evident that every one of them was in crying need of expansion. For capital formation better access to loan funds than the Japanese cities now enjoy is clearly needed. Funds could come either from central authorities or their agencies (such as the British Public Works Loans Board) or through the Market, by borrowing either at home or abroad. If the purposes for which loan finance was permitted were extended, and additional methods introduced, there would be little difficulty in borrowing. The Japanese cities are in a very sound condition financially with light debt burdens, relatively to the cities in most countries. It may well be maintained that a wider use of loan finance and the broader decision-making which it facilitates is complementary to autonomous finance on current account. More capital formation at home would ease rather than damage the international position of the yen.

We have seen that the budgeting methods used by the Japanese local authorities are very conservative. The recent experience of Osaka is an interesting demonstration of the difficulty of breaking out of the present system into more forward looking development. At present expenditure plans tend to be considered piecemeal, on a micro basis. A more general forward-investment policy

would call for the adoption of methods which would
convert the budget into an instrument of policy for
decision making. The situation would be much clearer if
separate current and capital accounts were kept.
Cost/benefit and feasibility studies are really necessary,
not merely to identify the optimum techniques for
particular projects, but also for checking the balance
between services, broadly considered. Finally regular
performance checks, in real terms, can most usefully
supplement the financial reports of progress. The
adoption of some such modern techniques should make a
city's plans not only more coherent but also more
intelligible and interesting to the citizens. This is the true
path to effective local autonomy.

The Japanese are only at the beginning of the
campaign for the modernisation and rehabilitation of
their cities. There is a lot to do. The Japanese people now
have incomes fully up to the level of Western countries;
they have a right to modern living standards, and indeed
they are demanding them. Yet their local public
institutions and finances are still essentially Victorian. As
Nagoya states in its Report, the whole attitude towards
public goods needs to be altered. Much could be learned
from the experience of some Western countries: by
administrators and executives making visits and perhaps
attending courses in city management and planning.
Above all leaders will be needed. The achievements of
Governor/Mayor Minobe in Tokyo or Mayor Sigetu in
Nagoya suggest what can be done. There are not enough
such men at present; but as the campaign gathers
momentum there is no doubt but that they will appear.
Given the will, there is not the slightest doubt but that
the Japanese can carry through the urban battle to a
successful conclusion. It will take time – Tokyo will not
be rebuilt in a day; but it is potentially one of the world's
finest cities as well as the largest.

Part III – The Less Developed Countries

8 The Management of Urban Development

In the less developed countries the cities play a vitally important role. Although urban centres are only a minor sector of the whole economy they stand out as belonging essentially to a different – more advanced – type of economic organisation than the rest of the economy, where the (more or less primitive) agricultural sector is predominant. The cities call for modern services of the types provided in advanced countries. In L.D.C.s it is common to find one or a few very large cities which are focal points for population. The remaining urban areas are more normal and more homogeneous in size. In fact some of them may be growing quite fast and others shrinking, even in a country with a high net reproduction rate.

The giants in the L.D.C.s are often very large. If we consider not only the historic (core) city but also the surrounding Metropolitan area, from five to seven million inhabitants is not exceptional. Populations of this order far exceed those of a number of full voting members of the U.N. Yet there is no one to speak for them and their special interests in world councils.

By the 'Metropolitan area' I shall imply the area within daily commuter range. There is little doubt that this is the operational unit of the future. The organisation and administration of such huge conglomerations of the human race would be a very difficult exercise in any event. With underdeveloped administrations and finances it is wellnigh impossible to make a real success of it. The results are often deplorable even given the best efforts of local and national governments. Much help is needed, especially in management and the mobilisation of resources.

We may presume that the basic objectives of the 'good' city are the same the world over: adequate space for homes, offices and shopping; provision for education and health services, open spaces for leisure pursuits, reasonable speed of circulation between home, work and entertainment, and finally a high level of employment opportunities. (This last implies some factory development within commuter distance.) To make the grade adequately the city must look attractive and possess amenities of which the citizens can be proud and which will foment community feeling which is itself an element of stability. In the L.D.C.s (as contrasted with the A.C.s) the large cities tend to be somewhat isolated: it is a long way from one to another. Partly for this reason they have a special significance as the growing points of the economy, both socially and economically.

From one point of view the problems of the great cities are the same the world over, in spite of constitutional and political differences and vast disparities in per capita incomes. We may emphasise in particular four of these common problems:

(1) *Rapid population growth* at a rate substantially exceeding that of the country as a whole. This is nourished (if not dominated) by immigration. In the A.C.s the immigrants may come from long distances away, (as Rome has been inundated by southerners and Paris by Algerians). In L.D.C.s the immigrants are more likely to come from the surrounding countryside, partly because of lack of communications – and communication – and hence ignorance. They come in the hope of earning an income, of a more interesting life and especially to get education for their children. In Rome the rate of annual immigration is said to have 'settled down' at 50,000. In Bombay between 1951 and 1961 it averaged 122,000. Immigrants are normally poorer than the existing population, and their fertility rates are higher.[1] This gives rise to further problems of additional

[1] This appears to be no longer true in Bombay.

health and education services as well as housing.
Eventually the position should improve as the tide of
immigration slackens, as it already has in the A.C.s where
the worst manifestations had political causes arising out
of the war. In time also the immigrants will conform to
the lower fertility rates of the city. But for the L.D.C.s
that is a long way ahead.

In many L.D.C.s problems concerning the immigrant
population are complicated by disparities between the
sexes – always a preponderance of males at the first
round. Thus in Bombay city of the intercensus total
immigration the proportion of male immigrants was almost double that of females. This sex disparity brings
with it a number of difficult social problems. It may have a
variety of causes. In India many men leave their wives and
families behind in their villages, but keep in close touch
with them. In some parts of central Africa the system of
indentured labour virtually confines immigration to unac-
companied males. In other parts of Africa, for instance
Nigeria and Uganda, young men come to the towns in
order to earn and save enough to marry (including bride
prices). Thus in framing policy not only the numbers and
age grouping but also the sex distribution of the immigrants has to be considered.

(2) *Congestion and pollution* are the lot of all Metros.
These two evils need to be carefully distinguished,
although they are closely related – in fact congestion may
also lead to pollution. Congestion is almost wholly a
community created evil and can only be cured by
community effort. It is a social cost caused by the action
of many rather than by the irresponsibility of
individuals. Those who give rise to congestion are
commonly themselves also sufferers. (This is particularly
true of commuters, one man to a car.) Congestion consists
of overcrowded streets and too great a density of
population with inadequate housing. Pollution is caused
by the action – or inaction – of particular individuals,
who may not necessarily suffer from it themselves. This
is obviously not true of air pollution caused merely by
congestion (see below).

In the A.C. Metros, congestion is especially a traffic and communications problem and there are known ways of mitigating it. The traffic is on the whole homogeneous; awkward vehicles such as transporters and heavy trucks can be forbidden the main arteries. Strict circulation and parking rules with a limited number of over- and under-passes and reserved bus lanes can make an immense difference at no great cost of time or money. In the L.D.C. Metros, traffic is far from homogeneous. Besides the normal city traffic of cars, buses and delivery vans many thousands of bicycles weave their way in and out. Bullock carts, rickshaws, and other slow moving vehicles cling to the centres of main arteries. Almost all are without lights. Neither the operators nor the animals understand or are inclined to pay attention to modern traffic needs and signals. There is also the human congestion problem. Millions of pedestrians throng the streets (not merely the side walks) largely because they have nowhere to go. Immigrants unbelievably overcrowd once good houses and set up their dwellings (of sacking and cartons) not merely on the outskirts of the city where at least they would have some room and better air to breathe, but also in any open space within the city (such as along railway lines).

In the last generation air pollution was largely due (especially in the U.K.) to the burning of crude coal in open grates and factory furnaces; this was the genesis of the 'London Particular'. This cause has now largely been eliminated by the enforcement of 'smokeless zones' and the change to other fuels. But its place has been taken by the worse menace of fumes from internal combustion engines – worse because it is both more lethal and more subtle, being largely invisible. (This too can be controlled but to do a thorough job is expensive.) In the L.D.C. Metros all these smog generators are working at once. There are a surprising number of private cars even in poor cities, most of them not conspicuous for their modernity. Fumes belch from factory chimneys and from diesel engines in antiquated buses and trucks.

The density of the resulting smog depends partly on

the Metro site. Manchester has special difficulties
because the Pennines to the east catch the prevailing
south-west winds and precipitate their dirt on the city,
while Liverpool's sea breezes keep it clean and sweet.
Delhi's inland smog is much worse than Bombay's
although it is a much smaller city (2 m. against 7 m.).
Mexico City is another unfortunate because it lies in a
basin surrounded by high mountains (which the smog
generally renders invisible) and consequently has no
cleansing prevailing wind.

The seriousness of water pollution in the A.C.s has
only recently been realised. The extension of water-borne
sewage which is discharged untreated into rivers, lakes
and the sea has not merely killed the fish but made the
water unsafe for human health and enjoyment. Again,
increasing numbers of factories discharge untreated
effluent into rivers. To some extent Metros in the A.C.s
have taken water pollution more seriously in hand than
air pollution. Factories which discharge untreated
effluent can be heavily fined. Even pretty bad water can
be purified and made potable. But it is a long and
expensive exercise, largely beyond the means of L.D.C.
Metros. It is not surprising to find that 80 per cent and
more of their hospital patients are suffering from
water-borne diseases.

(3) *The administration of Metros.* In most countries
(both advanced and less developed) administration is
made more difficult by the existence of a large number of
separate political jurisdictions within the area. Usually
this is merely the result of the tide of urbanisation en-
gulfing small towns and villages as it advances. These
latter are not necessarily opposed to being absorbed,
balancing some loss of independence and perhaps higher
local taxes against better services. Hence there would
probably not be much opposition to the establishment of a
formal Metropolitan area, especially if this is fostered by a
higher level government. I have yet to learn of any Metro
in an L.D.C. that shares the passion for separate jurisdictions on high democratic principles that one finds in the
U.S.A. This is not surprising since only in India (and to

some extent in Bangladesh and Pakistan) is there any well
established tradition of representative government.

Even if a successful Metro area government is
potentially feasible there will be many problems to solve,
due to the disparity in wealth and size of the absorbed
entities. In the U.S.A. as we have seen there is a marked
tendency for the rich to move out of the city seeking 'tax
havens' or merely more room and better air. This
tendency for out-migration is much less marked in the
L.D.C.s. The consequence of this migratory difference is
that the spread of incomes tends to be greater in L.D.C.s
than in an American city. The poor are very poor indeed
but there are districts of rich people who are very rich
indeed (and their tax payments are likely to be
negligible). The combination of interlocal and interpersonal disparity is very noticeable for instance in districts
like Malabar Hill in Bombay, Lomas in Mexico City, the
new developments up the hill in Tehran and their
respective slum neighbours.

(4) *The financial needs* of Metros everywhere are
enormous, on current and even more on capital account.
Most of the services which they provide are if not capital
intensive (such as construction and public utilities) at
least heavily capital using (such as schools and
hospitals). We shall have later to discuss the financial
implications of the resulting need for capital formation.
In almost every country, rich and poor, city financial
resources are grossly inadequate in relation to their
commitments. In the A.C.s where there is no real
shortage of command over resources, the main cause of
lack of funds for urban purposes is paucity of
independent revenue sources, taxes or public profits
which they can themselves control. Sweden and Finland
are perhaps the only countries in which local funds
appear to be adequate. There the local authorities have
control of a powerful local income tax as well as a range
of profitable trading services.

In the A.C.s this shortage of Metro funds could be
relieved in a number of ways, especially by the award of
additional tax rights or grants from higher level

governments. The applicability of these in L.D.C.s we shall examine later. In the L.D.C.s there is always an absolute shortage of funds. Higher level governments can to some extent come to the rescue but it is difficult for them to do so since they are themselves poor. In both A.C.s and L.D.C.s shortage of resources may well be exaggerated by low administrative standards and poor management. But in the L.D.C.s high standards are very difficult to obtain both because of the shortage of educated high-calibre potential administrators and by the greater attraction of the national civil service.[2]

While there are thus a number of common problems facing Metros everywhere, from another point of view the problems of every city are *sui generis* and call for careful individual study, taking all factors into account. Even then it is possible to identify certain group differences. The first distinction that has to be made among the L.D.C.s is between the very poor countries (such as Pakistan, Bangladesh, India, Sudan and several African countries south of the Sahara) and the not so poor (for instance in the Caribbean, Middle East and Latin America). Some of the not so poor (for instance Mexico, Argentina and Iran) are within measurable distance of the A.C.s. Within a large country there may be substantial differences in wealth between one Metro and another; contrast the difference between Bombay, a flourishing seaport with growing industrialisation and lying between two go-ahead states (Maharashtra and Gujerat) and Calcutta, deprived of its commercial hinterland by Partition and lying within the abject poverty of West Bengal.[3] The fact that some important Metros in not so poor L.D.C.s or areas could in principle

---

[2] In India the Civic Commissioner (Chief Executive) is on the national (I.A.S.) roster and is sent down to a Metro for a seven year term. On the whole the system works very well, although naturally difficulties sometimes emerge.

[3] The Planning Commission has sought to locate heavy industry, including steel works, in this area; but since these industries are so very capital intensive the local effect on the employment and other multipliers has been negligible.

have funds within their reach unfortunately does not imply that they can realise their potential. Resource mobilisation and management are major stumbling blocks all along the line.

Metros in L.D.C.s tend to enjoy a much greater prestige than in A.C.s largely due to the fact that they are unique; there is a big gap between them and the next range of cities. Nevertheless in a heavily populated country like India the second and third line cities are extremely large in relation to those of less populated L.D.C.s (for instance Shiraz and Isfahan in Iran, Tolucca and Monterrey in Mexico) which are not very large. The evaluation of these and other differences is unfortunately severely handicapped by the statistical blackout which shrouds alike their activities and their finances. Assistance on getting these into order would be a most beneficent sort of aid.

In examining the prospects of Metros in L.D.C.s four points distinguishing them from Metros in A.C.s need specially to be emphasised:

Firstly, basic services: in very many Metros even of relatively wealthy L.D.C.s basic services which are taken for granted in A.C.s are very imperfect or even entirely lacking. Thus Tehran, a Metro conglomeration of over five million, has no underground sewerage system, nothing but cess pits and open water-courses by the roadside. The water supply is also very inadequate, notwithstanding the presence of mountains with high rainfall immediately to the north. In Mexico City the water supply is inadequate and so mixed up with the sewerage system as to be highly dangerous, although small amounts of purified water are available to special customers.[4] Gas and electricity supplies are often of poor

---

[4] It must be admitted that both of these cities have some special difficulties. In Tehran an ancient system of Quanats (underground water courses) complicates the situation; but plans are in the making for both a sewerage and water system. In Mexico City whole areas which are heavily developed are sinking into the soft ground of what was formerly a lake.

quality. Efforts to abate air pollution or to regulate traffic are virtually non-existent.

Secondly, although quite wealthy Metros such as Buenos Aires – and Rome – have colonies of shanty dwellers for whom they have not yet found accommodation, the inhabitants are not really poor. They can buy radios and at least motor cycles; their main lack is moderately priced housing. In the poor L.D.C.s on the contrary the shanty town dwellers are miserably poor, undernourished, underclothed and without means of washing or sanitation. The birth-rate is very high but so also is the infant mortality rate. They are lucky if they are not diseased and if their children receive any education.

Thirdly, unemployment: largely as a result of these conditions (themselves the child of mass immigration) the level of unemployment tends to be very high. There is no work to do and little will to do any. Too often body and soul are precariously held together and the government's conscience salved by meagre cash grants. Thus it comes about that unemployment is a major, perhaps the major, preoccupation of most L.D.C.s, above all because of its political implications. Urban unemployment is a national problem; the cities cannot solve it themselves. Real jobs are not available for all and are not likely to be in the foreseeable future. Yet right now there are better ways of first-aid than cash grants, ways in which shanty dwellers could be shown how to help themselves and which would not cost the taxpayers much more than the cash grants. Some of these we shall discuss in Chapter 12.

Finally, education: the rate of illiteracy among shantytown immigrants is understandably high. But in many Metros it is high even among established families. High birth-rates imply a broad-based population 'pyramid' and a consequently inflated demand for, and cost of, education relatively to the advanced countries. Although the urban literacy rate is generally higher than the rural it is still low, and this is particularly true of the women. The shortage of citizens with any substantial schooling, and especially those with a sound secondary education, is a handicap that runs right through the efforts of the L.D.C. Metros. On the administrative side it makes it difficult to find the right man for the job, and when the search fails it means a waste of manpower, two or three men being employed inefficiently and the job badly done. On the social side illiteracy greatly increases the difficulty of communication, and hence of participation, whereby the citizen could help not only his own family but his neighbour's also.

When planning how Metros in L.D.C.s could best be helped there is a fundamental difference (as there is in A.C.s) according as the country's constitution is unitary or federal. In the latter case local government will be a state matter. This does not necessarily imply that the national government cannot help the Metros. It can do so indirectly, for instance by specific grants (for education, health or roads and so on) awarded through the states, or more directly through the choice of location for projects of national interest. In India (as in the U.S.A.) the volume of funds disbursed locally for national projects much exceeds those allocated in grants for other purposes. Although the national projects may not be located actually within a Metro they are likely to help the local situation, if only to the extent that the additional incomes created will put the receiving states into a better financial position.

Fundamentally Metros in a federation are a national responsibility as well as a state commitment. They are an L.D.C.'s window on the outside world and are important in making its image. This is especially true of the capital city, which has problems of its own. The extent to which national and state governments interest themselves in urban problems varies substantially from country to country; it also varies within a federation from state to state. Thus in Canada Ontario has been outstanding in promoting Metro organisation, and also in 'after care' by making grants for services which may not be popular with local taxpayers, such as low income housing. In Australia state interest goes even further; it might almost be said that the states run the cities, doing their planning and augmenting their resources.[5]

In L.D.C.s the fiscal interest of the states in their Metros is less pronounced, mainly because they are themselves so poor. But India is a federation with a strong 'states rights' ideology and considerable state assistance has been given, for instance for higher education. The Union government also makes grants for Works in Metros, via the states. In the former Nigerian federation where the states (Regions) were strong and the centre weak, most of the assistance to the larger cities (apart from Lagos) came from the Region. The all important education grants however came from the central government, being distributed on a broadly promotional formula, irrespective of Region.[6]

With given potential resources the effective wealth or poverty of a Metro hinges largely on the commitments it has to undertake in respect of the social services, such as education, welfare (public assistance) hospitals, environmental and preventive health. The key service in this respect is school education, including lower technical. It would be unusual for a Metro in an L.D.C. to find money for a university, which would be a state matter. Few L.D.C.s practise such localised school finance as exists in the U.S.A. under the School Board system; although in some areas local contributions are very important at the primary stage.[7] In most L.D.C.s education is not a

[5] The Commonwealth government is prohibited by the constitution from helping any state – and hence Metro – differentially (apart from the statutory grants). Nevertheless projects of national interest do in practice assist particular towns, for instance in developing mining areas. The Commonwealth government also makes large grants for hospitals and higher education, most of which are of special benefit to the Metros (which are in fact the state Capitals). *Cf.* U. K. Hicks, 'Current Problems of Federal Finance in India and Some Comparisons with Australia', *Public Finance* (1967).

[6] But in practice for many years very little of the grants went to the Muslim north which resisted funds which might aid Christianity.

[7] In the former Eastern Region of Nigeria educational finance depended to a substantial degree on the 'assumed local contribution', which was a semi-voluntary levy collected through churches and schools.

separate system (except in so far as it may be run by religious organisations) but is a direct and heavy responsibility on local authorities. There are however several ways in which the situation may be eased; by central grants, as in Nigeria, or by the assistance of religious bodies, especially for secondary education. In Nigeria also a large part of school construction is undertaken voluntarily by the parents and others. This appears now to be happening in Bangladesh.

A word must be said concerning the finances of the capital city in L.D.C.s. In a federation the establishment of a new city 'neutral' between the states is a common device (Ottawa, Canberra, Islamabad). It may take many years for this to reach Metro proportions (Canberra attained 200,000 in 1967); but Delhi, which preceded independent federation, had passed two million by 1967 and is growing fast. If no *ad hoc* federal city is established the capital tends to be just the largest city, the commercial and business capital (Buenos Aires, Lagos, Mexico City, Tehran). This complicates the problem because the capital city acts as a special magnet, drawing in more immigrants than other Metros. Since the capital city is the country's showpiece for the outside world the national government is usually anxious to see a better standard of service than elsewhere. Thus the education and housing standards of Lagos were long the envy of the western Region with which it was contiguous.[8]

There are however two possible disadvantages for the capital city Metro. First, its government is not really independent so that the city Council finds itself in an ambiguous position, not knowing quite how far it can go in various directions. This uncertainty is not productive of efficiency. In some respects there will certainly be overlapping services and divided responsibility. For instance in Tehran traffic regulation falls between the two stools of the city police and the national (quasi-military) force. Secondly, in countries where a new capital has been created the citizens will probably

[8] The new state of Lagos now covers these areas.

be to some extent disfranchised, and unable to introduce the improvements they seek. These difficulties are not insuperable; they merely illustrate the ways in which a capital city Metro needs special attention, although it is probably the centre of wealth in the whole country.

In spite of areas of slum and grinding poverty, by and large in L.D.C.s Metros are concentrations of wealth as compared with the rest of the country. Some Metros however are really poor, due perhaps to a historical accident or to the decline of the area in which they are situated. (Calcutta has had both these disadvantages: loss of her hinterland on Partition and decline of the jute industry.) For such unfortunate Metros the prospects of improvement, which must come from outside, depend partly at least on the degree to which interlocal and interpersonal redistribution are considered important as a matter of national ideology. In India for instance *interlocal* redistribution is certainly considered important. It is promoted by such means as grants, loans and direct investment, but there is still room for a more active policy. On the other hand in India in spite of much talk of the Welfare State *interpersonal* redistribution within the cities seems to arouse little interest. It is left to religious and private agencies to fill the gap as best they can.[9]

In contrast to India, Mexico does not appear to take much interest in interlocal redistribution, unless one can include recent efforts by the Development Bank to use its grants to persuade firms to set up in poor areas or areas of high unemployment. On the other hand the excellent 'national health' hospitals in Mexico City as well as some low income housing, are signs of a constructive policy of interpersonal redistribution.

Interpersonal and interlocal redistribution are complementary sides of the same problem. A country which is interested in the advancement of all its people will be anxious to find ways and to receive help in order to improve them both.

[9] For instance the excellent work of the Indian Social Institute, run by Jesuits.

We may now summarise our rapid overview of the problems of Metros in L.D.C.s. First come those which are common to Metros the world over: mass population movements, especially immigration, and consequent additional need for housing, schools, hospitals and protective services, over and above what would in any case have been necessary to raise standards. Secondly we must put congestion – in the streets and in the number of persons per house, especially in the central areas, coupled with inadequate means of cleansing and control, leading to pollution of air and water. As a result health hazards are serious and there is a high incidence of pollution diseases, almost all preventable. Thirdly, the situation is complicated by a large number of separate jurisdictions within the Metro area. Some of these are poor, some richer, but with a preponderance of poor in the inner 'core city' districts. Great difficulty in formulating a policy is inevitably experienced unless it is possible to establish land-use planning throughout the Metro area. Metros in a federation share a further jurisdictional problem in that the states within which they lie and to which they must look in the first instance for help, tend to be both poorer and less interested in the fate of the Metros than national governments would be.

Metros in L.D.C.s share all these difficulties, but they are manifested in an exaggerated form because there is more to be done and less money with which to do it. There is a lack, sometimes a complete absence, of basic water services, especially pure water supply and sewerage. Their population 'explosion' is heavily weighted with very poor immigrants, many hardly employable even if there were jobs for them. Hence the unemployment problem tends to occupy a central place in public consciousness. A government which has done much to raise the standard of living in general may still cease to command the confidence of the electorate if it is considered not to have done enough for the unemployed (as at the last election in Sri Lanka). In the educational field the illiteracy rate is high and there are many obstacles to establishing a wide coverage with adequate buildings and teachers, even at the primary level. At the same time there is often a distressing amount of graduate unemployment. But the greatest obstacle to improvement is lack of finance, coupled with lack of managerial ability to make the best use of such funds as may be available.

Our next task is to examine on what financial resources the great cities draw.

9 Fiscal Practices and Potentialities

Before settling down to discuss the financial resources available for urban development it is desirable to pause for a moment to consider what the total orientation and image of local finance should be. Local finances are part of a national tax system and their potentialities depend on (or are heavily influenced by) the fiscal policies and practices of higher levels of government, as well as on what they are formally permitted to do under the Constitution.[1] For instance heavy use by the national government of income, profit, general sales and turnover taxes may virtually squeeze out any use of these taxes by local governments, even by Metros. Again, in a federation the states frequently have the right to taxes on land, and it is only by their grace and favour that local governments can have an independent stake in these most useful taxes.

On the expenditure side the current account commitments of local governments are very regular and unvarying. Consequently they require a good steady revenue which will obviate the necessity in bad times of either borrowing in order to pay teachers and other public servants, or letting the standard of services fall. It follows that the extent to which lower level governments can practise 'compensatory finance' is very limited. In fact it would be a mistake for them to attempt to do so. This is the special province of the national government,

---

[1] Following the lead of India it has become customary in new federations to draw up specific lists of central state/local and concurrent tax powers and expenditure duties. Cf. R. Watts, *New Federations* (O.U.P., 1966).

since it is responsible for the level of economic activity in the economy and for the health of the balance of payments. In pursuance of these aims it has the right to control important taxes; and in case of need it can devalue the currency. Cities cannot do this and neither can they be allowed to go bankrupt. Nevertheless if they possess a good steady source of revenue they should be able to avoid 'fiscal perversity': reducing services and raising taxes and charges in bad times. This is the most that can be expected of them in this field.

From the local standpoint the most important consideration is that the cities (and so far as possible less powerful local authorities also) should have sufficient resources which they can exploit independently, allowing for national constraints; sufficient that is, so that the content of their budgets and the priorities which they enshrine are basically of their own choice. Not merely should their resources be sufficient in the present, they need a good upward elasticity, since all the services for which they are responsible are rapidly expanding. Good elasticity is especially necessary for Metros in L.D.C.s due to the present under-development of public services within their areas. The raising of these services to an acceptable standard implies progressively rising costs, quite apart from the effect of population expansion and the probability of rising wages and costs of materials. These conditions are more easily satisfied if there is a variety of resources available (at least for Metros) than if they are confined to a single tax source, however reliable.

A high degree of budgetary freedom need not be incompatible with 'guidance' in the choice of priorities in the interests of national policy. Such guidance can take a number of forms, such as differential grants or subsidies, low interest rates for a particular type of project or for special areas, in short any means of persuasion (not compulsion) that seems relevant. So long as the assistance offered is moderate it should not distort a Metro's budgetary choice and incentive should still be active. How large a bait a national government will have to offer to attain a desired reaction from Metros depends

to a considerable extent on the interest which Metros – or
a particular Metro – display in the matter. If there is a big
local demand for the objective then a small amount of aid
will suffice. But if the subject is one of little interest in
terms of local politics a large grant will be needed if the
national government thinks the objective important. The
grant must however stop short of 100 per cent if efficient
implementation is to be assured. The optimum amount of
assistance can often only be ascertained by trial and
error.

These considerations are common to Metros in every
country that values local initiative and regards its Metros
as essential leaders in the economy. Even in countries
with an authoritarian form of government a degree of
democratic freedom is not infrequently to be observed at
the local end (we might instance Taipai and Athens).
Unfortunately in L.D.C.s the attainments of these
principles is made more difficult, firstly by the low
standard of literacy, necessitating a greater need for
personal contact with taxpayers and others; secondly the
scarcity of reliable and trained tax assessors and
collectors is a continual handicap; thirdly, partly arising
out of this shortage, is the virtual impossibility of using
certain tax sources which are normal in A.C.s. Thus the
range of fiscal opportunity is narrowed, which sets up a
tendency for the over-use of bad taxes. As a result taxes in
L.D.C. Metros tend to be unnecessarily regressive. For
instance valuations for property tax are especially
inaccurate on large properties (perhaps more through
inefficiency than through political favour). Again,
general turnover or sales taxes tend to fall most heavily
on the wage goods of the lower income groups.

Finance for urban purposes can in principle be
obtained from four different sources: (1) income – rents
or profits – derived from capital assets or rights owned by
the Metro, (2) taxes, (3) grants or subsidies from higher
level governments or from abroad, and (4) investment
loans from higher level governments or from public
agencies at home or (less frequently) from abroad. Let us
consider each of these in turn.

(1) A number of Metros own considerable amounts of real estate: land, office buildings, garages, domestic property. From most of these they should be able to derive some net income. The main exception is low income housing which inevitably has to be subsidised both as to construction and as to maintenance. Not many Metros in L.D.C.s have ventured far into this field and when they have done so the results have not been particularly auspicious.[2] Reliable contractors and housing managers are hard to come by. Research into locally appropriate building methods and materials has been very meagre.[3] This is a field in which foreign experts could contribute a great deal, and it is one which is essential for urban reform. In respect of income from other forms of property the results are often disappointing due to poor management and maintenance. It has to be faced that monsoon climates are unkind to buildings and correspondingly more maintenance is required if the property is not to deteriorate. Opportunities for increased income undoubtedly lie in this field and should be exploited.

We next come to profits from trading services and public utilities. Those most commonly managed by Metros in L.D.C.s are the usual: electricity, gas, water (including sewerage and waste disposal) and public transport. In principle all of these could bring in some return from user charges, and some of them should be capable of making a net profit on the whole undertaking. In practice they rarely do so; in fact they are more likely to be operating in the red. This is in strong contrast to

---

[2] A bold slum clearance and re-housing scheme in Lagos was marred (1) by the use of more substantial and expensive construction material than the climate required and (2) by a system of subsidised rents which gave a differential advantage to the largest accommodation, thus inflating demand and costs in respect of the whole scheme. The project formally belonged to an *ad hoc* Board, a device adopted to 'keep it out of politics', but financially the government was heavily involved.

[3] Nairobi is an exception. A light but durable sheeting of pumice and coral cement was evolved which enabled construction to be carried out quickly and cheaply.

some A.C. Metros such as those in West Germany, Sweden and South Africa. In the case of West Germany and even more so in South Africa, such a policy has been more or less forced on local authorities by the paucity of local tax rights. It need hardly be said that from an economic point of view this is not an optimum situation. But Sweden is different, for there the local authorities have better tax rights than in almost any other country (as we shall discuss below, p. 175). In addition however a number of local authorities have a stake in valuable industries such as timber products. These can clearly sustain commercial prices if they are well managed.

In the L.D.C.s it is common to find that public utilities and trading services which should be making a gross profit at least sufficient to cover interest charges, are instead operating perpetually in the red. For this state of affairs there are a number of explanations which recur again and again, revealing mismanagement which could often be put right with relatively little trouble if once the situation were properly understood.[4] A common explanation is that the services are working at too small a scale. Most public utilities work under conditions of increasing returns to scale, and until the scale is considerable unit costs will be high. This situation may be merely a transitory phase; but it raises the question (so much debated in the U.S.A.) of over- or under-provision of public services. In most L.D.C.s governments, national and local, are anxious to undertake public services whether or not conditions for their success are likely to be realised. It is common to find public utilities working at less than full capacity either because the initial installation was larger than could be efficiently supplied with the necessary complementary parts, or because the equipment itself was poor, old or inappropriate. This condition is made worse by poor maintenance,[5] so that

[4] Cf. Burnell and Vince, Modern Transport Consultancy, *Report on the Tehran Bus Company*, June 1970.

[5] Thus when Lagos took over the public transport system from a private operator it was found that the buses had been badly maintained; apprehensive that they would not be able to get them started in the morning, the drivers kept the engines running all night.

up to 25 per cent of the equipment may well be out of commission at any moment. In many situations the leading trouble is with the administration. Friends travel free on the buses; user charges for gas and electricity are not collected.

On the other hand in some circumstances the management could do better if it were allowed to raise prices to a remunerative level, but is prevented from doing so by a higher government, for political reasons. The management then cannot meet the demand, since its deficit rises with every additional passenger carried, or unit sold, as the case may be. The supply of water essentially falls into this category although it is usually not expected to cover its running costs for fear of curbing demand on health grounds. The original installation is found to be extremely expensive, so an insufficient supply of good water is planned. As population expands and demand rises it is then found necessary either to make an entirely new installation or to introduce expensive purification works[6] which are at best no more than a palliative. Similar troubles are encountered in sewerage and waste disposal works. In respect of all these services running in the red implies that the deficit must be carried on the general budget (unless a higher level government is – improvidently – prepared to come to the rescue.) Thus those who do not enjoy the service are penalised.

The capital requirements of the social services, schools, offices, hospitals and so on, are normally financed by borrowing, either by the Metro itself or with help from a higher level government. Once established there should be a modest income available from fees and rents. But from the nature of the services charges cannot be pressed. The greater part of current finance and maintenance must come from taxation, in so far as it is not possible to bring charitable organisations into the picture. The protective services – law and order, police,

---

[6] Tehran is a prime example of this, see below, p. 252.

prisons and fire services – again must mainly be financed from taxation, although court and police fees and fines in some L.D.C.s are often far from negligible. There is also the possibility that higher level governments will make grants for police and other protective services. This however may be a mixed blessing since the grant-giving authorities may insist that the personnel shall enjoy remuneration and terms of service at national standards which may be quite unnecessary in local conditions.[7]

A final potential source of income in this category is from the Metros' right to grant licences and permits to carry on certain activities. The majority of true licences are of a regulatory nature and cannot be pressed as a source of revenue without having undesirable effects. Certain trading licences (such as for tobacco and liquor or for stalls in the market) may bring in small returns, but the chance of stimulating black-market sales is high.[8] Similarly licences for radio and television are usually kept low because the authorities wish to use them for communication and educational purposes. 'Licences' and other charges related to motoring are in a different class and are best considered as indirect taxes (see below).

It emerges that the contribution to Metro funds of all our first group of incomings are unavoidably meagre in L.D.C.s. That is not to say that with improved management considerably better results could be obtained; but for substantial funds we must look to taxes.

(2) Taxes suitable for management by L.D.C. Metros may be levied on any or all of five broad groups: (a) property – personal and impersonal, (b) transfers of certain kinds of property, (c) consumer outlay on general sales and turnover, or on selective commodity sales,

---

[7] States and cities in India have much experience of this disadvantage.

[8] Nigerian Local Authorities used to operate some picturesque minor licences, such as for drumming and for exercising the profession of a wandering minstrel. With the onset of modernisation these revenue sources have tended to decline.

or on transport of goods and people, (d) on incomings – personal and impersonal – such as realised
income, imputed income or potential income, (e) on
capital, either total or incremental (capital gains, estate or
gift taxes). Many of these are only suitable for operation
by very large Metros and where the whole area can be
made subject to the same tax. Moreover the majority of
these taxes are unlikely to be reserved for the exclusive
use of Metros. Thus their scope is limited and their
independence doubtful. We should nevertheless have a
look at them all before condemning any of them as
non-starters.

The leading tax base for local purpose (formerly for all
purposes) is land. Normally this would include any
buildings thereon. This base has three merits not shared
(or not shared fully) by any other. First, the base is
completely localised; secondly, values do not fluctuate
violently and unpredictably as do commodity sales and
incomes. The main cause of fluctuation in revenue
receipts is generally difficulty in collecting revenue in
bad times. The base could expand or contract in an
intervaluation year through the demolition of buildings,
the addition of new buildings or by change of user. But
the revenue effects of such marginal adjustments are not
likely to be great. Thirdly, presuming that the valuation
is fixed for a term of years, both assessment and
collection are very economical. These advantages are
shared by all real estate taxes, whatever their type and
whatever degree of development of the country in which
they operate. Both in A.C.s and in L.D.C.s they are
almost universally in use in one form or another. They
are generally known as property taxes, but must be
distinguished from true capital taxes since there is no
attempt to include every form of asset. In order to reach a
judgment on the best type for Metros in L.D.C.s we must
briefly examine the main types.

Property tax may be levied on a capital value base, and
in fact this is the usual practice.[9] Capital value may be

---

[9] Outside the British Commonwealth.

defined as market selling price, ascertained from the
record of sales or imputed by analogy where there are no
actual sales, on the basis of what a willing buyer would
offer and a willing seller accept. Alternatively capital
value may specifically include expected appreciation,
looking further ahead than the market, and including
probable change of user, according to the judgement of
the valuer. The base may be confined to land,
disregarding buildings. Or alternatively it may be
confined to buildings, disregarding land. Most commonly it covers land as developed, including buildings. The
tax may also attempt to cover certain other durable
consumer goods such as automobiles, watches, works of
art or luxury. In addition intangibles (such as stock
exchange securities) may come within its purview. The
tax may essentially be directed to personal property only,
or it may also include industrial and commercial
buildings and equipment. In this case it is common to
find that the impersonal property is more heavily valued
than the domestic (we return to this point below, p. 167).

The alternative to a capital value base for a property tax
is annual value. This is derived from rents, and its
plausibility largely depends on a sufficiency of market
rent evidence. The base may be actual rents, or it may be
attempted to estimate a fair or average rent, on the basis
of what a willing tenant would be prepared to give and a
willing landlord to accept. (These characters, it may be
observed, are as elusive as the willing buyer and willing
seller, especially in conditions of rent control.) In point
of fact in L.D.C.s renting is not very common, other than
the ephemeral type of 'bed space', which is in no way
suitable as a tax base. Where some sort of formal rents do
exist they are usually heavily rent controlled.

The shades of difference in the interpretation of these
two bases for the property tax reveal the Achilles heel of
this whole family of taxes: the process of valuation.
Whatever base is adopted it is clearly necessary that it
should be adhered to, and that initially there should be a
comprehensive and objective valuation of all the
property to be included. In some ways it is better to have

relative values more correct than absolute values, since the amount of tax due depends on both the valuation and the rate at which the tax is levied upon it. This is a difficult and costly process; but it is only the beginning. To preserve the equity of the tax (and especially the relative equity between different types of property and different localities) it is necessary that there should be regular revaluations, say every five years. Normally land values are stickier than other prices; but where inflation and speculation are rife they may rise quickly and dramatically, although probably at substantially different rates from one area to another. These difficulties are especially likely to be encountered in L.D.C. Metros with their ultra-rapid rate of expansion. It is to be hoped that inexperienced administrators and valuers can overcome these hurdles and make a good job of the tax.

However it is undertaken a true valuation is a difficult and expensive exercise. It demands the services of experts who have not merely the right training but also the right experience; for only long experience can produce the sound judgement on which the equity of the tax largely depends. Initially it would be wise for an L.D.C. Metro to hire a team from abroad for the first valuation. It should be insisted that they would demonstrate to the Metro officials and Council members the method by which they are proceeding, in order to convince them of its equity. Promising young officers can then be trained for subsequent revaluations. Even a large and wealthy Metro will find it a great easement if a higher level government will look after the valuation exercise. This may well be in its interest since if more tax is raised locally there will be less need for aid from central funds. Unfortunately it is common experience that while a Metro may succeed in screwing itself up for the initial valuation it is much more difficult to keep enthusiasm going for subsequent revaluations, although technically they should be a great deal easier. Unless valuations are kept up to date the equity of the tax will deteriorate and the revenue become eroded. It is important for administrations to realise this from the start.

The feasibility of a good property tax depends very much on the type of base chosen. Given a reasonably free and active capital market the easient to manage is the selling-value capital base. In a rapidly expanding Metro there should be no shortage of evidence. All that is then required is that careful maps and records of all sales should be kept. As values rise the base will automatically expand: directly where there have been sales and by analogy in the neighbourhood. The recorded sales will provide the information for increased valuations quite reliably, although naturally the values cannot rise by the full amount of the additional sales price, on the consideration that an individual sale may be unique, whereas if a large number of houses in the street had been for sale lower prices would probably have been realised. The capital based tax should subsequently exhibit a fair amount of elasticity. In fact it can be regarded as a method of taxing capital gains as they accrue, not merely when they are realised.

By contrast the annual value base is much less suitable for L.D.C.s. Not only is there likely to be a shortage of usable rent evidence, but the base has less natural expansion, since values can only reasonably be increased when there is a new rent contract. Britain has used the annual value base since the start of the local 'rate' in the thirteenth century. British colonial officials found it easier to introduce the base with which they were familiar and could explain to the people. (It appears that in some ways it is easier to 'get across' the idea of a tax based on an annual payment than one based on the more difficult concept of capital value.) Once governments have got accustomed to one base it is difficult to persuade them to change to another.[10]

[10] In India it is sometimes argued that the capital value base would be impossible for a local tax since capital taxes are on the Union list. But the best opinion appears to be that a property tax is not a true capital tax. Some parts of the Commonwealth have adopted the capital base, for instance the three East African and two Central African (now independent) countries. Rhodesia also uses this base. In all these countries the originator of the idea was South Africa which was directly influenced by Henry George. Most of them use (at least partially) the unimproved value base.

Two other problems in the valuation field require brief mention: the level of assessment to be aimed at and the relative rates of tax to be assessed on different types of property. In an ambitious Metro with few other good revenue sources the property tax is likely to be pressed hard so that on certain categories of taxpayers it becomes a substantial burden. It may consequently be thought politic to discriminate in favour of some classes of taxpayers. Thus domestic property may be charged lightly or, more rarely, it may be discriminated against in relation to commercial or industrial property. Again in respect of domestic property it may be decided that owners of larger property should pay at a higher rate than the little man. One method of introducing discrimination is by varying the level of assessment. So long as a comprehensive, non-discriminatory, 'full and fair' (to use the American phrase) valuation[11] has been carried out there is no great harm in this.[12] Although the motives for discrimination are often suspect, since they depend on social, economic or political judgements, they are presumably acceptable to the taxpayers. For instance it may be desired to encourage industry to come to – and remain in – the area. Or again it may be observed that personal taxpayers (who have votes) scream louder at a rise in rates than business or industrial firms who look to pass on the extra charge in enhanced selling prices.

By and large property taxes levied at the same rate, according to their relative valuations, are in principle a more or less proportional tax, whether on a capital or on an annual base. In practice they are to some extent regressive (although too much is often made of this)

---

[11] Some U.S.A. authorities try to please their taxpayers by decreeing a fractional general level of assessment. Such a tampering with what should be a reliable yardstick can set up a very bad ravel. I know of no L.D.C. Metro which uses this method. Their trouble lies further back with faulty valuation.

[12] Thus British 'productive industry' was taxed at only 25 per cent of the official valuation from 1929 until a few years ago. Some of the benefit of this easement was lost through the growing under-valuation of domestic property, fundamentally due to rent controls introduced in two wars. Cf. U. K. Hicks, *The Valuation Tangle.*

primarily because accommodation is a larger item in low income family budgets than in higher income households.[13] Statistical investigations in A.C.s have shown that the degree of regression is considerably less serious than that of some sales taxes on wage goods.[14] But payments for accommodation are an overhead and in special circumstances, such as temporary failure of the family income, or out of the lowered income of old age pensioners who do not reduce their housing costs *pari passu,* the tax may become a serious burden. Metro Councils are specially sensitive about the burden of the tax on lower income groups, partly no doubt because they form a large body of taxpayers. If the tax is on an annual value base an easement can very easily be written in the form of a 'rate rebate' for which taxpayers can apply.[15] A similar rebate could presumably be introduced into a capital based tax; but it would less certainly reach the people for whom it was intended. It may be questioned however whether such sophistications would be in place at all in an L.D.C. Metro.

An alternative method of bypassing any regressive effects of the property tax is the so called 'sliding scale' or assessment of the tax at rates progressing with the size of the property. This idea is popular in a number of L.D.C.s. In the absence of an effective national system of progressive taxation this seems to present one way of making the rich pay more, and so furthering social policy while benefiting the revenue. It has been very noticeable in rural areas where the sliding scale has been in operation that it leads to the splitting up of properties in

[13] Small property also tends to be more homogeneous than large and so is easier to value.

[14] Cf. R. Netzer, *The Economics of the Property Tax* (Brookings Institution, 1966); Hicks, *The Incidence of Local Rates in Great Britain* (N.I.E.S.R. Occasional Papers, vol. VIII (1945) and the (Allen) Report of Committee on the Impact of Rates on Housing.

[15] A rebate of this nature became a feature of the British rate system under the first Wilson Government. Applications for it have been less than expected suggesting that the hardship was not in practice very great.

order to escape the higher rates,[16] but this could also occur in urban areas. Consequently the hoped for additional revenue is not realised. In any case a partial property tax is not an appropriate medium for implementing a policy of redistribution. The consideration that in A.C.s any regression in the property tax is much more than compensated by highly progressive income and capital taxes, while in L.D.C.s the progression of the tax structure exists more on paper than in practice, does not justify the attempt to introduce a progressive element inappropriately.

In addition to regression there is a further drawback to the forms of property tax so far discussed. Both on a capital base (as described) and on an annual base they exhibit some disincentive effects on building and property improvements. In principle anything that enhances the value of the property makes it liable to a higher valuation and hence to additional tax. The answer to this difficulty has been sought by exempting buildings and other 'improvements', confining the valuation to so called 'unimproved value'. Strictly speaking in this case the tax base should be the original condition of the site including only its location and natural amenities. This should be aggregated up to a certain point of time and discounted to the present, allowing for foreseeable changes of user. Accurately valued this would amount to a very considerable sum, which in principle should check speculative price rises in land values.

The attraction of this base, properly assessed, would be that as and when development took place there would be no rise in tax. Thus larger and better buildings could be erected at a profit than if they had a rise in tax coming to them. Unfortunately all the problems of valuation show up in an exaggerated form in respect of the U.V. base. There is no inherently 'right' way of valuing what is never sold: a built-up site without its building. Consequently valuations tend in practice to include such development as has already taken place. Some more or

[16] Cf. J. R. and U. K. Hicks, *Finance and Taxation in Jamaica*, 1954.

less arbitrary dichotomy is then made between the value of the site and the value of the building[17] – perhaps on the basis of estimated replacement cost of the building. What emerges is simply a more or less complete 'detaxing' of the building. In itself this should give some stimulus to building; but there is no guarantee that the most appropriate erections will occur in the places in which they are wanted. The best stimulus is likely to be for large buildings in expensive areas where the differential advantage of the base is greatest. This will add to the prosperous and modern appearance of the Metro; but it will be laying up future trouble with congestion and parking problems. More serious, it will accomplish very little for the regeneration of bad areas.

There remains the problem of which tax base will best promote both improvement at the centre and orderly development on the fringes. This problem is closely related to the much debated question of compensation for damage and charge for betterment of property values as a result of the action of public authorities. Since this aspect is likely to have special importance on the fringes it should be of great interest in L.D.C. Metros. As we have seen, there seems as yet to be less out-migration of the wealthy seeking more air and less taxes in L.D.C.s than in the U.S.A. In places such as Mexico City and Tehran the level of taxation is so low that tax havens are hardly necessary. But the situation might change at any time, especially if better assessment and collection of internal taxes were to be established.

Even with the degree of integration that is now foreseen, the rise in land values on the fringes will probably be dramatic. Until development actually takes place these areas will probably continue to be valued at agricultural levels. Hence unless or until a fringe owner apprehends development in the near future, and consequent extension of the Metro tax area, it will pay him to keep his land off the market until he judges that the net gain from disposing of it will be maximised. Thus

[17] Thus Jamaica was advised to adopt the ratio used in New Zealand, itself an arbitrary figure.

there is likely to be spotty and incoherent development, costly to supply with communications and basic public utilities – in other words 'urban sprawl'. There are two possible answers to this problem. A comprehensive Land Use Plan can be prepared with estimates of potential betterment (development) charges which will be payable when development takes place. Clearly this exercise will be much easier to carry through if the whole Metro area has been brought together administratively.

Alternatively, areas considered likely to be developed within say the next five years, can immediately be given a double valuation, one on a rural and the other on an urban basis, which would be announced at once. The higher one would come into operation retrospectively on the start of development. For this to work well valuations would need to be kept very much up to date, since it is in just such areas that land values would be changing most rapidly. Such a procedure might well act as a curb to speculative holding. The valuation would include both betterment charge and compensation, as appropriate. (In principle both of these would be allowed for automatically in an accurate valuation on the base of market prices; but in practice this cannot be relied upon.)

There is however in many countries a strong feeling that it should be possible to tax betterment more specifically, and a number of attempts have been made to do so. While everyone agrees that betterment exists it has proved a 'will o' the wisp' exercise to identify, isolate and quantify it, and then to determine to what extent it is due to public activity.[18] L.D.C. Metros would be well advised to reserve their scarce staff for more important

---

[18] In the U.K., under the Attlee Government's Town and Country Planning Act, 1947, this was attempted through the principle of confiscating all development value; but the definition of this proved unworkable. More recently the Wilson Government set up a Land Commission to evaluate betterment. This occupied much time and personnel chasing little bits and pieces of betterment, to the detriment of the Income Tax administration from which the personnel had been drawn. The Land Commission was an early victim of the Heath administration.

investigations, relying on the change in market values to pick up most of the betterment.

We have seen that it is possible to introduce a modicum of interpersonal redistribution into the property tax, or at least to reduce its regressive effects. The question of interlocal redistribution is perhaps more important when we contemplate the relative riches of one Metro (say Delhi) and the poverty of another (say Calcutta). There is not much that individual Metros can do to reduce this imbalance; it is the business of higher level governments, state and national, to attend to it through their fiscal policy.

Within a single Metro however there may be very great inter-district differences in wealth. The same rate of property tax will bring in very different amounts of revenue per capita from one area to another. Internal redistribution at this level should be well within the competence of the Metro government and its sub-units. It depends on how much interest the Metro itself has in the matter, and on how far it can persuade the richer areas to help the poorer in the interests of the whole. Precedents for intra-Metro redistribution are not wanting. In London there has been a common poor law fund in operation from well back in the nineteenth century. The system is now in course of being extended to take account of the larger area of the Greater London Council as compared with the former London County Council.

From our discussion it will emerge that the property tax is a levy of great flexibility. Metros can operate it in whatever way suits them best. It can be a powerful tax capable of covering up to 80 per cent or so of their tax needs. Advisers and aid givers would provide a very great service if they could help Metros in L.D.C.s to make full use of it. We may pass more quickly over other tax sources because although they may in themselves be powerful revenue raisers they are not reserved for Metros, who must consequently take second or third place in their exploitation.

As has been said one great advantage of the property tax is that its base is unequivocally located within the area. There is a further small number of taxes which share this advantage, for instance taxes levied not on property itself but on its transfer from one owner to another. These can simply be collected by means of stamps on the relevant documents. The most likely candidate for such a tax would be transfers of real estate. Their base would also be unequivocally localised. Information collected for the tax on real estate and for transfers would mutually assist in the operation of both taxes. Transfers of automobile ownership might also be included in the tax if there is (as there should be on other grounds) an efficient system of registration and identification of ownership. Subject to the concurrence of higher level governments any Metro that had a stock exchange within its area could levy *ad valorem* duties on all transactions. (This would presume that there was not another stock exchange near at hand to which investors could easily transfer their operations.) Another possibility would be fees for registering trusts and corporations.

Levied in every case on the seller, stamp duties are equivalent to a modest capital gains tax. It is unlikely that any Metro could operate successfully a general capital gains tax. In any case such possibilities that exist for such a tax would probably be pre-empted by the national government. It cannot be pretended that even in the best circumstances and imposed at worthwhile rates, stamp duties would bring in a large revenue. But an ambitious Metro might well find them worth its while.

We now come to the large family of taxes on outlay (indirect taxes). We may start with those on transport and communications since in principle they can be controlled satisfactorily by Metros, subject of course to the concurrence of higher level governments. By far the most useful and potentially expanding tax in this group is the annual registration duty on motor vehicles. Small amounts of tax can also be extracted from other means of transport (as they put it in Jamaica from 'horsekind and wheels'). In view of the enormous numbers of pedal bicycles a small tax on them will bring in some revenue and will be useful in enforcing traffic regulations (for instance lights). Charges can also be made for the use of city car parks, garages and parking meters. (London experience however demonstrates that parking meters are too easily robbed if not watched.) 'Terminal taxes' on travel by rail and road have a long history in India. To these sources can now be added air passengers. While there are objections to taxes that reduce mobility of persons or freight, the elasticity of demand is likely to be fairly low.

In some Indian states the old Mahratta tax on goods entering the area still lingers. It is a thoroughly bad tax and 'octroi' (as it is still known in India) has long been abolished in the country which presumably gave it its name. Collection (and evasion) are impossible to check because of the many points of entry, and it is extremely disruptive of interlocal trade. It is lamentable to observe long strings of trucks loaded with perishables standing hour after hour in the broiling sun, waiting to be passed through the check point. Yet octroi remains in the states where it is traditional because it has the virtue of bringing in quite a sizeable revenue. This underlines the necessity of developing more modern taxes to enable bad traditional taxes to be withdrawn.

In India, as in many parts of the U.S.A., the pillar of state finances is a retail sales tax; in the U.S.A. it is also used by some cities. It is questionable whether a general retail sales tax would be feasible for Metros in L.D.C.s. The range of an Indian sales tax cannot be so wide as in America, due to the difficulty of including small traders who do not keep accounts and many of whom are illiterate. Even at the state level the tax is not operated very efficiently. When not long ago the Union government took over the administration of certain sales taxes from the states (distributing the revenue more or less on a derivation base) the revenue increased threefold, due merely to better administration. In the more advanced L.D.C.s prospects would no doubt be better; but it must be remarked (for instance) that the very large city of Tehran has very few department stores or self-service establishments.

Other taxes of a similar nature such as turnover taxes or taxes on value added would labour under similar difficulties; but would not necessarily be completely impossible. More promising is the imposition of surcharges on particular indirect taxes operated by national or state governments for instance on cigarettes or gasolene.[19] These would be easy for a Metro to manage; and if the higher level government allowed the Metro to have a fairly free hand in choosing the rate of surcharge, could be a not inconsiderable source of nearly independent revenue. The conditions and coverage would remain under the jurisdiction of the higher level government; but they would not necessarily be different from those that the Metro would have chosen itself. Under the heading of taxes on outlay we should perhaps also include lotteries in which people buy a chance of a large gain. These are popular in Mediterranean countries, especially in the poorer parts, and could no doubt be operated by some Metros in L.D.C.s. One would hesitate however to recommend them.

As we have seen, the country where local authorities seem to be most fiscally satisfied is Sweden.[20] This is largely due to their local (proportional) income tax, assessed both on personal and impersonal (profit) incomes. It is of long standing, actually preceding the progressive national tax, so that there is no question of ever withdrawing it. Formerly assessment was carried out by local voluntary committees who must frequently have based their findings on presumed or imputed income, since other data would not have been available. Recently it has been felt necessary to adopt more formal methods and both assessment and collection have been taken over by the national government; but it would not be surprising if some of the assessments at the lower end of the income scale were still made by primitive methods.

[19] Many countries operate a national tobacco monopoly and this would presumably knock out local government.

[20] For a good and up-to-date account of the Swedish local income tax, see Dr K. Knutson, contribution to a Conference organised by the Institute of Municipal Treasurers and Accountants, April 1970.

The change in the technique of operation does not necessarily render the tax any less independent so far as the local authorities are concerned; but there is a greater time lag before they receive the revenue that is due to them.

Local authorities in Kenya and Uganda operate an interesting type of tax, essentially on *potential* income. In rural areas the basis is the expected yield of the various assets (livestock and crops) under the control of the tax family. In these areas it is impossible to introduce the more obvious tax on land due to the fact that most land is in tribal, not individual, ownership. The assessments are graduated (rather unsatisfactorily on the 'slab' system) with a ceiling imposed by the national government.[21] In urban areas the Graduated Personal Tax (as it is called) does not work so smoothly in the absence of the easy rural indicators; but it is well worthwhile. In parts of Nigeria there is now a tradition of direct, slightly progressive, local taxes based directly on income. In so far as they can be collected by current withholding systems (which actually include day labourers by means of stamped cards) they are by no means unsuccessful and could well be copied elsewhere. Both the Swedish and the African local income taxes are available for all senior local authorities; but the revenue is naturally greater in large cities than in small ones or in villages. In the more sophisticated L.D.C.s there is no inherent reason why such a tax should not be a paying proposition, in so far as national governments would be prepared to allow lower level governments to operate it. Many national governments (and not only in L.D.C.s) make a very poor showing themselves at operating a progressive income tax; it might even be easier to work successfully for a more limited area.

The Indian constitution denies the use of income taxes at the state or local levels; but there is a sophisticated system of revenue sharing, which we shall examine below. Were it not for this constitutional prohibition it

[21] Cf. U. K. Hicks, 'Rural Taxation and its Contribution to Development', *Development and Change*, 13 (1969–70, The Hague).

might be possible to impose surcharges on the national tax. There is some precedent for this arrangement. In West Germany the local authorities have recently achieved this step forward. When the new arrangement has been run in it will give them a share in a rapidly expanding and elastic tax with a minimum of administrative bother; but shared taxes of this nature cannot be regarded as fully autonomous, any more than can local sales taxes. In India local governments have rights in a tax described as on 'trades and professions'. Some authorities have discovered that this can be developed into a sort of income tax on presumptive or potential income. It is a primitive form of tax, but it does bring in some badly needed revenue, and could bring in more if the very low pre-war ceiling on assessments were to be raised.

Few of the local taxes which we have been discussing are truly autonomous, although they may embody a certain independence if the rates can be determined locally. But by and large they will probably be being exploited by other levels of government. In the case of surcharges on state or national taxes it is the tax *source* which is being shared. It must be asked whether it would not be simpler to collect the tax at a single rate (or rates) for the whole economy and then to share the *revenue*. A percentage could be fixed nationally for the shares respectively of the national government and the state/local governments. Although assessment and collection would be still simpler than under an arrangement of surcharges on national taxes, it would obviously provide no autonomy or independence for lower level governments.

The trouble about this simplification is that the method of revenue sharing that is to be used raises very awkward political and social questions. The basis that appears to be the simplest is that of 'derivation', which may not be the same as 'revenue collected'. On this base revenue accruing (derived) from a particular jurisdiction would be returned to it in the proportion that it bore to total revenue collected by the tax, in so far as it was possible to

measure the relative shares correctly (often by no means
an easy matter). The result of revenue allocation by
derivation is that the richer the area the more it will get.
Poor areas, in any country which has an ideology of
interlocal equalisation, will not be prepared to accept
this. A simple alternative is to distribute the revenue on a
straight per capita basis. This will have an equalising or
disequalising effect according as the poor areas or the
rich areas have the denser population. One would expect
Metros to do relatively well out of this type of allocation.
A more sophisticated policy of equalisation calls for the
construction of an appropriate allocation formula; but
this is to anticipate the discussion of grants from higher
level governments as a source of Metro revenue.

It may be concluded that the tax systems of L.D.C.
Metros leaves a good deal to be desired. A fair part of this
can be ascribed to inefficient and corrupt administrations; probably better personnel was just not available, or
not available at the price the city was prepared to pay.
But taxpayer resistance is also an important factor. Since
the taxes are not heavy in terms of what local taxpayers in
A.C.s are accustomed to, this suggests a lack of
community consciousness and interest. This is indeed
very widely true; but we must reflect that social group
consciousness as understood in A.C.s is a very
sophisticated idea, far removed from the familiar tribal
group consciousness, it can only be expected to emerge
gradually. This generalisation needs qualification for
some Metros. The community feeling in Bombay seems
to be a good deal stronger than in other Indian cities.[22]
The growth of community consciousness depends a great
deal on the close co-operation and participation of
executive, council and citizens. In Metros with much
poverty and a low rate of literacy this is hard to bring

[22] The community feeling in Bombay is exceptionally good, due I
suspect to the influence of substantial Parsee and Ismaili
communities, both of whom have a strong social sense. Yet it was in
Bombay that I saw a notice strung across the street in a fashionable
area: 'The Society of Reluctant Taxpayers Welcomes You'.

about; but generally speaking a good deal more might be done to foster it.

The question is sometimes asked whether earmarking of certain taxes for particular purposes may not help to break down taxpayers' resistance. Taxpayers feel that the money they part with is really going to finance some desired objective. Thus in a number of countries motoring taxes are earmarked for road works. In principle the earmarking of taxes is not a good idea since the rate at which it would be appropriate on general grounds to tax the consumers of the taxed good need not bear any close relation to the amount which it is appropriate to spend on the service.[23] If nevertheless it is proposed in an L.D.C. to impose such a tax, the best candidate would undoubtedly be for education. This has indeed been tried in a number of places.[24] In a community which greatly values education this may give good results for a time; but it is less flexible than planning and financing development from the general tax pool as the necessity arises. A policy of an earmarked tax for education is more likely to succeed in a community of fairly homogeneous income levels. The richer citizens and firms are allergic to paying for the education of the poor. Hence the policy of earmarking would probably not be very useful in Metros.

(3) As we have seen revenue sharing between the different levels of government amounts to a type of grant rather than to an independent source for the lower levels. It differs however from a true grant (the amount of which will be fixed at the beginning of the grant period) in that the amount available for transfer fluctuates with the total

[23] Perhaps the most famous case of inappropriate earmarking was the English nineteenth century tax earmarking the revenue from certain liquor duties for the development of higher education. There was a heavy demand for more education just when people were becoming more moderate whisky drinkers.

[24] For instance in some Indian states the tax is designated a 'cess' to indicate the special benefit it is supposed to produce. The word 'cess' is widely used in British taxation to indicate a levy whose revenue will be wholly devoted to the interests of the payers.

revenue collected. This creates a difficulty for the lower level government's budgeting since it has no means of estimating in advance what is coming to it. How much difficulty will be caused depends naturally on the importance of the amount to be transferred in the local budget. On the other hand if the revenue to be shared is derived from a rapidly expanding tax source the grant-receiving government will have a more elastic revenue than it would be likely to get under a straight grant system, where the amount of grant would be fixed for several years at a time. It is possible to write into the grant formula a rate of expansion for the later years; but higher level governments are unlikely to allow for much increase, lest it should encourage local extravagence.

Grants from higher to lower level governments can take many forms. Before discussing their relative appropriateness for the different needs of L.D.C. Metros it will be as well to consider briefly just what they are wanted for. In the first place there is in every country whose constitution is not entirely centralised a basic imbalance between fiscal resources and commitments at different levels of government. National governments must necessarily control the taxes that are needed to implement national policy – internally as respects economic and social balance and growth, externally in respect of relations with other independent governments, above all in the fields of defence and trade. These needs imply that national governments must have control not only of taxes on imports but also of income and profits taxes.

On the other hand lower level governments (especially Metros) usually have the major responsibility for national social service commitments, especially for education and health. In all countries social service expenditure is expanding very rapidly. It is virtually universal experience that over the last two decades at least lower level government outlay has been growing faster than central government budgets. Lower level governments have not the resources to finance these services unaided in ordinary circumstances, hence it is implied that the need for aid is rising rapidly. Even in

Sweden, where as we have seen local governments have relatively ample resources, grants have been expanding fast, although they are still small in relation to total local expenditure. Not only do lower level governments have growing needs on current account (especially Metros), as we noticed earlier most of the services which they supply require a good deal of fixed investment. Some of the funds for this can possibly be found out of their own budgets, but most will have to come from above, either by loan (which is costly) or by grants on capital account.

There are also matters of national policy to consider, for instance the development of particular medical services, improvement in the quality of protective services, or expansion of certain parts of the educational system. Local authorities (even Metros) may not be particularly interested in these developments. Far better than attempting to force their compliance is to work through the persuasive influence of promotional grants.[25] These however must have some sanction of control if they are to do their work efficiently. The carrot without the stick can be very expensive for the grant-giving government.

Finally, grants are one of the most serviceable instruments that national governments have for interlocal redistribution. In this respect they are an alternative and more flexible instrument than a revenue allocation. Interlocal equalisation grants can be awarded on current account by a suitable formula, either directly on the responsibility of a higher level government, or they may be determined by some independent commission such as the (Australian) Commonwealth Grants Commission (a perpetual body) or the Indian Fiscal Commissions which are appointed every five years for one grant[26] period.

[25] Cf. D. N. Chester, *Central and Local Government* (Macmillan, 1951).

[26] Formerly in Nigeria and in the Federation of the Rhodesias and Nyasaland the revenue allocation was made automatically from a 'distributable pool' derived from a number of taxes. The composition, size and method of allocation was determined by an independent Commission every five years.

If grants are required to serve all these purposes it is not surprising that there should be a need for more than one type of transfer. In fact it is normal to find that a number of different grants are in operation together, but that they have been awarded in a haphazard manner often emanating from different sources.[27] To get the best results it is clearly necessary that they should be integrated with each other, so that it is possible to estimate the total effect on central and local funds. It should also be possible to calculate the impact on each individual Metro. It would take us too far afield to go into this very complicated problem in any detail; but there are some generalisations which can usefully be derived from experience. For present purposes we can concentrate on three types of grants: (1) unallocated (block), (2) specific (carrot and stick) and (3) project (for a particular purpose). The first two would have reference only to current outlay but project grants might well include provision for capital outlay as well as for immediate needs.

(1) The basic purpose of an unallocated grant is to provide lower level governments with additional free income, in lieu of widening their tax rights. Being without strings it does not disturb the priorities of the local budget. From the point of view of the grant-giving authority the block grant is probably the easiest type to use as an instrument of redistribution. If an objective measure (which is not capable of control by the lower level governments) of relative needs and relative tax potentials can be found, the going is easy. A reliable comprehensive valuation for property tax is probably the simplest measure, unless indeed there are available estimates of local incomes. Failing a good and up-to-date valuation, resort must be had to indicators such as level of unemployment proportions of dependent population (children and geriatrics) which will serve as proxies. So far as the process of distribution is concerned an efficient method is to confine the grant to authorities with less

[27] Cf. G. F. Break and R. Turvey, *Studies in Greek Taxation* (Research Monograph Series of the Center of Planning and Economic Research, Contos Press, Athens, 1964).

than the average potential ability of their class (e.g. Metros) and among these to increase it by the percentage by which each area falls short of the average.

The history of the Australian Commonwealth Grants Commission demonstrates that a block grant system can also be used as an instrument for the improvement of budgetary practices among the grant-receiving authorities.[28] The full grant will not be forthcoming until the Commission is satisfied that the true budgetary position has been set out. It is also always necessary to ensure that the amount of grant does not rise above a certain proportion of the total (Metro) budget, since this may lead to slack budgeting and a reduction of tax effort. With this apprehension in mind some Indian states have made it a condition of grant that certain minimum taxes must be imposed.

(2) Specific grants are a much sharper instrument than block grants both for promotion and control. In fact they may be too sharp, because they carry with them a certain risk of budgetary distortion. Services that are not grant aided are discriminated against. Further, they tend to be interlocally disequalising, because only the wealthier authorities can afford to take full advantage of them. (This assumes that we are not concerned with 100 per cent grants since they would be a clear invitation to lax expenditure.) There are thus two difficult problems for grant-giving authorities operating specific grants: first how to select the optimum level of assistance in each case (especially if it is also desired to write in an element of equalisation); and secondly how to ensure that the funds are allocated in a satisfactory manner. The use of unit cost or performance data from which deviations can be measured, explained and remedied, is the shortest route towards solving these problems. Even a sophisticated Metro would probably need some help in developing the relevant statistics. In respect of the control element the grant-giving authority will probably find it desirable to insist that a particular form of accounts is kept in respect

[28] Cf. W. Prest, 'Federalism in Australia', *Journal of Commonwealth Political Studies* (University of Leicester, March 1967).

of the aided services; and these will need to be backed up by inspections. In view of all these complications in relation to specific grants it is as well that they should not form a very high percentage of the whole.[29]

It must be envisaged that (apart from the states in a federation) the main recipients of current account grants will be Metros in the L.D.C.s. They are the most likely to have both the most pressing and best articulated needs and also the administrative expertise to use the funds wisely. But who should be the grant-giving agencies? In a unitary country obviously the national government (in so far as some special Commission may not have been created to deal with part of the problem). But in a federation local government is a state subject, so that they have the prime responsibility. In L.D.C.s in particular a very common situation is that while the states have a rather wide range of tax powers, they are loath to use them fully. They have not the authority of the national government, but they are still too remote from the taxpayers to convince them that the taxes will definitely be applied to things they really want. Thus taxpayers' resistance tends to be serious and the state governments are apprehensive of the political results of raising taxes. The national government will consequently find it desirable to bring what pressure it can on the states to see that they shoulder their responsibilities adequately.[30] There are a number of devices open to national governments for this purpose; but it would take us too far afield to consider them here.

(3) A project or capital grant is similar to an ordinary specific grant in that it is tied to a particular purpose. Consequently it raises parallel problems of the appropriate amounts of aid to be provided, in respect of effectiveness and of timing and also concerning techniques of control. It differs however from a current

---

[29] The Shoup Mission to Japan suggested 18 per cent of total grants as the maximum for specific grants.

[30] For an account of essentially the same problem in the U.S.A., see The American Assembly, op. cit.

account specific grant in that it is not intended to be a permanent feature of the grant structure. The grant may have reference to a single project, such as the setting up of an agricultural experimental station, building a hospital or specialised school. If the project is a large one it may take several years to complete, so that the timing of the transfers becomes very important. If the objective to be aided is a programme rather than a project (for instance low income housing, school building or the setting up of a chain of clinics) long-period planning will be required in respect of choice of site, type of buildings and time profile of the whole exercise. Thus different types of project call for different types of grant aid.

The first problem is the selection of projects and the arrangement of their priorities. This will naturally take place along broad cost/benefit lines but paying attention at this stage to the externalities rather than attempting close quantification. If the idea of the project emanates from the potential grant receiver a good Metro should itself be able to prepare a well reasoned scheme. Nevertheless the grant-giving authority may well wish to reassure itself by providing for a feasibility study by experts. If the transfer is to be made in a series of annual sums, estimates of the time profile of the inputs will also have to be made. Although as a result of experience it is now possible to define in general terms the probable time profile for works of different types, unexpected snags (such as delays in receiving necessary components) are always liable to turn up. These may not be in any way the fault of the implementing authority. It is of first importance for the grant-receiving government to have an assurance that it will not be penalised for this kind of delay (for instance by being made to return unspent balances at the end of the year). The whole process of construction of the project needs to be taken as an integrated exercise if the best results are to be obtained.

An alternative method for a higher level government to give assistance with capital programmes is for the implementing Metro to be put in a position in which it can borrow, and for the grant-giving authority to undertake to give an annual sum to cover the whole or part of the interest charge for the duration of the loan.[31] This however brings us into the field of methods whereby Metros can raise loan funds, and with it the problem of the relation between grants and loans for financing long term investments which are beyond the capacity of even the wealthier Metros.

(4) As we have discussed, cities have more need of investment funds than any other level of government, not excluding national governments. Almost all the services which they provide call for substantial fixed investment: in schools, hospitals, water and sewerage systems, housing, offices and road works. Most of the public utilities which they may undertake are also heavily capital using. There is very little scope for financing any of this from current surpluses, although certain programmes can sometimes be arranged so as to call for a steady annual charge (such as road works and school building) which can be covered in the current budget. If it were to be attempted to finance a large amount of capital works out of taxation their big requirements are so fluctuating as to be unmanageable in face of the inevitable rigidity of revenue receipts. Moreover financed out of loan the works are likely to be completed more quickly. This has to be set against the very considerable additional cost of loan finance, depending on the rate of interest which has to be paid and the length of loan required.[32] It is for the grant-giving authority to decide in each case whether, if assistance has to be offered, it should be in the form of a loan or a grant (or more likely what grant/loan mix will be optimum in particular circumstances). It does not promote good management to allow poor authorities to accumulate a debt burden they can never hope to repay, whereas for a richer authority a loan carries more

[31] For over 50 years in the U.K. large programmes of slum clearance and low income housing have been financed in this manner. The system is not proof against inflation and rising interest rates but it has undoubtedly been very effective.

[32] See my paper for the Toronto Conference on Metro Problems, 1967, for illustrations of the differences in costs for loans of different lengths at varying rates of interest.

freedom of management and choice of time profile in implementation, so that it may well be preferred. If a choice of this type has to be made it should be carefully considered and the decision made on economic and social grounds, not on rule of thumb methods.[33]

In principle there are a number of ways in which Metros may be able to have access to capital funds. The availability of these depends largely on higher level governments; but generally speaking it is easier to find lenders for trading services which should be self-sustaining in respect of debt service, than for social investment where the debt service will have to be found out of taxation. This proposition certainly seems to be true of contractor's credit (which we shall discuss later). But as we have seen the chance of trading services in L.D.C.s being really self-sustaining is not very high. It is consequently important to lenders to have an assurance that higher level governments would come to the rescue in case of local default. Even this may not be completely reassuring. We must consequently examine possible sources of loan funds which might be generally available.

In the first place a limited source exists for at least the larger Metros in the accumulation of internal reserves (sinking funds attached to loans, pensions and other commitments maturing in the future). So long as there is a reasonable certainty that in case of a sudden call the funds can be replaced temporarily by short term borrowing there is no reason why they should not be used for immediate capital formation. In the U.K. this is an important source of investment funds; but they are not likely to be so useful in L.D.C. Metros if only because they will have had much less time to accumulate.

In the past the larger Metros in the British Commonwealth had access to the London Stock

[33] The policy of the Indian Planning Commission of following rule of thumb methods (depending on the type of works) led to a very heavy debt burden in some of the poorer states, largely on account of Metro investment. This alarmed the Reserve Bank which had been under an obligation to provide the funds. See the Terms of Reference of the Fifth Finance Commission and my Memorandum thereon, 'Memorandum for the Consideration of the Fifth Finance Commission', *Indian Institute of Public Opinion*, x 3 (1968).

Exchange at very reasonable rates (under the Colonial
Stock Acts). These carried a British Treasury guarantee.
But this and similar sources have now largely dried up,
due on the one hand to the increasing control of new
issues by the lending countries in the interests of
national fiscal policy, and on the other to investors'
doubts concerning the release of funds for dividend
payments and eventual capital withdrawal. Project
borrowing from foreign governments (either in cash or
more likely in kind) has expanded rapidly; but it would
probably be only as a by-product of a national loan that it
would come the way of a Metro. The same is true also on
loans from international Agencies. There is also no
assurance that the finance offered would fit the Metro's
own priorities.

Where a Metro has set its heart on a particular project
and there seems no other way of getting hold of the
necessary funds contractors' credit may well come
forward to fill the gap. The Metro is of course under no
obligation to accede to the contractors' terms, but few
Councils (or city managers) can refuse what seems a good
offer and the chances are that they will not look too
closely. Even if the project has been wisely chosen and
correctly estimated on cost/benefit and feasibility lines,
the Metros will have virtually no control over the process
of implementation, particularly over the quality of the
work put in.[34] Experience of this source of finance in
various parts of the less developed world has tended to
reveal it as a 'borrowing of last resort', to be used only

[34] Two examples that have come within my experience are: (1) the
use of a French contractor to repair the major streets of
Tehran – within a year the pot-holes were back again; (2) use by the
city of Brisbane of contractors for various projects. When the costs
were totalled up they far far exceeded the sums originally mentioned.
Use of this source of funds by Brisbane was wholly the result of the
very tight rein kept on local authority borrowing by the Australian
Loans Board and hence by the State of Queensland. Nigeria is
another country which has made large use of contractors' credit, see A.
A. Ayida, 'Contractor Finance and Suppliers' Credit in Economic
Growth', *The Nigerian Journal of Social and Economic Studies* (July
1965), and Kathleen Langley, 'The External Resource Factor in
Nigerian Economic Development', ibid. (July 1968).

when more reliable sources are unavailable, and even then with great circumspection. It is the business of higher level governments to see if better ways of borrowing at home cannot be made available for the legitimate needs of Metros.

Consider first loans from the private sector. In a number of the A.C.s (especially Germany, Australia, Japan and the U.S.A.) commercial banks and insurance companies have proved a prolific source of funds, mainly for moderate sized and medium term loans. This source is likely to be less useful in the L.D.C.s, if only because most of the companies have their head offices and decision-making units outside the country asking for aid. Indigenous banks (for instance in Nigeria) are only too willing to lend but their funds are scanty. They also prefer investment in commercial enterprises to loans for social service development. In principle in L.D.C.s where stock exchanges have been started Metros might expect to float loans on them; but if such a demand were to develop it would be more likely that the national government would itself float the loan and relend to the Metro. In most L.D.C.s borrowing by lower level governments is very strictly controlled. Under some constitutions it is virtually prohibited.

Formerly British Metros found a ready source of mortgage-type funds among their own citizens, who were proud to have 'something on the Town Hall' by depositing their savings over the counter. This useful source has rather dried up since other openings (such as unit trusts) have developed for the small saver; nor is it likely to be much use in L.D.C.s where there is not a large body of small savers, just a few wealthy citizens and a mass of families who hardly save at all. The wealthy citizens might be persuaded to do something for their cities; but they would probably prefer to finance some conspicuous project bearing their name, or perhaps a school or hospital intended primarily for their own community.[35]

[35] For instance the 'Aga Khan's Maternity Home' in Dar-es-Salaam. Service is (I believe) not confined to members of the Ismaili community.

For longer-term funds L.D.C. Metros must rely on the national government, probably operating through the central Bank or Planning Commission. One method, which has been tried successfully in Kenya, is to set up a Public Works Loans Board on the lines of a very well established British institution. The Board is in a much better position to borrow than an individual Metro: it then relends to local authorities. Some L.D.C.s have established public savings funds of various types some of which are virtually compulsory and almost partake of the nature of a tax. These make loan funds available to Metros through a Development Corporation or Bank. One of the most successful organisations of this type is the Indian Life Insurance Corporation. It has a complete monopoly of life insurance business and has emerged as a major source of funds for urban development and renewal.

There are thus in principle a number of ways in which Metros in L.D.C.s might have access to capital funds. In practice however their investment funds are wildly inadequate for the tasks which they should be doing. Given better management,[36] more realistic choice of priorities and adequate project evaluation, much more use could be made of the sources of investment funds already available. This is a line in which international technical assistance could help enormously with advice and training in management.

[36] Although Indian states and cities are chronically short of funds, so that they can accomplish little, yet some of them have accumulated an unmanageable burden of debt at the Reserve Bank. A good deal of the blame for this state of affairs must be ascribed to the rigid policy of Delhi concerning loan and grant finance. (See above, note 33.)

10 Urban Problems in India*

As is now evident, the present troubles of the cities are a world-wide experience. The causes are everywhere fundamentally the same: the growth of urban populations well above that of national averages, the extreme mobility of the population, both in respect of the daily tide of commuters and in the longer run through change of base. City growth is largely due to rural/urban migration: but where the net reproduction rate is high (as it is in most L.D.C.s) the expansion of the initial city population may be an important contributory factor. As we have seen, the main weight of the population explosion falls on the large cities, which exercise a magnetism lacking in the smaller towns. This is general experience. The purpose of this chapter is to explore and discuss the particular aspects of the urban crisis which most affect India.

The population of India is still expanding at a fairly high rate. In the 1961/71 intercensal period the rate was 2·12 per cent per annum. This was not by any means the highest, when we recollect that, for instance neither

* A version of this chapter was included in *Indian Economic Thought and Development* (first Nehru Memorial Volume). In preparing it, I was greatly indebted to the works of Abhijit Datta, especially 'Financing Urban Development', *Economic and Political Weekly* (July 1969) and 'Financing Municipal Services', *Indian Journal of Public Administration* (XIV, no. 3); and also to Abhijit Datta and Mohit Bhattacharya, 'Centre-State Relations in Urban Development', *Indian Journal of Public Administration* (February 1966) and 'A Functional Approach to Indian Federalism', *Indian Journal of Public Administration* (1968); and finally to helpful discussions with friends at the Institute in December 1969.

Mexico nor Iran have yet got their growth rates below 3
per cent. It is forecast by the Indian Registrar General's
Department that in the 1971/81 intercensal period it will
prove to have fallen to 1·85 per cent, and thereafter will
gradually decline, reaching 1·30 per cent in the period
1981/2001. In India the major problem is thus not so
much the rate of growth (although this is obviously
important) as the sheer number of people that has to be
dealt with. Although India is relatively well provided
with good administrators, their work is much hindered
by the diseconomies of large scale with which they have
to work, both in rural areas and in the cities. In 1961 the
total population of India was 442 million; by 2001
(according to the most favourable projection) it will be
near 870 million. Less optimistically, it may reach 1000
million. The key factor in this respect is the success of
the family planning drive. This again (as appears clearly
from the statistics) is much influenced both by the level
of family incomes and by the level of parental education.
Both of these factors are improving.

The large Indian cities are indeed very large. The three
ancient 'Presidency' cities of Calcutta, Bombay and
Madras, and Delhi, the federal capital, have each
between two and seven million inhabitants. Delhi, as the
capital, has typically been growing fastest of all, but
Hyderabad, Ahmedabad and Bangalore were all over one
million at the 1961 census and they are still growing fast.
The average rate of city growth in 1961/71 seems to have
been 4·4 per cent, but in the large cities it was
considerably higher. Moreover the rate will most
probably accelerate: 5 per cent is forecast for the
following intercensal period. The rural sector in India
still comprises over 80 per cent of the population,
although it is slowly declining. In a country which will
eventually have a substantial manufacturing sector this is
clearly only a transitional phase. As in every country, it
makes a big difference whether we are measuring city
size according to traditional boundaries or by their
metropolitan areas. No formal Metro areas have yet been
designated in India, but it is evident, in Bombay at least,

that plans far exceed the city boundaries. (There is a Bombay plan, not yet formal, to establish a series of satellite towns of some 250,000 inhabitants to relieve congestion at the centre.)

The problems of the cities are particularly difficult in India from several points of view: first and foremost, the general poverty and low level of incomes throughout, although obviously not equally serious everywhere. Poverty has both rural and urban aspects which are quite distinct. The former is basically due to the unproductive nature of the soil and the uncertainty of the monsoon, when only it comes to life. In some areas the poor quality of the soil is largely due to overcropping, but the real villain of the piece is shortage of water. Adequate irrigation could enormously increase fertility, but it is very expensive, for where is the water to come from? It is estimated that at present no more than 30 per cent of the land that needs irrigation has been provided with it. It is recognised as an urgent priority to step this up to 50 per cent at least.

The generally poor achievement of Indian farming has two results. In the first place, rural incomes are very low, particularly among the landless families. Hence most rural families have a strong incentive to migrate to urban conditions. Secondly, it is difficult to assure a good regular supply of food at reasonable prices for urban dwellers, many of whom also have very small incomes. Opinions differ as to whether rural or urban poverty is the more pressing problem. A thoughtful Indian once said to me 'Rural poverty is pitiful, but urban poverty is horrible'; but a good deal of urban poverty derives directly from rural poverty. Consequently policy needs to be directed to both aspects at once: urban poverty being more visible tends very often to absorb attention. What is needed is to improve rural conditions and incomes and so reduce the incentives for mass rural/urban migration, while at the same time to tackle existing urban conditions on the spot. Important as the rural problem is, it must be with the urban aspect that we are here most concerned.

A second difficulty lies with the federal structure of the
Indian constitution. The fact that local government is a
state concern (as it is in all federations) makes it difficult
for the national government, which alone has the funds,
to help the cities directly. But as we have seen, national
governments in other federations (such as the U.S.A. and
Australia) are increasingly developing ways of doing so.
In this respect, India should be in a better position than
the other federations because of her strong national
Planning Institutions and their succession of Five Year
Plans. To some extent this is so, but as we shall see
below, the practical working out of central assistance to
local entities often leaves much to be desired.

Rapid urban growth is by no means a new
phenomenon in India.[1] In the intercensal period 1951/61,
of the seven largest cities Delhi expanded 63 per cent,
Bombay 46 per cent, Ahmedabad 45 per cent, Bangalore
35 per cent, Hyderabad and Calcutta 15 per cent. In
several of the Metro areas there are now signs that the
pace is beginning to slacken; but although the percentage
rate of growth may be falling in absolute terms, the cities
are growing faster than ever. Calcutta had its most rapid
percentage growth (85%) between 1931 and 1941.
Greater Bombay's (58%) was in the decade 1941/51, but
it has again accelerated. Madras grew by 82 per cent also
in the decade 1941/51. In this same decade Delhi set up a
record of 106 per cent, but it is still (it seems) the fastest
growing city in India (exactly parallel to Canberra in
Australia). Hyderabad reached its fastest growth in
1931/41, before its merger with Andhra Pradesh.
Ahmedabad also reached its highest rate (93%) in that
decade: the rate then declined, but picked up again in
1951/61 with the establishment of the new state of
Gujerat. Bangalore grew extremely fast (91%) in the
decade 1941/51, but then slackened, although it now
seems to be picking up again. In general, for many
although by no means all Indian cities the great decade

[1] Cf. Pravin Visaria, 'Growth of Greater Bombay 1951–1961',
Economic and Political Weekly (July 1969).

for percentage growth was 1941/51. The effect of state boundary changes is very noticeable.

The extent to which urban growth is due to immigration is important, not merely in terms of sheer numbers but also in respect of the type of immigrants, their sex and their intentions. In the A.C.s the immigrants have frequently come long distances. They may belong to different ethnic groups, thus creating racial tensions. In the U.S.A. the influx of coloured population from the south is a major cause of the urban crisis. In the U.K., similarly, there has been a certain amount of trouble with coloured immigrants who refuse to give up their traditional way of life and who consequently cannot be absorbed into their new environment (this trouble will almost certainly cease when the rising generation grows up). In India, in spite of language difficulties, this particular aspect of immigration is less noticeable. On the whole, the immigrants are similar to each other and to the initial population. Apart from the once and for all influx of refugees following on Partition, the immigrants have tended to come from near at hand: 'urban drift' seeking employment, a more varied life than that of the village and, in particular, education for their children.

There are some signs that this position may also be changing. On the one hand, with better knowledge and better communications, the rural emigrants are beginning to go further afield. For instance, Kerala is increasingly losing population to Bombay rather than to the neighbouring states of Mysore and Tamil Nadu. On the other hand, a certain (and increasing) proportion of the urban immigrants apparently do not drift vaguely into the cities, but attempt some crude but rational calculations of the probability of getting a good job in two or three years. In the meantime they are prepared to wait, picking up what odd jobs they can and perhaps having some small savings to help eke out over the short period. They reckon that, discounting the future income stream down to the present, benefits are likely to exceed costs. This would conform to Latin American patterns, where, however, incomes are in general larger and living standards higher. It is interesting that in Bombay of recent years the immigrants have experienced a lower unemployment rate, and exhibit a lower fertility, than the initial inhabitants. In so far as some such calculation is in fact made by potential immigrants, it could partly explain the failure of Calcutta to expand by immigration: in recent years in that city benefits have not looked like exceeding costs, but here again things may be changing, with the establishment of friendly Bangladesh on its frontier and the reopening of the vital water-borne commerce.

In very many countries, and certainly in general in India, the immigrants tend to be poorer than the existing residents, exhibiting more primitive social habits and a lower rate of literacy. Thus in the fast-growing suburbs of east Bombay, the immigrants' literacy rates (1961) were: males 55 per cent, females 33 per cent, compared with the well-established C Ward, where the rates were respectively 74 per cent and 66 per cent. The immigrants also exhibit a different sex ratio. In the whole Indian population there is a preponderance of males over females, but among the immigrants this is especially marked. Thus in Greater Bombay, the sex ratio of the population (1961) was broadly 6 : 5, but among the immigrants it was 8 : 4. But this may also be changing. In some Wards of Bombay female immigration was increasing more rapidly than male, so that gradually a more normal balance should be reached. In the meantime, the sex disparity produces social strain. It poses a problem of accommodation for single men in order to prevent them from becoming chronic 'footpath sleepers' with deleterious effects on their health. The vast majority are young adults who may easily become politically discontented if they cannot find jobs. But on the other hand, when once they are settled they will be starting or expanding families, and so inflating the future demand for education and health services.

In the U.S.A. immigration is to some extent balanced (fiscally far more than balanced) by out-migration. As the cities increase in unpleasantness, congestion, pollution and noise (and, it must be added, crime) the wealthier families tend to move out to less developed areas, say twenty or more miles away, so that they are lost to the city both as citizens and as taxpayers. In the U.S.A. especially their place in the inner city is quickly taken by negroes pouring into the abandoned large nineteenth-century houses. In India this type of out-migration followed by a different income level immigration is less marked, although there are plenty of examples of it in Bombay. The shady boulevards of New Delhi continue to appeal to the wealthy, and the large extensions to the south of the city are mainly for the occupation of middle and clerical class families. Decongestion in Old Delhi has as yet made little headway. The result of this difference between in- and out-migration in India as compared, for instance, with the U.S.A. is probably that there is a wider spread of incomes in an Indian Metro.

The ways in which the Indian approach to urban reform differs from that of other federations has already been mentioned – her planning apparatus, especially at the national level. Instinctively, as it were, the first step in dealing with a newly identified problem is to establish a national planning scheme or agency for it. This reaction is echoed more or less uniformly at the state level. But at the city level there is little or no planning even among the Metros.[2] The result of this tendency to concentrate planning at the higher levels of government, and to neglect it at the level where it is most relevant, is to cause both the centre and the states to distrust city managements and to entrust improvement works to special Boards or Agencies instead. The result of this policy is that planning and improvement at the city level tends to be fragmented. It is nobody's business to see it as a whole.

The most obvious effect of the population explosion is congestion. Masses of human beings wander about the

---

[2] As a quantification to this statement, Delhi plans come within the purview of the national planning organisation. Foreign teams of experts have also made some Metro plans, notably for Calcutta (C.M.P.O.).

streets mainly because they have nowhere particular to
go. They manage to exist in shanty dwellings of
cardboard and hessian wherever there is a little
unoccupied footage, and crowd incredibly into once fine
houses in the inner city (as in the Apollo Bunder in
Bombay). It is a teeming, shifting population with hardly
any income at all apart from meagre cash grants from the
government. Metros in many countries (and by no means
only the L.D.C.s) also suffer from shanty settlement
congestion. Even in a country with a high growth rate
such as Mexico, the rate of urban immigration is too fast
for the corresponding provision of more permanent
housing, even if the immigrants find jobs. But there, at
least, one does not see the crowds of urban unemployment which give rise to political apprehension in India.
The basic difference between India and most other
countries is that in India the shanty dwellers are all
poor. This may not be at all true in other countries:
for instance, in Italy, Argentina and Mexico they own
radios, motor bicycles and so on. The inhabitants are
able to practise a good deal of self-help and even to
establish a tolerable *modus vivendi* until such time
arrives when more permanent arrangements can be made
for them.

Traffic congestion is the second aspect of this evil
which needs to be considered. This is not necessarily an
accompaniment of human congestion, and tends to be
worse in A.C.s than in L.D.C.s. It is related, rather, to the
mobility aspect of the population explosion, placing
more and more vehicles on the streets, especially at rush
hours when all the commuters are going in the same
direction. In India and other L.D.C.s, while the volume
of motor traffic is not yet so heavy, it is growing rapidly.
But such motor traffic as there is at present is more likely
to cause congestion by its age and poor maintenance than
in an A.C. The most serious aspect of traffic congestion in
L.D.C.s is the variety of the vehicles concerned. Bullock
carts and other slow means of transport throng the
centres of the main arteries, while rickshaws and bicycles
in thousands weave their way among the rest; even today

the whole traffic flow in a street may have to deviate due to the immobile presence of an urban cow.[3]

In the U.S.A. many people consider that the basic evil of the cities is pollution. In L.D.C.s (and especially in India) water pollution would seem to be a greater danger than air pollution. Some years ago I was informed that 80 per cent of the patients in Bombay hospitals were there with water-borne diseases. Although the statistics are very defective, I am sure that this is by no means exceptional, for Bombay has a relatively good supply of water. The major safeguards against health hazards by water pollution are a good water supply and underground, water-borne sewerage. In very few places in India can it be hoped to have an adequate supply of pure water for all purposes in the forseeable future. The major rivers are, no doubt, extremely infected; but it should be possible to purify a sufficient quantity for drinking, at least in Metros. It would naturally have to be rationed. An adequate supply of water of any quality is as yet sadly lacking in most Indian cities. It was estimated that by the end of the Third Plan, 52 per cent of the urban population would still be without piped water supply, while 76 per cent would still be without underground sewerage. This is a field in which the general shortage of water makes it particularly difficult to meet basic needs.

For India, a very high priority must be the supply of piped water and underground sewerage, at least for towns of 100,000 or more inhabitants. For smaller settlements and fringe development sewerage need not be so elaborate. A system of modern cesspits, frequently inspected and regularly emptied, is substantially cheaper and should suffice for many years, but something much more elaborate than the traditional 'conservancy' service is called for. In 1967 the Rural/Urban Relationship Committee carried out for the Ministry of Health and Family Planning an analysis of the situation in seven representative-sized towns situated in different states. They found that one town of over 110,000 inhabitants

---

[3] We return to the problem of traffic regulation below.

had no piped water; in most of the others the flow was very meagre (12 or 13 g.p.s. in cities of nearly 150,000). The sewerage situation was typically very much worse; none of the seven had underground systems. This is a service which it is always difficult to provide: it is an unpopular subject, and potential suppliers of loans fight shy of it because they know it will not be self-sustaining.[4]

Although water and sewerage systems are the highest priorities, they are by no means the only 'musts'. The level of other municipal services in these towns was also not impressive. All reported some improvement in their preventive health and maternity services; five out of the seven reported some improvement in road facilities (the other two still complained of bullock carts). Compulsory free primary education was claimed to have been established in all; but no description of coverage or quality was available. None had achieved any distribution of electricity, domestic or industrial. Three of the largest had started to prepare 'Master Plans' but none was ready for implementation. These cities are not particularly poor, but it was very noticeable that the level of revenue was not closely correlated with the services supplied. Of the two worst in respect of services, one was the best-off, the other one of the poorest: in both, it seemed that poor lay-out and absence of any land use organisation were partly responsible, by making it more difficult to distribute services. By way of contrast, the smallest and poorest had a (relatively) good standard of services all round, and a water flow more than double that of any of the others: some of the explanation was almost certainly that it had been rebuilt after the Bihar earthquake, so that it had a more modern lay-out.

It was the opinion of the R.U.R.C. that (at then current prices) satisfactory minimal urban services could not be maintained below an average of Rs. 30–35 per head. This figure makes no allowance for development. Only the largest cities can hope to attain this standard, and even their outlay is below what is desirable. The smaller

[4] Cf. Paul Downing, *The Economics of Urban Sewage Disposal* (Praeger, 1969).

towns (up to 20,000) were found to be spending on average no more than Rs. 12·83 per head on current account. It is clear that their greater poverty, combined with the diseconomics of small scale, make their position very precarious. The Zakaria Committee (on the Augmentation of Financial Resources of Urban Local Bodies) estimated that the largest gap between desired and achieved services was in the two middle groups of towns (B population 110–500th and C population 50–100th) but in no class was the gap less than 41 per cent, except in the very highest group (A Special). It is worth noting, also, that per capita expenditure on education declined steadily from Rs. 6 in the A Specials to Rs. 1 in the small towns.[5]

On capital account the situation is no better. Whatever provision has been made, a heavy backlog of maintenance charges exists in every urban category. There is, as on current account, heaviest in the Class B and C towns and relatively lightest in the A Special. Failure to maintain assets leads directly to deteriorating services in the present, and to much higher costs in the long run. It is suggested that in respect of potentially viable services user charges could be raised to reduce or even to eliminate the shortfall; this would leave more of the taxpayers' money to finance social services such as education and health. We must return to this point later.

Poverty is not the only cause of the failure of Indian towns to provide better services. The absence of planning at the municipal level no doubt also contributes. Unfortunately, the standard of administration is low and in some places there is a high level of corruption. In no country in the world are these two weaknesses entirely absent in municipal government. But low pay and poor prospects aggravate the situation. Poverty reacts on officials directly, and also in general because it is a dispiriting exercise to try to bring about real progress in shoe-string conditions and stagnant circumstances. Yet there is a large number of central and

[5] See 'Report of Zakaria Committee, and Datta, 'Financing Municipal Services'.

state schemes to help them, and Indian local government has potentially as good a range of resources for local revenue as do urban areas in most countries. We must, hence, proceed first to examine and assess the national improvement schemes, and secondly the prospects for improving the local tax position.

In all, nine major schemes of urban development have been launched. Some have been in operation for a number of years, others have hardly reached the pilot stage.[6] The first was the National Water Supply and Sanitation Programme. Its objective is to improve these services in all communities of 5000 or more inhabitants. Implementation is in the hands of Agencies appointed by state governments and local bodies. Priority goes to municipalities with no protected water supply. Finance is by 100 per cent loan from the centre to the states. Since we have already discussed the major problems involved in these services, we may leave them for the present, save to note that the progress in respect of water is very much better than in respect of sewerage.

Next we come to no less than five separate housing schemes. It is worth going into these in some detail, as they are illustrative of Delhi policy both in respect of general provisions and of finance.

(1) *Subsidised housing scheme*, primarily for industrial workers with incomes up to Rs. 350 a month, but workers in similar positions with incomes up to Rs. 250 in Bombay, Calcutta and Delhi, less elsewhere are eligible also. (Presumably this difference represents the assumed difference between industrial and other wages.) A long list of bodies and agencies, including co-operatives and employers, are entitled to take part in this scheme. Financial assistance is subject to a ceiling cost per unit and the charging of a standard rent. Detailed professional plans of proposed projects and their lay-out must be presented, and they must pay regard to existing infrastructures. Finance is partly by loan and partly by subsidy, the percentages varying with the type of developers.

[6] Cf. Datta and Bhattacharya, 'Centre-State Relations'.

(2) *The low income housing scheme* can be used by persons having incomes up to Rs. 500 a month (not so very low). Loans are available up to 80 per cent of the cost, with a maximum of Rs. 10,000 per unit. Virtually any agency designated by the state or by local government is eligible to take part. The state government must approve designs, estimates and lay-out.

(3) *The slum clearance and improvement scheme* is in a different class. Its purpose is to upgrade shanty settlements, and to supplement them by the erection of hostel and dormitory type dwellings, including night shelters for footpath sleepers. Persons with incomes up to Rs. 250 a month in the three chief towns and Rs. 175 elsewhere are eligible for assistance. The scheme may be implemented by state governments and housing boards, local bodies or private landlords of slum property. The central government offers 50 per cent loan and 37 per cent grant, leaving the state government to find 12½ per cent of the cost, including that of land acquisition where necessary. Assistance is subject to a ceiling cost per unit and the exaction of a standard rent. It is stated that 'provision for water supply, street lighting, drainage and sewerage, schools and dispensaries, should be included in each colony'.

All these schemes are, wholly or in part, financed directly by the central or state governments. We now come to three related schemes for which (on account of their supposed greater viability) finance from the Life Insurance Corporation is to be sought. (a) *A middle income housing scheme* for those receiving between Rs. 500 and Rs. 1250 per month. Assistance may be up to 80 per cent of the cost, subject to a ceiling of Rs. 20,000 per house. It will only be given when designs and layout have been approved and essential services are already installed. Implementation may be undertaken by virtually any individual or co-operative society. (b) A somewhat similar scheme is available exclusively for *rental by employees of state governments,* with preference given to those with lower salaries. This is to be financed 100 per cent by loan from the L.I.C. and implemented by any agency approved by a state government. (c) The whole housing programme is rounded off by a *land acquisition and development scheme,* also to be financed by 100 per cent loan from the L.I.C.; but it is confined to rapidly growing towns. This is not (as might be expected) a scheme for orderly fringe development: the highest priorities are for slum clearance. It appears to be optimistic to expect the L.I.C. to contribute to such an objective; it certainly would not be an investor's first choice.

Taking account of all these schemes, the Indian National Housing Programme is indeed impressive and any country might be proud of it. Yet there are a number of comments that seem to be called for. Only the slum clearance and improvement scheme is directed to those in real need, for whom the public sector must unavoidably provide most of the finance. For much of the 'subsidised housing' scheme it should be possible to charge something like economic rents. It should consequently be questioned whether other sources of loan finance would not be available, for instance Building Societies and the L.I.C. The case for *not* using the taxpayers' money for the remaining housing schemes is even stronger. There is a danger of the less well-off (who contribute heavily in indirect taxes) subsidising the better-off. There is also a danger of over development of potentially self-supporting schemes, since this tends to encourage even more immigration.

There are special difficulties about the 'slum clearance and improvement' scheme, difficulties that have been encountered in every country which has experimented in this line. Where 'clearance' implies demolition of substantial houses, great care needs to be taken to see that the net result is not to reduce the value of low rent accommodation in the areas, substituting better and, of course, more costly accommodation. This is a real temptation to slum property owners. (If 'clearance' merely implies the removal of debris from a shanty area, the problem hardly arises.) It should be a rule that families should not be moved, even from very inferior accommodation, unless or until adequate alternative accommodation has been found for them. This is now a strict provision in the U.K. In many of the U.S. states a lack of any such provision, in the naïve belief that private enterprise would provide the necessary accommodation, has led (for instance, in Chicago) to nothing better than shifting slum conditions to the next area. In Indian conditions it should be possible to erect good cheap blocks of flats, such as have been built by the P.W.D. in Hong Kong, without subsidy apart from the fact that the land was free.

There is a further difficulty in providing accommodation for shanty dwellers. They have probably been 'squatting' rent free. Transferred to any sort of building they would have to pay some small amount of rent. They may not be willing to leave their shanty accommodation for such a prospect. An alternative worth exploring is to follow a less ambitious programme of improving minimal services to the shanty settlements together with the means to improve their accommodation (we return to this point below, p. 220).

Another difficulty with the housing programme is that local authorities will be faced with a great deal of trouble and expense in providing the infrastructure, which is a necessary condition of receiving grants under several of the schemes. It is also doubtful whether the land acquisition scheme will make it much easier for local authorities to get hold of the land they need. Modern legislation would seem to be needed, simplifying the purchase procedure and providing machinery for the independent determination of compensation of dispossessed landowners. Local authorities will need to be armed with the ultimate sanction of compulsory purchase, although it is to be hoped that they will not often need to use it. Since the L.I.C. is supposed to come forward with 100 per cent grant under the scheme, it would seem likely that they would prefer potentially remunerative investments rather than slum clearance.

Two other schemes in the Urban Development Programme call for brief comment, although they are so recent that there has hardly been time to observe how they will work out. They are concerned respectively with the preparation of Master Plans and with the establishment of an Urban Community Development organisation. The idea behind both these schemes is admirable. As we have seen, there is at present far too little planning at the municipal level. Save in one or two cities there is little feeling of social solidarity or of willingness to work and think for the good of the community; such as does exist, is more the work of charitable organisations than of a getting together by the citizens. It may be doubted, however, whether the schemes as set out are likely to prove suitable instruments for their objective.

Marvellous-looking plans have been produced in a few places, but they are mainly the work of outsiders and do not spring naturally from the administration and organisation of the city, nor take much account of its financial potentiality. It would seem that even making such plans (let alone implementing them) is likely to be an expensive luxury in present Indian conditions. All that is really necessary at present is a simple land use plan to which the needs of all services are integrated in outline. There must naturally be sufficient detail so that we do not have houses without schools, nor buses without suitable streets for them to run on.

Similarly with community development. There is ample experience of the working of rural community development to suggest that it is only a success in exceptional circumstances, for instance where there are good outlets close at hand for agricultural produce and for the output of small industries. The development officer also needs to be an exceptional leader. In the villages the officers have very definite objectives, such as persuading farmers to adopt more productive methods with their crops. In urban conditions one might expect that there would be less opportunity for this pragmatic sort of instruction. Certainly urban community feeling needs to be fostered, but it is not so certain that this would be the best method of inculcating it. There is a possibility that more might be accomplished by assisting particular districts with self-help schemes. We must further consider this line of approach presently.

Looking more generally at the urban improvement schemes, there are a number of points that might be emphasised, although most of them have already been made by committees appointed to examine their progress.[7] Indeed, the number, scope and coverage of these committees cannot but raise the suspicion that something is not quite right. Is it the organisation, the legislation under which the schemes operate, or the want of financial opportunities available to the cities? Most of the programme was launched in the 1950s, so that real results should by now be visible. With every year that passes progressive urbanisation aggravates the problems.

The authors of *Centre-State Relations in Urban Development* collected some specimen time-flow charts for particular projects: the delays recorded are lamentable. Much time is evidently wasted in negotiations with Local Authorities. The absence of any system of decentralised decision-making is no doubt one of the reasons which causes higher authorities to prefer to deal directly with specialised Agencies, Housing Trusts, Local Boards and so on (we noticed this tendency at an earlier stage, see above, p. 197). While this procedure may well give quicker results in particular directions, it is inimical to balanced and integrated development. The delays seem to be equally frustrating the other way round. A small town puts in a request for a water supply for which it would be eligible for a grant. The first authority to which it applies passes the papers to another,

[7] For instance, Report of Seminar on Financing and Management of Water and Sewerage Works (Ministry of Health, 1964); Report on National Water Supply and Sanitation Schemes (Committee on Plan Projects, Building Projects Team, New Delhi, 1961); Report of the (Thacker) Committee on the Integration of Urban Housing Schemes and Land Acquisitions Proceedings (Chandigarh, 1965); Reports of Five Sub-Groups on Housing and Urban and Rural Planning for the 4th Plan (Ministry of Works and Housing, 1965); Rural-Urban Relationship Committee (Ministry of Health and Family Planning); Report of Committee on Urban Land Policy (Ministry of Health, 1965). Also Annual Reports of the Ministries concerned.

which repeats the exercise, and so on. No one seems to be in a position to take a quick decision.

From the list of committees appointed to examine progress (see note 7), it is evident that at least four Ministries and the Planning Commission are involved in the programme. Moreover, the scope and content of ministerial responsibility is frequently changed. The division of function and responsibility is repeated at the state level. Potentially many of the schemes are 'open ended' in the sense that if all the authorities which were eligible for a particular grant were to apply there would be no ceiling on the centre/state commitment. Probably there is little danger of this occurrence because of widespread shortfalls in expenditure. But this brings in its train another difficulty, because *virement* of funds from one purpose to another is not allowed. Unspent balances must be handed back. In practice this necessity does not worry local authorities too much, since they have been able to satisfy their needs through the 'back door' of a General Development Loan allocation. Clearly these arrangements are far from optimal. (This point belongs to the financial discussion which we shall presently reach, but it is worth mentioning here because it aptly illustrates a major difficulty with the whole programme: too much inflexibility on the one hand, too much generosity on the other.)

The evidence strongly suggests that the most difficult and time-consuming negotiations are concerned with land acquisition, or rather, with the determination of the compensation to be paid to dispossessed owners. This is a very troublesome problem in any country, but it is made more difficult in India by the circumstance that population pressure and the want of any strong local tax system that includes capital values have combined to raise Indian urban land values to unprecedented heights. Those in Calcutta are said to be among the highest in the world. Land acquisition at inflated market prices is very costly to the local authority: yet this is the equitable price to use in order to avoid the destruction of legitimate expectations. This is a universal dilemma. It has been much discussed in the U.K., where also there is no tax on land values (although the local rate is a tough tax on the *occupation* of land and buildings). The Town and Country Planning Act of 1947 attempted to solve the problem by imposing a 'development charge' over and above the agricultural valuations of the land when developments occurred. The assessment of these values proved extremely difficult, with the result that the real estate market almost ceased to function. The next government repealed this legislation, and made valuation (and hence compensation) depend on market values as determined by an independent tribunal.[8]

In Indian conditions it would seem sensible to proceed cautiously with land purchase except on the outskirts of cities, where land values have not yet risen extortionately and where land is needed for orderly fringe development.[9]

Perhaps the most serious weakness of the Indian urban programme is its interlocal rigidity. This affects both its administration and its finances. Although precise figures of state per capita incomes are not very satisfactory, enough material is readily available to demonstrate very large differences on the one hand between the financial potential of states and on the other in the cost of living and wage levels in different urban areas. Yet in the terms of grants offered, there is scarcely any differentiation. The whole programme is also extremely centralised. Thus, for the water supply and sanitation scheme, the Federal Government imposes standards and regulations, formulates programmes, scrutinises and approves all

---

[8] Datta and Bhattacharya, 'Centre-State Relations'.

[9] The problem of the valuation of fringe land has given rise to much controversy in the U.S.A. The best solution appears to be to make a double valuation: at present agricultural use, and at urban developed value. On development the higher valuation would be payable retrospectively. This would help to steady prices, to reduce speculative forward buying on the one hand, and retention for a rise on the other. In Indian conditions special valuations would presumably have to be made, since neither the Land Revenue nor the urban rate valuation would serve.

projects. For urban housing and related activities it sets
standards and regulations and formulates schemes. Most
rigid of all are the Master Plan and Community
Development schemes, where in addition to the
regulations similar to those for the other schemes, staffing
and wage rates are fixed by the centre (notwithstanding
that planning and community development are constitutionally on the state list).

The result of all this centralised procedure, when
combined with the necessary complementary investment
by the states and local authorities, not to mention the
maintenance costs (which when the project grant comes
to an end can be extremely heavy) is that only the
wealthiest states and urban authorities can take full
advantage of the programme. It is thus anti-
redistributional. Moreover, this amount of regulation is
inimical to the growth of initiative and sense of
responsibility at the local level. Before its reorganisation
the Planning Commission heightened the confusion (and
probably increased the delays) by giving direct orders to
Trusts and other development agencies.[10] Since the
Planning Commission is not itself a constitutional body,
this would seem to be going beyond its powers, however
great the provocation.

Turning to more financial aspects, it will be observed
from the particulars of schemes given above that there
are bewildering differences in the type of assistance
offered. The 'mix' of grant and loan is apparently
fortuitous. This affects a number of aspects of
centre/state financial relations.[11] The mix of grant and
loan is certainly not related to wealth differences. Indeed,
it has added to the difficulties of poor states by imposing
debt service liabilities which they cannot meet.[12]

[10] Datta and Bhattacharya, 'Centre-State Relations'. Cf. also the
central distrust of municipal administration, above, p. 61.

[11] See my 'Memorandum to the Fifth Finance Commission'.

[12] Hence to the Terms of Reference of the Fifth Finance
Commission, a rider was added for them to find a solution to the
problem of state indebtedness to the Reserve Bank.

A further cause of confusion lies in the categories into which projects are divided. First, we have the distinction between 'Plan' and 'Non-Plan' projects, the latter qualifying for less central assistance. In fact the definitions are not watertight. They also become slurred by the maintenance charges for completed Plan projects, which fall on the states and hence on the local authorities. Further confusion is caused by the classification of projects into 'centrally sponsored' and 'centrally assisted'. Centrally sponsored in particular implies a considerable inroad into states' powers and responsibilities as set out in the Constitution. The formal distinction is that centrally sponsored projects belong essentially to the Central Plan and are supposed to cover only those projects which are either of the nature of demonstration pilot projects and research, or projects which have inter-state (regional) or all-India reference. But the distinction becomes blurred when the pilot projects have passed the experimental stage and become generalised (as has occurred with the water supply and sanitation scheme) but nevertheless continue to be included in the more rigid centrally sponsored category. The extent of central control has led to the establishment of very close relations between the central Departments concerned with particular schemes and their opposite numbers at state level. Thus the latter tends to become mere creatures of the central Departments, deprived of the incentive to take the initiative themselves; and so a type of 'vertical federation' is established.[13] To some extent this must be to the detriment of horizontal federation, and tends to increase the difficulty of attaining horizontal co-ordination at state or local levels.

In 1935, when the Government of India Act was passed (which effectively became the Independence Constitution of 1949) the idea of planning in India had not yet seen the light of day. The establishment of the Planning Commission was announced in Lok Sabha in 1950. It continued to be assumed at first that no further

[13] Cf. K. Santhanam, *Union/State Relations in India* (Bombay, 1960).

transfer of resources from the centre to the states would be required beyond what had been allowed for in the Constitution. This comprised only allocations from the Distributable Pool (fed mainly from income tax) as advised by a Finance Commission to be appointed every five years. Planning altered all this. The allocations of Plan funds came (at least by the third Five Year Plan) enormously to exceed the revenues which successive Finance Commissions had within their competence, notwithstanding that these were increased somewhat from time to time. The funds for Plan Projects were largely derived from the Reserve Bank under article 282. This was interpreted as giving Lok Sabha (or for that matter, state governments or the Planning Commission) rights of spending virtually on any good cause. It is clear that this interpretation of article 282 was stretching it far beyond the intentions of the Constitution.

It has been noticeable that the inter-state location of Plan funds has tended to be substantially different from the Finance Commission's proposals for allocation of revenue between the states. The Planning Commission has endeavoured to locate projects in poor areas so that the result was (in intention, at least) redistributional.[14] The effect of the Finance Commission's allocations were on the whole anti-redistributional, due to the heavy weighting given to straight population. The Finance Commissions are tied down by their constitutional commitments; not so the Plan Authorities, since the Planning Commission has no constitutional status, and hence no limitations on its actions.

Unfortunately, there is little sign that these confusions and contradictions are getting nearer to solution. It has become urgent that a great effort should be made to straighten them out, no matter what legislation is required. In the first place, the offers of grants and loans from various sources and for various purposes need both streamlining and improved flexibility. These changes

---

[14] Although if the projects were very capital intensive, such as steel, or heavy electric the effect on local incomes was slight. Eastern Bihar provides a good example of this.

should succeed in making it clear what allocations are in
fact being offered to each state, and how far they are
related to the relative financial potential of states.
Secondly, the status of the Planning Commission itself
needs to be regularised. Reforms have indeed been
carried out, but they are hardly sufficiently fundamental.
If the Commission were to be placed firmly within the
Constitution, Lok Sabha would have much more
authority in discussing its activities and the amounts and
allocations of its grants. This arrangement might, indeed,
lead to political log-rolling to a greater extent than at
present; but at least the Commission would be less
detached in its own 'back room'. It has been suggested
that inter-state location of loans and grants might be
broadly agreed between the Finance Commission and
the Plan Commission; the latter would then proceed to
implement this in its plan policy. Some such arrangement would be much facilitated if the Finance
Commission were to be given permanent status, as in
Australia. These are not matters on which an economist is
competent to pronounce. Nevertheless, unless some
fairly drastic steps are taken, one cannot be too hopeful
that things will be better in the future than they have
been in the past.

So much for the general relation between central and
state finances. The urban problem belongs more directly
to the relation between state and local finances. In this
field the urgent problem is to get the cities (and
particularly the Metros) standing on their own feet, doing
their own planning and working out their own destinies.
Clearly they cannot be expected to be independent
financially. But with the resources within their
competence, together with grants coming to them from
the centre (via the states) they should have a better
supply of funds than up to the present they seem to be
able to absorb. In addition, there are some grants coming
directly from state finances. Unfortunately these are not a
very reliable source; if anything, they are less
co-ordinated than grants from the centre to the states.
They are also more uncertain, since they depend on the

vagaries of state finances; but they are nevertheless not useless.

If the cities are to become the local centres of decision-making, as they should be, they have need both of more autonomous current revenue and of better opportunities for capital finance. In respect of current revenue two possibilities need to be discussed: (1) the better utilisation of existing sources (tax and non-tax) and (2) the discovery and exploitation of new sources. Turning first to potential non-tax revenue (largely the profits of public utilities and enterprises): apart from administrative obstacles, such as mismanagement and attempts to conduct an essentially business enterprise on too small a scale, a common cause of failure to make profits, or even avoid losses, is to control selling prices or rents at so low a level as to make it impossible to cover even running costs, much less secure adequate maintenance and replacement. This trouble frequently occurs in respect of electricity undertakings. The result is that taxpayers who have no opportunity of using the service contribute to those who do. This generally implies that the poor are subsidising the better-off. Something very similar occurs in respect of housing schemes. For any but the really low income groups there is no case for subsidised rents. On the other hand, there is no hope that sewerage projects can be viable. Due to their extreme urgency this has to be faced and adequate subsidisation provided. This emphasises the need of economising on subsidies where they are not absolutely necessary.

Water is a more marginal question. Initially it was anticipated that the scheme would be self-supporting; but this has not happened and subsidisation has gradually crept in. Calcutta and Bangalore (perhaps others) have given tax powers to their independent water undertakings in an attempt to relieve city finances. It is not desirable that non-government bodies should become taxing authorities; but the action of these cities does seem to indicate that user charges could well be higher. Especially in India, water usage is probably closely correlated with family income, so that additional charges (geared, for instance, to accommodation enjoyed) would not be socially undesirable.

Another instance of mistaken policy concerning user charges is concerned with municipal bus services. A service of modern, well-maintained buses plying frequently (especially at rush hours) is of enormous benefit not only to commuters and their employers but to the whole community. The fixation of ceiling fares at too low a level on the one hand leads to an inefficient supply of buses which cannot be properly maintained and cannot be expanded because every additional passenger is carried at a loss; on the other hand, poor and infrequent buses mean enormous queues with all the frustration and additional physical strain which these impose. At the same time, their slow and uncertain progress contributes to traffic congestion and pollution. A more sensible policy would be to sanction the imposition of higher fares, making sure that they are really collected, even if this is not in the best tradition of theoretical welfare economics: it may, indeed, promote welfare in the long run.[15]

Turning to the exploitation of existing taxes, the first candidate for reform is the local rate. Since in Indian urban conditions this is based on annual supposed rental values, inherently it has only a low elasticity. Valuations can only be raised (apart from additions) when a change of tenancy or user occurs. This rigidity is enhanced by faulty valuations, especially of the larger houses and office buildings, which tend to be much undervalued. It is well known, also, that there is evasion, and even collusion between the taxpayer and tax-collector or local politician. If the base were a capital, instead of an annual, value – say, market price – it would automatically expand as land values rise. We must return to this point later.

Whatever may become possible by way of taxing land values in the future, here and now it is urgent to improve

[15] Cf. The Commission investigating the bus service in Tehran, Burnell and Vince, op. cit.

the valuation, assessment and collection of the local rate. It would almost certainly be a mistake to transfer responsibility for valuation to the central government. This has been anything but a success in the U.K.[16] In the U.S.A., as we have seen, a few states have taken over responsibility for valuation for the Property Tax (the corresponding levy to the local rate) and this has been a success. This does not prove that if the transfer were to be compulsory and universal it would still be a success; the situation varies greatly from state to state. A more promising approach for India would seem to be to establish independent valuation bodies or tribunals at state level. Cities would be entitled to representation on these, it would be well to co-opt some professional valuers from the private sector, at least at first, and some use might be made of voluntary effort. A similar suggestion has been made in the U.K.[17]

The two other urban taxes of any importance now in use in India are octroi and the tax on 'trades and professions'. It is otiose to discuss the reform of octroi, since, as everybody knows, the only possible reform is to abolish it completely. But this cannot be done in states which make heavy use of it unless or until there is something else to put in its place. On the other hand, some steps might be taken to improve the local tax on trades and professions. It is widely realised that this is a limited type of income tax. It cannot function very fully for two reasons: first, its coverage is not fully comprehensive; secondly, there is at present a constitutional ceiling of Rs. 250 on each assessment. It would be only reasonable that this should be raised at least in conformity with the fall in the value of money. It might be possible to extend the coverage of the tax also. In addition to this tax there is no compelling reason why the

[16] Experience has shown that the central authorities are far too busy with central taxes to attend properly to the local rate; valuations have been slipped, and when made, skimped.

[17] Cf. my 'Report on a Conference on the Financing of Local Government', *Local Government Finance* (Dec. 1970).

larger towns, at least, might not have a share in the
national income tax, channelled through the states. Just
this privilege has recently been won by the West German
government by the Association of Local Authorities.[18] If
this could be accomplished (and it would need a great
deal of fighting to achieve) it would give the cities a most
useful and expanding source of revenue, although clearly
not so much as in an advanced country. Also it could not
properly be regarded as an autonomous tax, since the
cities would have to accept the national rules and rates. It
would nevertheless be administratively cheap for them.

The closest substitute for octroi would be a share of
state sales taxes, at least for the larger cities. This has
been suggested both by the R.U.R.C. and the Road
Transport Taxation Enquiry Committee. This privilege
should naturally be extended to the whole country and
not confined to the states at present using octroi. State
sales taxes are not very efficient, as was demonstrated by
the immediate increase in revenue from those levies
which were transmuted into Union excises. Nevertheless,
they do produce revenue. In fact, they have been one of
the most elastic sources of revenue in India in recent
years. An overwhelming part of state tax revenue must
always be derived from the larger urban centres. It would
seem only fair that they should enjoy a share of it. This
could be arranged by means of a surcharge which they
would be free to levy, or by a percentage of the state
revenue collection, transferred, perhaps, on a derivation
basis.[19]

Whatever means can be used to produce more revenue
for urban authorities, a very great effort should be made
somehow to include land values in the base. Not only
would this secure a much more elastic revenue, it should
contribute to curbing the rise in land values by acting as
a species of capital gains tax. The gains would be taxable
as they accrued, and not only when they were realised, as
in a straight capital gains tax. The problem is, what is the

[18] Ibid.

[19] Ibid. This improvement also has recently been achieved by the
West German Association of Local Authorities.

best method of approach for India to a tax including land values? There is a very wide feeling in many countries that it should be possible specifically to tax betterment, or the increase in property values which occurs without action on the part of property owners, mainly arising from the activities of public authorities. To tax betterment has been attempted more than once in the U.K., but, it is fair to say, with no success. Everyone knows that betterment exists, but to identify it, much more to quantify it, merely wastes the time of Inland Revenue officers; they can be much more productively employed than in chasing up little pieces of possible betterment.

In principle, the simplest way to include capital values in an Indian local tax would be to turn over the local rate from an annual to a capital value base. It is anomalous that outside urban areas the local tax (land revenue) always had a perfectly good capital value basis, although it was essentially a tax on income. But when the urban boundary was reached, valuers had to turn over to the inferior annual base. Valuations for the capital base should in principle be easier than for annual value, since in most urban areas there is probably more ownership than substantial renting. Alterations of the rate base would require lengthy negotiations, possibly a constitutional change (although it would not be a 'capital tax', from which the states are constitutionally debarred). It would, nevertheless, be well worth the trouble.

A short cut for immediate use would be to impose a new tax, specifically on land values. Although this would in principle be in addition to the rate, it would probably be possible to reduce somewhat the height of the local rate (although remembering that it is part of the object of the exercise to raise *more* revenue). The new tax could either be assessed on the market value of the site plus building (which should be quite simple) or, alternatively, an attempt might be made to confine the tax to the value of the land. The aim of taxing land only is to encourage building, since improvements will be tax free. The taxation of land only (the so-called unimproved base) greatly increases the difficulty of the valuation process, unless one is satisfied with mechanical rule of thumb methods, since in built-up areas there is no satisfactory way of separating the two elements of site and building, as they are never sold separately.[20] The most likely type of buildings which will be encouraged are large and expensive structures, where the exemption from taxation of buildings gives the biggest gain. It would seem that this is not really what India needs. Nevertheless, the use of either the improved or the unimproved base should contribute to curbing the rise in land values and so greatly facilitate the redevelopment which municipal authorities wish to make.

Once the cities are assured of a regular and reliable source of current income it should not be too difficult to get their governments to think out projects that they themselves could initiate. In every city there are a number of improvements which can be implemented quite quickly at no great expense. What is needed is to breed a 'healthy and constructive discontent' with existing conditions.[21] Space does not permit us to go into this fascinating and rewarding subject in any detail. I will concentrate briefly on two aspects which especially call for action: (1) traffic decongestion and pollution abatement, and (2) improvements of a minor sort to make life in shanty settlements more tolerable. That is not to say that there are not many other urgent calls on a city's short-term finances, for instance better street repairs and much better maintenance of all publicly owned property: neglect of the former aggravates traffic congestion, skimping the latter greatly increases costs in the long

[20] There is an immense literature on the taxation of land values, dating from the time of Henry George in the last century. For a useful summary, see J. R. Hicks in *Essays in World Economics* (O.U.P., 1959).

[21] I owe this phrase to a very successful District Officer developer in East Africa, cf. my *Development from Below*. The Commission endeavouring to reform the Tehran buses found that a great obstacle to improvement was the acceptance of existing conditions as inevitable.

run, besides giving a city a shabby and unattractive appearance.

As discussed earlier, traffic congestion in less developed countries stems much less from sheer number of vehicles on the streets than from mismanagement and want of control in the little things that interrupt the smooth flow of traffic. Heterogeneous traffic is much better segregated, for instance by providing bicycle tracks (stolen, perhaps, from both road and foot-path – this would be easy in Delhi). Bullock and other carts, rickshaws, cows and other slow-moving objects need to be confined to the sides of the streets instead of as now hugging the centre line. Making up alternative routes and designating some of them one-way would help to reduce the crowds on the main arteries. Especially it should be sought to eliminate time-consuming level crossings. Owners of vehicles which emit clouds of diesel fumes should be prosecuted; these are almost certainly the result of bad maintenance. Identifiable industrial polluters of air or water should be heavily fined. From the social point of view this should be considered a first charge on the profits. Improved services from the roads would require a substantial force of traffic wardens, for it is a waste of money to employ highly trained police on the job. The wardens need not be highly skilled nor very highly paid, but it is important that they should have distinctive uniforms to improve their self-confidence and to increase their visibility. It is essential that they can be relied on to act promptly and entirely without favour.

Turning to the improvement of shanty settlements: since there is little hope that the dwellers can be absorbed and the settlements eliminated in the near future, it is well worth while to consider whether the living conditions could not be improved so as to make them more tolerable and less of a health hazard. A first step might be to provide better materials for the construction of dwellings: timber and plywood if nothing better were available. The inhabitants would need instruction and demonstration in their use, and also

the loan or rental of simple tools. But there should be no
inherent difficulty; one family could help another.[22]
Secondly, cotton cloth could be distributed with
instructions for the mothers on how to improve the
clothing of the children. Another important improvement
would be to apply some surfacing and to align the
alleyways between the dwellings. Rows of latrines with
adequate cesspits (or better still, drainage) could be
cheaply erected. It should be possible to arrange for
regular rubbish collections, the inhabitants leaving
receptacles (which were publicly provided) at some road
main enough for trucks to get along. A considerable
number of additional standpipes would also be needed,
so that all could wash readily without going a long trek to
some river. Whenever possible electric light should be
made available so that the day does not stop at six in the
evening. If that is done, many new interests are opened
up. To these physical improvements might be added
simple community services: literacy classes where
necessary, basic health and nutritional instruction,
sewing and other simple handicrafts. No elaborate
organisation would be required.

Most of the improvements which we have been
considering should be able to be financed out of current
revenue, at least in the larger Metros. For more ambitious
programmes some loan funds would be necessary. But
where are they to come from? The Reserve Bank cannot
indefinitely act as a milch cow. Some of it might, indeed,
be economised if fewer loans and more grants were
available from the national budget for weak states. These
have no prospect of servicing loans adequately. The
L.I.C. and perhaps Building Societies and Trusts, might
be prepared to lend more to 'good' borrowers if, for
instance, they came to realise that some cities really did
know how to tax themselves regularly and fully. Other
countries in India's present stage of development have

---

[22] As was the practice in Uganda, the government supplying only a
concrete floor and a latrine pit. The rent and period of tenancy
arranged when the house is completed depends on the type of
house – up to 15 years for solid construction.

relied heavily on foreign borrowing. It would be worth considering whether a single All India Agency on the lines of the Australian Loans Board might not be a useful institution. Both the Union Government and the states would be represented on it and it would determine the total foreign borrowing to be undertaken in the financial year, as well as its distribution between states. This should serve to encourage potential lenders and also to give an opportunity to examine the relative merits of the schemes put forward by the states, or the Metros through their states.

These various suggested improvements require an administrative and still more a management backing. Anyone who attempts detailed urban research discovers at once that it is normally impossible to find out what has been spent, either *in toto* or on particular items, still less what has been achieved. The researcher consequently has to pick a sample, hoping that it will be representative, and then proceed to analyse the accounts in detail. This was the procedure adopted by the R.U.R.C. committee and by countless others; but it is a very poor second best. In fact there is a considerable amount of research on urban finance being currently undertaken in the universities, but mainly at no higher than the candidate Ph.D. level. Such studies as have come my way (and they must be only a small fraction of the whole) have been very interesting; they reveal what a rich field exists for harvesting, and also that the necessary talent could be made available. But it is the cities that need to do this sort of thing for themselves.

A basic reason why more regular material is not readily available is, I suspect, because urban and even Metro budgeting and accounting is on a low level. The traditional, and at the early stages of reform still essential, system of accountability or stewardship control is not properly followed through, so that the completed accounts exactly mirror the estimates.[23] Municipal budgeting is not inherently different from national

---

[23] Cf. J. R. Hicks, *The Problem of Budgetary Reform* (O.U.P., 1950).

budgeting. Indeed, many Indian cities dispose of much larger sums than a number of independent nations. The annual accounts need to display a stretch of three or four years: far enough back to reach firm 'actuals', with careful details of the year just ending (both Budget and Revised Estimates) as a preface to the year just beginning. There is no alternative means nearly so effective in uncovering mistakes and malfeasances. As a supplement, performance or achievement checks should be introduced wherever quantifiable. Period (or Programme) budgeting is really only useful in the operational sense when stewardship accounting in the urban budget has been firmly established. I return to this in a moment.

The Municipal Development Plan (on which great emphasis has been laid) should, of course, cover a period of years. Preferably it will have more the character of a rolling than of a rigid Five Year Plan. Changes that are small from a national point of view, such as the shutting or the opening of a single factory, can be of shattering importance to an individual city. Hence flexibility is essential. The more the city budget can also take 'forward looks'[24] to match, the better founded the Plan will be; (it is implicit in this suggestion that Plan and Budget should follow the same accounting period). These forward looks should, in the first place, display estimates of the (no doubt growing) costs of existing services, including maintenance and replacement of existing assets. As a result, the scope for expansion should become evident. Forward looks concerning potential revenue from existing sources and possible exploitation of new fields are no less essential.

The adoption of full-fledged Programme budgeting calls for a thorough reorganisation of the existing lay-out from an input (subjective) basis to an output (objective) basis.[25] In place of subjective/input items (wages and

[24] The phrase used by the Plowden Committee on The Control of Public Expenditure (1959) to indicate something less formal than a Plan.

[25] See my article 'Current Experiments in Budgetary Organisation', *United Malayan Bank Review* (Dec. 1970).

salaries, travel, telephoning and so on) there will be grouped activities such as roads and transport organisation, education and children's services, environmental and leisure activities, arranged on an output or performance basis. This revolution, for such it virtually is, can fortunately be approached gradually, by first adopting a more meaningful arrangement of the existing items, so that it is possible to read across from one Department to another, and so obtain the costs (although not the performance) of a complete service, say, education and its subsidiary activities. It is important, in this as in many other walks of life, not to throw out the water you have until you are assured of a regular improved supply, and not to run the risk of being left with empty vessels.

11 City Transport and Circulation*

In every sense the great cities are the growing points in the economies of the less developed countries. On the physical plane their populations are increasing much faster than those of the country as a whole. This is true everywhere – in Latin America, Africa and Asia. A common rate of population growth in the less developed countries is 2–3 per cent per annum. For the cities it is likely to be about 5–6 per cent or even more. Moreover the large cities (which I shall refer to as Metros) are growing points in the dynamic impulse which they impart to the economies. They tend to acquire a higher level of civilisation and incomes than the rest of the country, where real incomes may be stationary or declining. This is especially marked in the developing countries. For instance per capita Bombay income level in relation to the national level is 3 per cent above, in Rio 5·2 per cent, Caracas 2·0 per cent. In Tokyo it is no more than 1·5 per cent and in New York 1·4 per cent.[1] This phenomenon when it emerges in the developing countries is sometimes referred to as the 'dual economy', with the implication that all urban incomes tend to be higher than rural incomes. The intended dichotomy is misleading in two ways. First, not all urban areas are growing richer, and secondly the higher standards realised in some part of a city are by no means universal. They coexist with slums and shanty settlements where conditions are more miserable than in many rural areas.

* Written for All India Conference on Roads and Transport, Mysore, 1972.

[1] Information from World Bank.

Nevertheless the wide spread of incomes poses problems of transport and circulation which are less apparent in the advanced countries.

Rapid and dynamic growth is especially marked in the very large cities, the Metros, which exercise a power of attraction superior to that of smaller cities. This is largely on economic grounds; they are considered more likely to produce jobs for immigrants as well as other amenities. A potent cause of immigration also is the desire for better education and large cities are normally more likely to be able to produce this than small ones. Typically immigration is the major cause of urban population growth. Thus of the addition to the population of Bombay between 1951 and 1961 of 1,207,000, 522,000 were immigrants. In Lagos the percentage was 75, but it is a much smaller city: in San Paulo, Brazil, (between 1960/67) out of a total growth of 2,543,000 the percentage due to immigration was 68. Mass immigration of this order cannot quickly be provided with jobs even in a city which is rapidly industrialising. Nor can satisfactory accommodation be erected for them. As a result slums and shanty settlements increase very fast (if total city population is growing at 10 per cent they may well be growing at 15–20 per cent). Within the last few years, across the world, the rate of expansion of slums is accelerating. In Calcutta 33 per cent of the population live in miserable conditions, many just on the streets. Karachi is no better. But this is not unique to the less developed parts of Asia; in Turkey the proportion of big city slum-dwellers is even higher. This growth of the big cities is partly the reflection of their rising wealth; but it is also closely related to the increasing mobility of populations as both communications and means of transport improve. It is not too much to say that this increasing mobility is altering the whole character of cities, especially Metros. It is even claimed by some American sociologists that the city as we know it and as our forefathers knew it, no longer exists.[2] It has become a mere 'node of communication' without a life of its own.

[2] Cf. *The Regional City*, Senior (ed.), and *Daedalus* (autumn 1968).

The implications of this claim for the transport and communications problem hardly needs emphasis. Fortunately the change is by no means universal. Nevertheless it is becoming evident that the urban unit of the future, for which we now have to plan, is the Metropolitan Area, consisting of the old, perhaps anachronistic and often very much decayed, 'core' surrounded by two or more rings of suburbs, leading out to the developing fringes, eventually merging with the countryside. This situation throws an entirely new light on the required policy for transport and circulation. The changes which need to be brought about in the inner areas, the suburbs and the outer districts of the Metro area in the system of street structure and usage are essentially different, and need individual policies if the transport system is to give best possible service to the community as a whole.

The volume of motor traffic is nowhere in the world (apart from Tokyo) so dense as in the cities of the United States, and in the less developed countries it is still much less than in most of the advanced countries. But conditions of street congestion and poor circulation may be just as bad in the L.D.C.s. This is due partly to the extreme heterogeneous nature of the transport and the large numbers of erratic and slow moving units. Even now in some cities of India traffic may have to deviate to allow a cow to take its ease in the middle of the street. Moreover the amount of pollution produced per motor vehicle tends to be higher because many of the cars and trucks are extremely old and often of obsolete design. Although the absolute number of motor vehicles in the L.D.C. Metros is not yet very high, all over the world it is expanding rapidly, new registrations doubling or trebling within a few years. The influx has come about so rapidly that there has been neither time nor opportunity to make preparations to face it. In the A.C.s the rate of new registrations is much lower and some of the largest Metros that have been experiencing the phenomenon for some time (for instance London and Paris) have taken action in a number of ways to improve the traffic flow. The writing on the wall for the L.D.C. Metros is perfectly

clear. They are following surely in the footsteps of the
A.C. Metros. It is vital for them to devote attention to the
reduction of congestion in their streets and to improve
the traffic flow while it is still relatively easy to do so. The
situation is naturally most serious in the large Metros,
both because they experience the most rapid increase of
population and because the greater part of motor
transport is concentrated in them. Thus 14·5 per cent of
the car population in India is concentrated in Bombay
while only 1·2 per cent of the population live there.[3]
Bangkok has a maximum 72·8 per cent (Thailand is a
country with few big towns). To look at the future from
another angle, the number of persons per car in Bombay
is 91. In the U.S.A. very many families have more than
one car. A middle class teenager reckons himself a
deprived child if he is not given a car by the time he is 17.
It is clearly in respect of the large Metros of the L.D.C.s
that the most urgent steps have to be taken.

Transport and circulation policy is intimately related
to infrastructure decisions not only in respect of the
street 'network' (throughways) and 'reticulation' (feeder
streets) but to the whole range of questions concerning
urban renewal and development, especially housing.
Both these lines of policy are in fact complementary
aspects of the general planning exercise. Neither traffic
circulation nor urban structure can satisfactorily be
considered in a self-contained isolated manner. Instances
where the mistake of decision-making in watertight
compartments have been made are conspicuous in many
countries: new ports and docks are constructed without
considering access, no attempt is made to absorb the
traffic entering the Metro from a new motorway; housing
estates are built on the outer fringes without thought of
public utility need nor the effect of extended journeys to
work on street congestion. Not only is such partial
decision-making costly and wasteful, investments made
in one direction in the short run, to relieve an immediate
problem, may well stand in the way of more fundamental

[3] Automobile Manufacturers Association and World Bank.

improvements at a later date and so may actually be more costly. So far it appears that few Indian cities have made use[4] of the Union Government's proferred help for town planning. This may well be because the exercise suggested is very detailed and complicated, and consequently expensive. In the first instance all that is required is simple land-use planning and zoning to make a framework into which more detailed decisions can be fitted as need arises. But the Metros should quickly get down to this.

Problems both of transport and infrastructure are embarrassingly dynamic in the sense that the conditions with which they are concerned are continually changing: traffic volume and flow, expansion and decay in different quarters of the Metro, development of public utilities (such as water, sewerage and power) related to the streets, are some of the changes with which they may have to deal at any moment. The durable assets which play an important part in the provision of these services can normally be less easily adjusted to change than can for instance school curricula or medical practices. Moreover because these services operate very largely on capital account they call for more complicated finances than other municipal services. This is not to say that certain aspects of road and infrastructure may not be heavy employers of labour from time to time. Little financial help from higher level governments is likely to be forthcoming for urban road problems. These governments' main interest in transport and communication problems is concentrated on intercity routes or rural development. Hence the cities must be prepared largely to act on their own;[5] even so, it is abundantly worth while. Few changes can do more to improve the efficiency and attractiveness of a Metro, especially to industrialists, than good transport circulation and an up-to-date road structure.

[4] Cf. Datta and Bhattacharya, 'Centre-State Relations'.

[5] There are welcome signs nevertheless that the World Bank is increasingly showing interest in loans for urban transport and road structure.

The overriding objective of transport and circulation policy must be to get traffic moving smoothly and regularly at all hours, (although obviously at peak hours the pace will be reduced), and to make it possible to travel with ease between home and work place, shopping centre, schools and other purposes. As the city and its traffic expand there will need to be constant adjustments to the street structure in order that flow may be maintained. Street reorganisation is not a once for all exercise, but a continuous challenge.

The transport/circulation complex of problems has three aspects which need to be considered separately, in spite of the extent to which they depend on each other. (1) *Traffic:* the volume and variety that has to be accommodated, setting out from the present provision of means of transport whatever it may be and assuming that no more than limited adjustments in the road structure are possible. (Even within this limited range it will be argued that very great and by no means all costly improvements can be made.) (2) Problems of the urban *street structure:* renewal and major improvements and development for the foreseeable future; and (3) the *financial and administrative* arrangements which have to be made to underpin road policy. In planning a new town the architects have a delightfully simple task in that they can arrange for all the latest traffic designs and inventions to be incorporated:[6] but they have to face the basic difficulty of forecasting what the various demands on the system will be. In replanning an old city there will be much less liberty of action; but in compensation there are definite ascertainable facts concerning traffic flows and volume at different times of day, which can be made to provide a relatively firm foundation for forecasting.

It must be clearly recognised from the first that no plans or regulations will be effective unless they are strictly enforced, without discrimination or favour. Hence a first necessity for reform is a sufficient force of traffic police who are paid enough to deter them from

[6] Cf. Report on the Master Plan for Milton Keynes, Buckinghamshire, March 1970.

accepting bribes to condone offences. It is most important that the force should owe allegiance to a single authority, preferably the Metro itself. It is desirable, but less essential, that the whole of the police force should be under Metro control. This is sometimes difficult, for security reasons, in a capital city. Nevertheless the problem seems to have been satisfactorily solved in London since many decades, with the national government (Home Office) paying half the salaries of the Metropolitan Police, but the London government responsible for their administration. Thus the national government retains control over appointments and other matters of discipline, but leaves the rest for local arrangement. The whole force is unarmed, so that there is no question of a para-military force operating in the capital, as occurs in many countries. Whatever arrangements are made, the professional traffic police need to be supported by a body of wardens to enforce parking and other regulations. They need to be reliable but need not be highly trained. Their very appearance will act as a deterrent to the erring motorist. In the U.K. the wardens are personally selected by the police; a great many of them are women. There is also a cadre of 'lollipop wardens' who operate stop signs outside schools when the children are coming to or leaving school.

The *traffic* problems divide naturally into two: (i) those concerned with the provision of the streets themselves and (ii) those concerned with the street users. All over the world both these aspects of policy are in urgent need of action. With every year that passes the accident rate, the congestion, pollution and delay get worse. But in the few large Metros which have tackled the problem of traffic flow seriously the results have been quite encouraging. There is no doubt that traffic flow can be improved substantially by relatively minor and economical adjustments. In respect of circulation the first step is to segregate the different modes of traffic. This is especially necessary in L.D.C.s where slow and primitive means of transport are still in use, and it is more than likely that the drivers cannot understand traffic rules. Side by side with the bullock carts, donkeys, camels or even elephants are thousands of bicycles and rickshaws. Motor vehicles have to force a way through the jungle; this is especially difficult at night since lighting regulations are seldom enforced, even if it is possible to apply them. Slow traffic and heavy trucks and containers should ideally be kept in separate lanes, or banned from main thoroughfares. If the streets are too narrow for lanes they can perhaps be kept to alternative routes. 'U' turns on busy thoroughfares must be strictly forbidden.

The second step in the respect of circulation policy is concerned with street intersections. Railway level crossings have no business on the streets and probably the streets will have to be carried over them, as it will be difficult to get the railway authority to take any steps since they are already assured a priority. Cities have inherited their street structure and initially they must take it as part of the data, although the initial set-up differs very much from Metro to Metro. Only Washington and perhaps New Delhi seem to have been planned with some prescience of the needs of the motoring age. Important intersections require special treatment since all forms of traffic (not excluding pedestrians) have to be given rights of transit. Depending on the volume of traffic, lights may be sufficient, or more ambitiously a roundabout.

If these are not sufficient protection for the pedestrian (and this largely depends on their enforcement) the optimum solution is a system of underpasses with escalators, as has been established with great success in Vienna. This device is especially useful at multiple intersections. A little underground plaza with shops (whose rents will help to pay for the construction) can also be built; tram and perhaps truck terminals can also be brought into the picture, as in Boston, leaving traffic to move along the streets above without interception. For less important intersections, and to deal with the problem of traffic entering from side streets, traffic lights will probably suffice, so long as the lights are linked from street to street. This is especially essential where the blocks are small. In respect of traffic entering it is essential that it should halt well back from the intersection. The use of traffic 'boxes' has proved very successful for this purpose. The actual intersection is ruled off, and no vehicle must enter it until the exit is clear. This entirely eliminates the chaos which results when the lights change before the traffic has been cleared.

The opposite side of the circulation problem is parking. Want of control of stationary traffic is the cause of at least 50 per cent of delays and congestion in some Metros (for example Naples). The first necessity is to confine on-street parking to a limited number of very wide streets, and even there it needs constant monitoring and revision as the volume of traffic increases, or else to little-used side streets where it can be reinforced by parking meters which can be adjusted to different lengths of stay, according to the probable type of demand. The difficulty about meters is that they are very easy to rob (as has been found in London) so that frequent visits by wardens are necessary, and this is inevitably costly. A difference between drivers who wish to stay only a matter of minutes, an hour or two, or all-day needs to be made. For the short stay 'disc' parking during working hours seems to be quite successful and is now well established in most Western countries; the time allowed can be adjusted to the traffic density. Disc parking also needs inspection but there is less provocation for overstaying than for robbing meters. For all-day parking the neatest solution is multi-storey structures either above or below ground, with appropriate charges. In respect of new buildings, whether for domestic or business occupation, it is wise to make it a condition of development permission that parking facilities should be built in for those who will occupy the building.

In discussing traffic segregation above, mention was made of the necessity of simplifying traffic modes on particular streets; but in this connection there are also major policy decisions to be made for the more complete avoidance of congestion. Congestion is by no means a new phenomenon. Large Metros like London, New York and Paris suffered badly from congestion by vehicles and pedestrians long before the advent of the motoring age.[7] The preferred solution at that time was to get as many as possible off the streets and into suburban railways (which might go underground as they reached the most dense areas). Commuters' suburban trains are only a limited solution, for two reasons. First it is necessary for travellers to make independent arrangements to get from their homes to the station, and, much more serious, to use the streets again to get to their work place at the end of the journey. The crowds spewed out from downtown terminals give rise to a succession of unmanageable congestion situations, especially in Japan, where want of inner-ring development has greatly enlarged the need for commuting. The second trouble with suburban mass transit is that in order to provide sufficient accommodation at peak hours it is necessary to acquire a large amount of rolling stock and permanent installations which are then wastefully out of use for most of the day.

For these reasons the ideas of both the traffic planners and the commuters are now turning to more flexible modes of transport. Nevertheless both suburban railways and undergrounds may still be the best solution in crowded low income districts where generalised car owning is as yet an impossibility. Bombay is probably the best example in the world of this situation; a quite exceptional proportion of its commuters travel by suburban railway. London is also still adding to its underground lines, with a good prospect of profitability. But to add one or two more lines to an established network is a very different proposition from starting an entirely new system. Yet not a few Metros tend to prefer this costly pseudo-solution to tackling street congestion directly. To possess an underground railway system has become a prestige symbol, indicating that your city is sufficiently advanced to require the solution of the great

[7] In the 1820s the Liverpool Improvement Commissioners (who operated before the establishment of an elected council) made regulations for traffic in the Dock area.

Metros. More often than not this is a myth, based on political desires and want of making fundamental analysis.

All the evidence collected by Inquiries points directly to the private motor car as now the preferred mode of urban transport; flexible and ready to hand at both peak and off peak hours, and for a great variety of loads. In the U.S.A., which is ahead of the world in this respect, 60 per cent of car usage is for the journey to work; for other uses also the private car proves to be by far the most convenient and economical, taking into account the different routes along which it will be required to travel, at different times of day and the different loads which will be needed. In the L.D.C.s the great majority of the cars are concentrated in the few big cities (as we have seen) and even there the density is much less than in the A.C.s. In Nairobi, a relatively wealthy and fast developing capital, there are 10·8 persons to a car. In Bombay there are 91, but in India as a whole there are over 1130.[8] In the A.C.s, not only in the U.S., more and more families are becoming multi-car owners. But the number of new car registrations in L.D.C.s is increasing rapidly at the rate of 10–20 per cent in a year. Doubling or trebling of the car population within a decade is commonplace. In Singapore in 1960 there were 63,000 cars; by 1969 they had become 130,000. This is the situation for which the L.D.C.s have to plan. There is no inherent reason why the cities of the L.D.C.s should pass through the nineteenth century phase of cramped streets lined with small houses, out of which the A.C. Metros are now trying to disentangle themselves and their traffic. With careful planning and with the greater ease of transport which the motor car provides they should be able to start out from a much better basis.

There remains the question of buses. In so far as commuters are prepared to use these rather than their cars, a single bus carrying 40 people saves the road space of 20–40 cars. Buses have a great deal more flexibility

[8] Information from World Bank.

than their predecessors, trams (street cars) or even trolley
buses. They can, like the railways, be treated as a trading
service, either belonging to the metro itself, or to a
corporation which is controlled by the Metro to some
extent, as to its routes and timing. But even a well
managed bus service has some of the rigidity of a
suburban train. It is still necessary to get to the nearest
bus stop before starting the journey and to walk from the
end stop to the place of work. Its timing is often very
uncertain and it gives rise to considerable congestion
itself, particularly at stops and halts. A way round this
difficulty has been sought in some towns by reserving
one lane of a street for buses; but in an unimproved street
this seriously reduces the amount of space available for
general traffic. (Elevated bus routes are a different matter,
but they are costly.) Finally at off-peak hours there will
be substantial waste of equipment and personnel not
needed – less equipment but more personnel than the
railways.

For the bus to be an effective means of reducing
congestion both the vehicles commonly used and the
roads they are to be run on need considerable
modification. As things are now, most Metros which own
or control bus systems experience heavy losses on them,
notwithstanding that they may have been making profits
under private ownership. As we shall see later a major
cause of loss is mismanagement – or want of
management. But it frequently happens that the policy
of the Metro government unwittingly puts the bus-
undertaking into an impossible position. Concessionary
fares are insisted upon, and these frequently take no
account of the length of journey. Hence on the one hand
every additional passenger is carried at a loss, on the
other urban sprawl is encouraged, giving rise to
unnecessarily long journeys. (This may well be further
encouraged by rent control.) In such circumstances there
is no incentive to increase the number of buses to meet
the demand; enormous and frustrating queues build up
at peak hours, adding further to congestion. Nor is it
possible for the bus-undertaking to renew or even

maintain its vehicles adequately, so that frequent breakdowns and interruptions occur. Much less can it hope to take advantage of the technical improvements in transport vehicles which are constantly being made. It is by no means unknown for half the bus fleet to be off the road at any one time, awaiting repairs and spare parts.

Troubles of this nature would occur under such a transport policy whatever the type of ownership or provision of streets, but in many Metros, especially in L.D.C.s, they are magnified by the inadequacy of street area. Street space is highly correlated with congestion. As the percentage of the built-up area devoted to streets falls below 20–30 (which is normal in the A.C.s) congestion progressively increases. Tokyo with 12 per cent, Bangkok with 14 per cent and Calcutta with 8 per cent clearly suffer from this cause; and it is essential that more street space should be made available. If entirely new streets have to be built in the core or inner suburbs the cost is high and substantial demolition may be required. (If as often occurs the exisiting 'improvements' are of very poor quality, this may not be a serious problem.) Frequently however there are in existence more or less parallel streets which could be made up to an acceptable standard and so take some of the traffic off the main thoroughfares. It may be possible to arrange for some amount of one-way traffic also; but to sanction a large amount of this device when it is not strictly necessary runs the risk of making congestion worse by increasing vehicle miles.

Going beyond the field of minor improvements to consider substantial extensions, the first necessity is a careful traffic analysis to ascertain the extent of congestion at different hours, and the length and direction of journeys on which road users are engaged. Broadly the streets require to be extended *pari passu* with the growth of the built-up area, but the rate of growth will not be the same in all directions, hence the need for careful traffic censuses. Where major through-ways exist it may be sufficient in the first instance simply to extend them until they reach the fringe. Tehran is a flagrant illustration of what happens when this has not been done. The carefully planned through-roads built by Reza Shah at the turn of the century end in a welter of new development which has occurred since.

In a Metro of any size orderly fringe development calls for a ring road, which will serve several ends. In the first place it will draw off through-traffic which has no particular business in the Metro, but merely wants to reach the other side. It will also serve as an exchange point for vehicles entering the city from different directions. The Rome Plan[9] (which after twelve years of inaction should perhaps be considered stillborn) gives an excellent sketch of how this could be done. Effectively the commercial and business elements would be moved east, to an undeveloped area bounded by a ring road. This would leave the old city with its priceless monuments relatively free for professional and financial offices, government and tourism. Within the new eastern enclave development centres would gradually be organised. It is necessary in any street extension or ring road development for the Metro authority to acquire the necessary land for the road and its immediate vicinity before speculation has raised the price disastrously. This implies good forward planning and the use of compulsory purchase or eminent domain. (This precaution was unfortunately omitted in Rome, greatly adding to the expense of the road.) If an effective property tax on land and buildings can be established this should also serve to check speculation.

The success of circulation policy in the built-up part of a city is determined by the street system and its management. For new development the road structure forms the skeleton round which the flesh of the new built-up area will be formed. Hence the road infrastructure must have a very high priority in land use allocation. But the skeleton will not be well articulated unless the other aspects of land use allocation and zoning – residential (including schools and open spaces) business and industrial quarters and so on – are integrated with

[9] Summarised in *The Times*, Sept. 1969.

the road plan. This calls for careful attention to the effects of different patterns of development. Thus the industrial quarter must not be placed to windward where its air pollution will fall on the city. On the other hand the factories must have good access and facilities for receiving their raw materials and disposing of their finished products. Again a housing estate intended for young couples needs extra allocation for schools and playgrounds. Housing development near to the factories will minimise the journey to work which otherwise may add anything up to four hours to the working day. Yet these simple commonsense precepts are neglected in city after city. This is partly because in many urban areas where no Metro authority has been established the streets and their traffic have to pass through many jurisdictions which do not find it easy to work together. Even where a Metro authority has been established trouble can arise because the different Departments do their planning in isolation from each other. A co-ordinating authority, whether or not a Metro Council, is thus an absolute necessity (I return to this point below).

Transport and circulation are one aspect of general planning and management, to consider which would take us too far afield. But there are some problems of the management and finance of transport that require separate discussion. A number of case studies have been made by outside consultants, for instance where either the municipal bus service was making inordinate losses or street congestion had become intolerable. Their findings clearly indicate that better management and administration would have made an enormous difference at no great cost. L.D.C. Metros are naturally in a worse position than others because of their poverty and because the population explosion and the impact of the motoring age fell on them together, with extreme suddenness. Metros in the more advanced countries have less excuse for failing to take action, but many of them are by no means blameless. In the L.D.C.s typically buses are irregular, overcrowded and work with a well established system of bribery to condone offences. For our purpose two typical investigations must suffice.

In Lagos, Nigeria[10] the bus system was taken over by the city from a private operator who had made handsome profits. Immediately after transfer losses began to be experienced. One reason undoubtedly was that nationalisation had been threatened for so long that the operator (not expecting adequate compensation) had allowed the buses to deteriorate. Hence the authorities took over a very doubtfully viable asset. No new buses had been purchased, and those that were still on the road were in such a bad state that the drivers feared that they would not be able to get them started in the morning, and so kept the engines running all night. It is well known not only in Lagos that one potent cause of loss is failure to collect fares from a large number of passengers who are friends of the driver. It may well be that better inspection in privately owned buses makes cheating more difficult than in a publicly owned utility. In Tehran, Iran, a team of consultants including a management expert, a transport engineer and an economist, examined the whole bus system minutely.[11] The undertaking was privately owned but subject to some control by the municipality. The usual failure to collect fares and to maintain the buses was found, as well as a flourishing system of bribery. About 50 per cent of the buses were off the street at any one time. This high casualty rate was found to be due partly to the absence of regular servicing, engine and tyre checks. These would incidentally have greatly reduced the cost of repairs when at last they could be postponed no longer. Reliance was placed on one large repair depot which was not well organised and was located so far from where it was wanted that delay was caused in bringing in buses. Yet the management of the undertaking had made considerable efforts to reach profitability.

One ingenious plan, which misfired, was to install a fleet of mini-buses as feeders to the big buses on the main routes. (It will be remembered that Tehran is a city which has failed to extend its main thoroughfares as the city

[10] Cf. Report by B. Keith Lucas for the Nigerian Government.
[11] Cf. Burnell and Vince, op. cit.

grew.) But passengers objected to having to change buses half way through the journey, so that minis got into the habit of running right through, for which they were not technically suited, so that they wore out prematurely. Thus they added to congestion in the inner city and deprived the standard buses of part of their trade. In all this muddle it was evident that there was no one at the top with overriding authority to plan or co-ordinate. Indeed the consultants found a disheartening readiness to accept the situation as it was and to make no effort to improve it. The recommended solution of the consultants was to select a small group of young men who seemed to have the ability to organise and had sufficient basic training in engineering, and to import for a few years two or three experienced personnel to give them on the job training until they had the knowledge and self-confidence to take over themselves.

In both Lagos and Tehran the major shortcoming was on the management side.[12] In 1970/71 Bombay asked the World Bank to conduct a thorough survey of the Metro. There had been no actual breakdown but congestion in the inner city, where most of the employment is, had become intolerable. The city felt strongly that the best solution would be an underground railway system. (This however was not the view of the Bank team, as we shall see.) Accommodation in the city is heavily rent controlled, so that a great deal of property cannot be adequately maintained and many once-good old houses are used as an alternative to a shanty settlement. (75 per cent of the population of Bombay live in rooms with five to ten other people; only 20 per cent of the houses have piped water). The Union government builds and operates the suburban railway system; this in itself is highly efficient, but under-cost fares are charged. This encourages suburban sprawl outside the rent controlled area, and where it is relatively easy to get a house. Bombay receives an immigration of 122,000 evey year so that the commuter problem is continually increasing.

[12] Cf. World Bank Report on Bombay, 1971. See also Pravin Visaria, 'Growth of Greater Bombay', op. cit.

The underground system on which the council had set their hearts was estimated to cost 500 Crs (U.S. $670 m.) and this was almost certainly an underestimate. As an alternative a scheme for Express Ways was put forward, estimated to cost $160 m. Considering the large number of small changes which could quickly and cheaply be introduced, and which it was estimated might increase efficiency by as much as 100 per cent (Bombay for instance has no linked lights) the Bank team judged that both these grandiose schemes were quite out of proportion to needs and to the resources available. Bombay's need, as will appear from the figures quoted above, is for housing. This is another example of the inadequacy of planning one service in isolation from others, perhaps more important. The population in central Bombay is 115,000 per square mile. This by itself makes congestion at peak hours inevitable. It is not at all clear that the crowds, who are largely its cause, would have benefited much by either the underground or the express ways. To them simple housing and clean and abundant water are a great deal more important.[13]

Road works give rise to one of the largest items of Metro investment, commonly amounting to 15–20 per cent of total expenditure (including capital and current account). Where a big project is being undertaken it may amount to very much more. Such costs cannot normally be met wholly by current finance; they call either for capital grants or loans from a higher level government or possibly from an international agency, such as the World Bank. In A.C. Metros, especially in the U.S.A., there are several possibilities for a Road Authority which is separately organised (not a department of the city government) to borrow for a term of years. The business community in both the U.S. and Canada are very conscious of the benefit of improved communications and so readily subscribe to Road Bonds. It is significant that it was the marked improvement in circulation

---

[13] This seems to be a suitable place to acknowledge the debt which I owe to the work of Dr D. N. Nanjundappa, who worked with me in England in 1970–71.

achieved by the Toronto Metro government in its first ten years which ensured its acceptability even when it started to branch out into more controversial (redistributional) policies.[14] In the L.D.C.s it is always more difficult to borrow, fundamentally because adequate funds are just not there to be tapped. Normally they must borrow from the Central Bank, in a federation through the states. In India there is the possibility that some funds might be available from the L.I.C., which has become an important source of finance for local investment. The only other possibility seems to be contractors' credit. When contract labour is employed either for street repair or development, this (as I shall discuss below) calls for very careful monitoring if the Metro is to get full value for its money.

For relatively minor improvements it should not be necessary to borrow, if proper use is made of financial opportunities. At the national level there are a number of opportunities for the specific taxation of motoring, such as tolls on motorways or earmarking of fuel and vehicle taxes. Unfortunately these resources are not likely to be available to Metros. They can however make charges for express ways with limited access, and also for all-day parks. There is a strong demand to develop ways of congestion charging by means of meters fitted inside vehicles; but no satisfactory method of operating these has yet been found.[15] They would appear in any case to be no more than a palliative until a comprehensive plan to reduce centre congestion can be put in hand. There is however a distinct possibility that a consortium of Metros might be able to wring from the national authorities some additional tax rights, such as surcharges on fuel tax, a limited sales tax on fuel, rights over vehicle licences and so on. (The West German local authorities have recently succeeded in getting themselves more tax sources after ten years of concerted effort.) It is not an

---

[14] Cf. Frank Smallwood, *Toronto Metro after Ten Years* (1966).

[15] Cf. J. F. Kain, 'Transportation in Metropolitan Areas', *Metropolitan Problems*, S. R. Miles (ed.).

easy thing to do, but it is possible. The best hope of concessions would be the demonstration that the Metros can carry through transport and circulation improvements, as was done in Toronto.

Whatever finance a Metro may be able to achieve for its road programme, the tasks of management will follow very similar lines. Road management has two aspects: road usage and road maintenance and development. The former implies taking decisions and making suitable by-laws concerning use of streets where some degree of rationing is called for, use of and charges for parking spaces and routes of public transport. Once the appropriate decisions have been made the main agents for enforcing them will be the traffic police, backed up by courts of First Instance. It is mainly for this purpose that it is desirable to have the traffic police wholly under the control of the Metro authority, so that there is no risk of the regulations being modified (or even countermanded) either by the Army or by a higher level government, as happens all too frequently.

A Metro Road Authority may take a number of forms. It will have to make itself familiar with the points at issue in engineering problems concerned with methods of maintenance, repair and improvement. Unless the Metro has a Public Works Department of its own which can undertake such works, it will have to rely on contractor service, probably engaged by tender. For this to work well much turns on the choice of contractor and on the drawing up of precise terms under which he will work, for instance as to grades of materials to be used, and dates of starting and finishing. Even then it is wise to monitor implementation carefully to see that the work corresponds exactly with what has been agreed.

So many troubles are commonly experienced with contractors that it will probably pay a Metro of any size to set up its own P.W.D. (or alternatively arrange for that of a higher level government organisation to be seconded to it for particular projects). It will still be desirable for the Metro Road Authority to keep an eye on the progress of its works, especially in respect of materials used.

Fairly frequent performance reports should be insisted on, which will detail not only man hours worked and materials used, but also actual performance[16] achieved in terms of projects, broken down into their components. If performance budgeting is in use these checks would fall naturally within its orbit. It is clear from all this that the Metro Road Authority will itself need to be familiar with management methods.

The precise form of the Metro Road Authority will depend on the local government system in operation. Obviously the Chief Engineer's Department will have a very important part to play, whether he reports directly to the Council, or to a City Manager or Burgomaster. He will have to keep close contacts with other departments which may wish to see works carried out on the streets, for instance for the insertion of public utilities. In respect of major changes in and extensions of the street infrastructure the closest possible contact will have to be kept with the Planning Department, especially in relation to land use, the siting of residential areas and the schools and clinics which they will need, no less than to the siting of factories and the reservation of open spaces. Whether it is possible or not to establish a single Metro area government (which is the neatest solution) it is clearly virtually a necessity for the transport and circulation problems to be tackled on an integrated basis agreed between the several jurisdictions.

[16] See Report of Administrative Reforms Commission, New Delhi.

12 Steps to Urban Improvement

In this last chapter an attempt is made to sketch out the most pressing steps that need to be taken towards turning a large city in an L.D.C. into a 'good city' as defined in Chapter 8. The difficulties are very great. They differ from country to country not only because of the relative availability of finance and management, but also according to the degree to which institutions are flexible, for instance in respect of the speed with which new technical methods can be introduced or new legislation passed. The task of urban improvement in L.D.C.s starts with two handicaps: first, that in every aspect it tends to get treated with indifference by the local élite, politicians, planners, councillors and also by most foreign advisers. Potential leaders are primarily interested in growth and hence in projects that promise to raise the G.D.P. Urban improvement seems to have no direct relevance to this. Concentration on growth implies that it is more difficult to get funds for urban improvement than for enterprises. Yet it is not really true that better urban conditions will not contribute to growth; they do so by improving the quality of the labour force, providing better living conditions, family planning and a reduction of health hazards, creating a better educated and more alert population.

The second difficulty arises from the need radically to change psychological outlooks: both of the citizens and of those who will be concerned with the implementation of change and with the administration of the reformed city. The majority of administrators may never have been outside their own country and never have seen a modern

city, or if they have done so it has seemed so incredibly
different from the conditions to which they have been
accustomed that they have difficulty in fitting it into the
familiar picture. Hence although they may vaguely sense
that things might be done better they accept the
traditional way as inevitable and even satisfactory for
their own country.[1] What would-be reformers are
effectively demanding is that the cities should be raised
to a new higher level of civilisation, and this is no easy
matter. The one aspect of urban conditions which really
disturbs politicians in many L.D.C.s is the spectre of
unemployment – on political and security grounds rather
than for social or economic considerations. Growth is
seen as the only effective way to deal with this. But
unfortunately many L.D.C.s grow only very slowly so
that it is highly unlikely that the unemployed can be
absorbed by growth in the foreseeable future. Other
means of dealing with this and related problems are
essential. Some of these we discuss below.

For the purpose of analysis it is convenient to divide
the projects and programmes of reform into two
categories: (1) those which are primarily concerned with
physical change in the environment – construction of
new assets, expansion and adaptation of old ones – and
(2) those which are primarily concerned with general
administrative changes. The needs of the physical assets
class are by no means confined to the construction of
assets and their successful operation (including the
necessary working capital and equipment). A large
amount of specific administrative development will also
be required, especially in the field of management.
Similarly, administrative programmes are likely to need
some new fixed investment: for offices, training schools
and the like. They will also be in need of much working
capital such as power supplies, computers and other
mathematical and statistical equipment. But whereas the
administrative changes will be for the most part a
continuous process of adaptation, the individual

[1] See Burnell and Vince, op. cit.

physical developments will have a more finite reference, a series of separate projects, albeit probably related, rather than a continuous process. A number of the environmental developments will call for heavy investment so that some time will probably have to elapse before they can be put in hand. It is useful consequently to divide the physical changes into (1) those which can be started at once and accomplished in a relatively short time, (2) medium term improvements in specific directions which, given reasonable flexibility of institutions, can be accomplished without fresh legislation or constitutional amendment and which present no insuperable difficulties such as the use of skills not easily available, and (3) long term improvements involving complicated engineering planning and legislation (especially in relation to the acquisition of land) training of town planners, engineers, cost accountants, and so on. Probably these cadres are as yet hardly represented. Substantial loan finance will be desirable and this will take time to arrange even if it is eventually forthcoming.

Although it is convenient as a first approach to divide the provision of physical assets in this way the process of urban regeneration is best thought of as a single process. The short term improvements should be complementary first stages of the more distant reforms. It would be wasteful to have to destroy them in order to make room for what is to come later, although this may sometimes have to be done. Such an integration of short and long term policy calls for careful statistical record from the start. It also implies that in view of the severe shortages of finance and personnel, project evaluation will have to play a very important part. Mistakes are too costly. Decisions will repeatedly have to be taken not only in respect of the relationship between short and long gestation projects, but also (even in the short run) between different techniques for obtaining the same objective – say improving the traffic flow through the city. These decisions will have to take account of the social opportunity costs of the alternative schemes. It will also be most necessary to consider the externalities: the social and environmental effects of adopting one scheme rather than another. We shall have to discuss these issues in more detail at a later stage.[2] These types of decisions may seem elementary; but in fact some of them involve a seemingly common-sense judgement which only comes of experience, while others involve quite sophisticated engineering and surveying problems. There needs to be someone at the head who will keep all these aspects in mind and will be continuously cost-conscious. This is another matter which calls for later treatment.

Among the physical environmental changes it is useful to distinguish between those which are primarily concerned with asset construction and maintenance and those in which the service element is uppermost. It cannot be expected that many assets which require a large volume of construction materials and skills can be created in the short period, so that when the service element is important it may be advisable to take decisions which are economical in this respect. For instance in an urgent schools extension programme it may be better to expand existing schools rather than build a large number of new ones (in so far as the old schools are well placed in relation to expected population movements). But generalisation is difficult: it may be quicker to build the schools than train the teachers.

We may classify under three heads the major environmental changes that deserve to be started at once: (1) decongestion, (2) reduction of pollution, (3) improvement in the housing situation. These are closely related, so that progress on one front will help the others. Thus decongestion of the streets – better traffic flow – will reduce air pollution, building new houses will not only be an improvement in itself but will aid decongestion in the inner city and shanty settlements.

An obvious way to relieve street congestion is to provide a good service of public vehicles. This is a utility which is very commonly attempted and should be remunerative. Yet it is common to find that the enterprise

[2] See below, p. 264.

is making heavy losses, while enormous queues line the
streets at rush hours. Investigation will probably reveal a
number of mistakes that could very easily be put right. It
may be that too low a ceiling is put on fares, so that every
additional passenger is carried at a loss, in this case the
utility has no interest in improving its vehicles. It may
also be that 50 per cent or more of the passengers travel
without tickets; in this case a system of inspection is
called for.[3] The vehicles may in any case be old,
unsuitable for the routes which they have to run, or so
badly maintained that some 25 per cent of them are off
the streets at the same time.[4] Bad maintenance also adds
to air pollution with diesel fumes. The traffic flow can
usually be improved by adequate control of different
types of vehicles, keeping the slow ones and bicycles to
the sides of the streets or even forbidding them the main
arteries. Selection and clear marking of priority streets
with traffic lights at intersections will also improve
discipline, as will better street lighting and enforcement
of lighting regulations on all vehicles, including bicycles
and bullock carts.

It is not likely that much demolition or realignment of
streets can be accomplished in the short period but in the
medium period it should be possible to widen and
realign some streets so that there are alternative main
routes both east and west and north and south.
Roundabouts, or better still pedestrian underpasses at
important crossings, will promote an even flow, which
naturally must not be interrupted by indiscriminate
parking. For effective traffic control it is essential to set
up a well-manned corps of traffic wardens (women can
equally well be used) who will be on the prowl at all
hours of heavy traffic to straighten out knots and deal
summarily with offenders; wardens need not be very
highly trained or paid. The main requirement is that they
should be responsible and impartial. A distinctive
uniform is a great help both to make them readily visible

---

[3] In the island of Tenerife an inspector appears to board every bus at
some point on its journey. Probably a wise precaution.

[4] See Burnell and Vince, op. cit.

and to increase their self-respect. (We shall return to this question later in relation to protective services, see below, p. 257.) In the long period it is not likely that a heavy programme of decongestion and street widening will have to be undertaken if the city is really to be modernised. It will be well to keep the likelihood of this in mind from the beginning.

In respect of pollution it should be possible (given determination) to make rapid progress, save in exceptional circumstances, as for instance higher level governments refusing to grant cities the necessary power to compel polluters to mend their ways, or in a particular Metro which is so located as to make it a major problem to keep the air clean. In respect of air pollution the worst culprits are likely to be factories and badly maintained trucks and buses, with the exhausts of commuter cars at rush hours coming a good third. In respect of factory smoke (or domestic smoke if that should constitute a nuisance) the most effective method in the U.K. has been found to be to enforce 'smokeless zones' while making it easy for polluters to acquire alternative equipment which will not be offensive. It is not possible in L.D.C.s to insist that all internal combustion engines should be fitted with gadgets which make exhaust fumes completely innocuous (as is contemplated in the U.S.A.) but more simple means should produce some results. For instance better maintenance can be insisted on for commercial vehicles, and better traffic flow at rush hours will also make a contribution.

Another aspect of air pollution which needs to be tackled quickly is the health hazard of domestic solid and semi-solid waste left about the houses or thrown into the streets. To deal with this nuisance effectively calls for a good deal of investment, but it should be possible to mitigate the effects by organising regular simple rubbish collections, the debris to be burnt (or better apparently baked) in some open spaces. In the longer period further disposal and treatment can gradually be developed well outside the built-up area.

Prevention of water pollution probably calls for more investment than air pollution; but even if the available water supply is initially very impure it should be possible to organise a small supply of purified potable water relatively cheaply.[5] This could be sold to householders by tanker delivery, or made available through taps with appropriate controls. A major difficulty about water (relatively to air) pollution is the greater degree to which it is unavoidably imported from neighbouring areas. Streams entering the Metro area of control may already have been polluted higher up by the discharge of factory effluent or untreated sewage. Clearly the best solution is to obtain the co-operation of the relevant authorities in a concerted policy. In the longer period it will probably pay to make more formal arrangements. Thus Toronto Metro has arranged a limited control over certain outside authorities for the purpose of protection of water sources.

Since pure water is a very high priority for health, in the medium period more extensive works are called for, if possible leading to a supply of pure water for the whole area. According to the circumstances of the Metro and in particular its location and the existence of a natural water supply not far away, this may or may not entail a large amount of constructional work. To take the case of Tehran where a better water supply is of the utmost urgency: abundant water is available in the Elburz mountains, just north of the city. Present reservoirs are insufficient, but although new ones can be constructed with little difficulty (although at not negligible cost) there are other snags. The uncontrolled flow from the mountains is already saturating the old city, dangerously flooding cesspits. The resulting effluent is a severe health hazard, and when at last the water leaves the town it is unusable for agriculture. Tehran thus has a double problem of reforming the water system and building effective underground sewerage. There is also the periodic storm-water problem to deal with.[6]

In a Metro where there is no convenient supply of natural pure water it will be necessary to make do with

[5] This is done in Mexico City.
[6] Cf. Report of team of consultants led by Sir Alexander Gibb.

intakes from any convenient source, even if polluted. Experience in London and other Metros similarly placed demonstrates that an ample supply of purified water can be made available from low down intakes; but the equipment required is naturally costly. Estimates of present unsatisfied demand and future growth will be needed; demand will rise rapidly with rising standards of living and modern housing. There is one merit in this method of dealing with the water problem. It can be proceeded with gradually. In contrast building a new reservoir implies massive construction right away. If the reservoir is going to be large enough in the medium and longer term, it will be unavoidable to start with over-capacity; indeed this may well be the cheapest in the long run. Obviously the costs and benefits of various alternative solutions and their location require very careful analysis.

The other group of major reforms that call more for construction than for personnel are in the field of slum clearance, housing and town planning. Some housing programmes will undoubtedly require loan finance and other assistance from higher level governments; but there are a number of minor (but by no means unimportant) improvements which could be carried out by local effort. These are essentially short period. In many L.D.C.s better repair and maintenance of publicly owned buildings (offices and dwelling houses) should be a high priority. Thereafter arrangements can be made for regular inspection and upkeep. To neglect this simple precaution is not only economically wasteful, but also psychologically harmful. It makes it more difficult for the citizens to be proud of their city if all the buildings are flaking.

A much bigger job which deserves to be started at once is to improve conditions in shanty settlements. Since there is virtually no prospect of their complete elimination in the foreseeable future it is well worth while to undertake improvements. These would not only make life more tolerable for the inhabitants but would remove a health and security hazard, not to mention an eyesore, from neighbouring areas. The process of reform can be cumulative if the inhabitants of the settlements are shown the way to self-help and further improvement. There are a number of ways in which shanty town rehabilitation can be started, depending on local circumstances. In the first place the dwellings themselves can be improved by supplying some better construction materials than hessian and cardboard. Instructions how to make better homes would probably have to be given and simple tools supplied. Neighbours can be encouraged to help each other. (In Africa this is a regular practice.)[7] It would greatly increase cleanliness if the alleyways between the dwellings were straightened and given some surfacing – in fact this is now being done in Calcutta. More standpipes and latrines are needed, with effective drainage into cesspits if no underground sewerage has been provided. Regular solid waste collections at some convenient place by a good road could probably be arranged.[8] If at all possible electric light should be made available so that the day does not stop at six. If this can be done many new interests can be developed. Finally for the women it would be most beneficial to introduce simple community services: instruction in sewing (with material supplied free for children's clothes), elementary hygiene, cooking and nutrition, and also in literacy for those who find reading difficult. Every effort should be made to encourage the participation of well-off members of the community in this process of regeneration. After all, for good or ill these people are now their fellow citizens and much deserving of help.

In the process of the rehabilitation of a shanty settlement no serious problem of demolition arises; but if slum clearance requires the destruction of large old buildings several additional problems have to be faced. In the first place a sufficient amount of demolition must be carried out to enable area rehabilitation to be

---

[7] For instance in Uganda, see my *Development from Below*.

[8] As is done in at least some shanty settlements in Mexico City.

undertaken. Attempting to rebuild old houses here and there is unsatisfactory in every way. Demolition should carry with it an obligation to rehouse the dispossessed slum dwellers. American experience (e.g. in Chicago) amply demonstrates that if this precaution is neglected the evicted families merely turn the adjacent area into a slum. There is the additional trouble that when the demolished area is rebuilt it will generally be found that the amount of low rental housing in the district has been diminished, making life more difficult for those who must live near their work. Special care needs to be taken to prevent this happening.

The reforming city is thus squarely faced with the challenge of low (really low) income housing. This is a very complicated problem which can only be attacked with public funds, either from the city itself or from a higher level government. The first stage is to see about minimising building costs by research into building materials, methods of construction, choice of contractors or an efficient P.W.D.[9] If the new accommodation is to house the really poor 'economic' rents cannot be charged, hence the need for subsidy. The trouble about this is that there is a widespread temptation to extend the range of subsidisation up the income scale. The better-off families are eager tenants, and more satisfactory to the authorities in every way; but there is a real danger that charging artificially low rents for this class will merely encourage immigration. It also fritters away public funds when it is not impossible that other assistance might be made available, for instance from Building Societies or Insurance Corporations. The taxpayers' money will then be available for more urgent needs in the social services. A case in point is that of India where the Housing Programme covers five different schemes. All are grant aided to some extent but only one (that for slum clearance and improvement schemes) is for really low income groups.[10] The nationalised Life Insurance Corporation

---

[9] Cf. The excellent flats erected by the Hong Kong P.W.D.

[10] Chapter 10 above and Datta, 'Financing Urban Development'.

provides some finance for the more expensive houses. There is no reason to suppose that this source could not be more fully exploited.

No very great progress with a housing programme can be expected in the short period; but a good deal should be possible in the medium term. The long term programme should aim to include not only large scale clearance and rebuilding in the centre, but also new developments. These may take the form either of fringe extensions (colonies in Indian terminology) or of satellite towns built some twenty to thirty miles away, so that they have time to develop a personality of their own before they are absorbed by the Metro. For these exercises two additional problems appear. First, land will have to be acquired. This is always a difficult and time-consuming process calling for negotiations both concerning the price to be paid and the compensation to be given to former owners. It will be necessary to have compulsory purchase powers in the background, although it is desirable not to have to use them. An independent tribunal can be set to adjudicate 'fair' market prices. In view of all these difficulties it is wise for a Metro to minimise the amount of land that has actually to be bought, and to 'make do and mend' in not so bad areas, at least in the short and medium periods.

The second new factor to be considered in a programme of extensive new development is that it is essential to have at least a simple land-use plan. By this is not intended an elaborate Master Plan, drawn up by a team of foreign experts and culminating in a handsomely illustrated 'glossy'. This does not really belong to the city. All that is wanted is for the Chief Executive to get together with his engineers and leading citizens to work out the next moves in the city's development: the traces of streets, simple (not necessarily rigid) zoning for the different types of areas; residential construction with their necessary complementary investments such as schools and health clinics, open spaces and entertainment areas, shopping centres. Commercial and factory development will equally have to be allowed for.

Probably in five to eight years' time the plan will want readjusting, and the need for this should be held in mind from the start. No one can foretell just how or where growth will take place. But for the near future the land-use plan will provide indispensable guide lines.

Much more might be said concerning local physically oriented improvements; but space does not allow. We can pass more quickly over the service oriented improvements, not that they are less important (since they embrace the major social services) but that policy will probably be largely determined at the national or state level so that the cities, even the largest, have only a limited role to play. This affects for instance education and curative health – environmental health is another matter. One group of service activities which is probably largely within the competence of local authorities is the protective services: police, possibly also courts, traffic control and fire prevention.

In this disturbed modern age there is probably no country in the world which deals with complete success with the twin problems of crime prevention and detection on the one hand and citizen safety on the other. It used to be considered that the problem was easier in the L.D.C.s because the criminals were less educated and ingenious. But with the reinforcement of local malefactors with drug traffickers it has become a very difficult problem indeed. Nevertheless in L.D.C.s crime remains predominantly a problem of civil violence. To meet this situation the aim should be to develop a highly trained (and inevitably highly paid) local police force which will have the confidence of the public. This will be costly if it is to be efficient; but it should be possible for a Metro to compensate itself to some extent by developing subsidiary services, such as traffic wardens and other assistants[11] to carry out duties usually undertaken by the police, whose time would then be set free for more exacting tasks.

[11] In a number of L.D.C.s there is a good tradition of these auxiliaries, cf. Native Authority Police in Nigeria, Revenue Runners in Jamaica.

Of all the social services education is by far the most extensive and the most costly. It is not uncommon for it to take up something like 80 per cent of local budgets. Generally speaking education is fairly heavily assisted by higher level governments, who consequently lay down the main policy lines. The purely local contribution is likely to be in the siting and building of schools. The provision of an adequate supply of schools requires long term planning and as we saw earlier (see above, p. 249) involves a number of difficult decisions between rehabilitating old schools and building new ones, always bearing in mind the prospective expansion of the school population both due to population growth in general (and especially in Metros) and to the need for improving educational standards. Local authorities can also make an important contribution by the provision of school meals, transport, school journeys and so on. These services can profit greatly by the co-operation of voluntary workers (including parents) so that the school becomes a real part of the community. For the siting of new schools the land use plan will be indispensable. A Metro will probably find it advisable to take advice concerning materials, layout, play spaces and so on.

Turning to health services: here again the strictly local sphere of operations is limited by national policy. Only in Metros are large modern hospitals likely to be sited, and the local authority will be able to exercise little influence over them. The main opportunity for local health services is preventive, in other words environmental. What can be done locally depends to a great extent on the water supply and sanitation situation, and on shanty settlement improvement, matters which we have already discussed. There is some scope for urban authorities to supplement curative services by organising a network of local clinics. These could deal with such things as minor injuries (which in the tropics must be treated immediately), family planning advice and pre-natal attention. If not provided by the big hospitals an ambulance service will need to be organised locally.

In all such ways health hazards should be materially reduced.

In this brief survey of urban improvement nothing has been said directly concerning the problem of urban employment. As mentioned above, in many L.D.C.s this is regarded as the most serious problem of all. Its basic cause is the flood of immigrants, which greatly exceeds possible employment opportunities even in fast growing economies. Urban unemployment cannot be tackled by the cities alone. It is a national phenomenon and calls for an integrated policy by all levels of government. Nevertheless the policy followed by urban authorities can promote or hinder success in several directions. As a first step it is very desirable to think up ways of curbing the tide of immigration. This is not primarily a matter for the cities. It calls for a national policy of rural development: improving the circumstances and incomes of farmers, providing them with as many as possible of the amenities that they would hope to enjoy in town – electric light, convenient shopping centres and so on.[12] This policy could well be supplemented by the transfer of selected urban families (not necessarily immigrants) to rural 'colonies' where they would be given holdings, taught modern farming techniques and generally put in the way of making a satisfactory income.[13] In this part of the exercise the cities could give substantial help.

Urban authorities could also help to stem the tide of immigration by a sensible housing policy (see above, p. 253). Moreover slum clearance and shanty settlement rehabilitation should help to improve the quality of the labour force. A programme of building low-income housing and schools would itself provide a substantial

[12] Cf. the Contribution by A. D. Moddie (Hindustan Lever Ltd.), 'Relieving Poverty Through Growth', *The Challenge of Poverty in India* (Indian Social Institute, 1970).

[13] After some not very successful experimentation this policy has been successfully followed in Sn'Lamka, and has contributed to the 'green revolution' in paddy growing. Rural colonies would be feasible in India although somewhat more difficult, since in India's drier climate a preliminary need would probably be additional water.

amount of worthwhile employment. Experience gained
in these exercises should enable the city authorities to
select and screen promising workers for settlement
schemes, factory employment and so on. Finally cities
can induce potential manufacturers to settle in the
neighbourhood by offering sites, buildings to rent and
information concerning the local labour supply and
potential markets. These are constructive measures; very
different from feather-bedding public offices or utilities
for the sake of disguising unemployment. That makes
efficient management impossible.

In most countries these suggested physical improvements could not be fully effective unless they were
accompanied by fairly drastic administrative reforms. In
detail these would largely depend on the political and
institutional organisation of the country. Nevertheless
some generalisations can safely be made. They concern
the organisation and conduct both of traditional
administration and of the new commitments which cities
have to undertake in the modern world. The need for
change is by no means only a problem for the L.D.C.s.
Many large cities in the A.C.s have deplorable budgetary
habits. Even those which have relatively good practices
could do with improvement.[14] This is not to be wondered
at since the new services make substantially different
management demands. Large cities have important funds
under their control. (It must be remembered that their
populations are many times greater than those of some
nation states.) Hence Metro budgets need to be as well
constructed and administered as those of the best
practices of national governments.

All investigators complain of the extreme difficulty of
finding out what has really been spent, even more what
has been accomplished, in relation to the estimates.
Indeed the estimates themselves are frequently little
more than wishful thinking. A high priority must
consequently be to improve the figures – as to coverage,
depth and speed of reporting. Without sound statistical

---

[14] Cf. Report by Dr Lennox Moak of Toronto Metro.

information planning and project evaluation cannot be effective. Full improvement in statistics can only be achieved gradually, as and when the departments can be made to produce the necessary details. Besides the departmental figures and the comprehensive budget (which should include all the outgoings and incomings for which the Authority is responsible) record charts of the progress of individual projects will be required.[15] For constructional departments reliable records of intake and withdrawal of stocks and shares will also be necessary.

A second line of improvement is that at the same time the standard of personnel at all grades needs to be raised, both as regards the level of education and methods of recruitment. Leading officers should have some kind of professional qualification, not so much for the extra expertise it may be supposed to give them, but even more to improve their self-confidence and reliability. They should then be more willing to take decisions, and not continually to pass the buck. The remuneration (of the higher cadres especially) should be on a scale considered satisfactory enough not to tempt them into illegal transactions 'on the side'. This precaution is particularly necessary in the case of tax officers who have big money passing through their hands. Senior finance officers would much benefit by a course in financial management such as is offered in a number of A.C.s.[16] Tax departments should be taught to operate with modern mechanical equipment, including computers when the scale of operation justifies their use. In the valuation department and for effective assessment for the Property Tax, detailed maps need to be available so that all changes can be recorded immediately.

A third line of advance is in respect of the organisation of the whole Authority's government, in a purposeful manner. This may call for greater power for the Chief Executive, and a more effective co-operation between

---

[15] Cf. my *Development Finance*.

[16] For instance the course on Government Accountancy & Audit, organised by the British Council in conjunction with the Ministry of Overseas Development.

him and the departmental heads and the councillors. Prompt publicity concerning the government's policy and achievements will improve the participation of the citizens. This is needed to promote ready acquiescence over policy decisions. The appointment of a 'management officer' responsible (under the departmental head) for such things as seeing that all officers are in a position to function optimally should also be considered.[17]

Some reform of budgetary content and presentation is a necessary accompaniment of administrative reforms. Space does not allow us to go into these matters in any detail.[18] If this has not yet been achieved the first step is to master the art of traditional accountability budgeting, with appropriations exactly matching the estimates so that deviations can be seen at a glance. The account needs to be shown for a term of years, far enough back to a year for which there are firm 'actuals' and forward to cover at least the year just opening. The 'statement' is naturally arranged on the traditional 'subjective'/input basis: so much for wages, purchases of goods and materials, cost of communications made and so on. It is true that in this form the account is not much help in policy decisions; that is not its purpose. But it should be possible to rearrange the votes (items) functionally so that the cost of particular services can generally be ascertained. In this set up the budget is much more useful for policy purposes. In addition great efforts should be made to put forward estimates on the output side, on the lines of a performance budget. But whatever can be achieved in this line must be regarded as supplementary, since only in a few instances are the achievements likely to be reliably quantifiable.

Some steps towards programme budgeting might also be attempted. This implies not only the introduction of a budgetary plan, with forecasts of outgoings and incomings over a term of two or three years, but also for

[17] As suggested by the Plowden Report on the Control of Government Expenditure (Cmd. 1432, 1959). Advisability depends on scale of operations of new Districts.

[18] But see my 'Current Experiments in Budgetary Organisation', *United Malayan Baking Review* (1970) VI, 2.

the rearrangement of budgetary categories into 'programmes' or basic objectives for services, such as 'crime
prevention', 'improving traffic flow' and so on. (We must
return to this point in a moment.)

The reform of budgetary techniques calls for a new
type of 'management' audit. Under traditional budgetary
practice there should be little difficulty in arranging for a
thorough *external* audit, since the figures are (or should
be) quite firm. This is a most important exercise, since in
the subjective/input arrangement the economic significance of the items cannot be readily perceived. If the
external audit cannot be carried out satisfactorily it is a
sure sign that the accounting is not good enough. At the
same time it is wise to put this to the test by subsequent
examination, for instance by a Committee of the
Council.[19] More advanced budgetary techniques call for
more sophisticated auditing, particularly for an *internal*
'management' audit. The auditors will want to look
carefully into the relation between targets and estimates
on the one hand and on the other between costs and
achievement over a term of two or three years. They will
also need to look at such matters as wage relations and
the effect of incentive schemes on productivity.[20]

In its simplest form a programme budget is a plan for
the city government, but without covering in detail any
enterprises it conducts (basically because they should be
keeping commercial and not administrative type
accounts). For steady and successful development a city,
especially a Metro, should draw up a period plan. The
techniques for such an exercise are too well known to
require discussion here. There is little in the technique of
planning which is inherently different at the Metro level
from the national level, apart from the constraint that a
local authority cannot freely indulge in deficit finance. It
is important that the plan should arise out of the existing

---

[19] On the lines of the British Public Accounts Committee, or, in a
small authority, the Finance Committee.

[20] Cf. H. C. Cotching, 'The Changing Role of the Auditor', *Local
Government Finance* (Oct. 1970).

activities of the Metro and not be completely alien to it, imposed from outside on general grounds of what is good for it. No project should be admitted to the plan unless it has first earned its priority with a cost/benefit test. This need not be elaborate at the initial stage. Detailed documentation may well be a hindrance rather than a help.

To repeat a point already made it is most important that externalities – relations with other programmes and environmental effects – should be carefully recorded and so far as possible quantified. To omit them because they are not fully quantifiable may give a wholly misleading conclusion. This is not the place to discuss what rate of interest should be used for discounting the alternative streams of benefits and costs; the optimum rate may differ substantially according to circumstances; but the same rate must of course be used for all the items in the programme at a given point of time. In general it would be sensible to employ a rather high rate, since the interests of the city are probably more short period than those of the national government. Citizen participation will be much encouraged if definite improvements are apparent, say within five years. The high rate will favour these.

Before implementation begins a closer project analysis and evaluation will be required. For this the Little-Mirrlees technique[21] (using 'world' shadow prices instead of local – probably distorted – prices) may be found useful not only for individual evaluations, but also for decisions between techniques over a wide range of projects.

One more question remains to be settled. For what area is the plan to be made? There are strong arguments for covering the whole Metro area as defined earlier, that is to say the range of regular daily commuting. At least as much as this is in any case necessary for water supply and sewerage installations, on purely physical grounds. It is better that the plan should also cover, at least in

[21] O.E.C.D. Manual of Industrial Project Analysis.

outline, communications and other aspects of land use. If the outlying parts of the area are fragmented between a large number of separate jurisdictions lengthy negotiations will probably be necessary before agreement is reached. The assistance of a higher level government may help to sort them out, and to reduce the number of separate authorities, especially those that are very small.[22]

The logical final step would clearly be the establishment of a single Metro area government. This would probably be easiest, at any rate to begin with, on a 'federal' basis so that the units retain at least their identity, although they form an integrated part of the organisation and government of the Metro. There are many signs that this kind of Metropolitan City is going to be the key element in the urban development of the future. Virtually this is determined by the growth of populations and their extreme mobility, as well as by the development of the technology of urban services with large economies of scale. On all this the literature is rapidly accumulating.[23]

---

[22] Thus the Ontario Provincial Government aided Toronto in reducing its units to a manageable number.

[23] Cf. Report of the Toronto Conference on Metropolitan Problems, 1967 (published 1971). U. K. Hicks, 'Economic and Financial Problems of Metropolitan Areas', *Zeitschrift für Nationalökonomie* (1969); Reports of the Maud Royal Commission on Local Government in England & Wales, 1970, and statements thereon by Labour and Conservative Governments. An extensive reorganisation of U.K. local government came into force in April 1974.

Index